W9-DCA-727

TURN
OF GLORY

TURN OF GLORY

★

AL LACY

Multnomah Books, Sisters, Oregon

With the exception of recognized historical figures, the characters in this novel are fictional. Any resemblance to actual persons, living or dead, is purely coincidental.

TURN OF GLORY

© 1998 by Lew A. Lacy

published by Multnomah Fiction
a division of Multnomah Publishers, Inc.

Cover design by D^2 DesignWorks
Cover illustration by Vittorio Dangelico

International Standard Book Number: 1-57673-217-7

Printed in the United States of America.

ALL RIGHTS RESERVED

No part of this publication may be reproduced, stored in a retrieval system, or transmitted in any form or by any means—electronic, mechanical, photocopying, recording, or otherwise—without prior written permission.

For information:
Multnomah Publishers, Inc.
Post Office Box 1720
Sisters, Oregon 97759

LIBRARY OF CONGRESS CATALOGING-IN-PUBLICATION DATA
Lacy, Al.
    Turn of glory/by Al Lacy.
    p.cm.—(Battles of destiny; no. 8)
    ISBN 1-57673-217-7 (alk. paper)
    1.United States—History—Civil War, 1861–1865—Fiction.
    2. Jackson, Stonewall, 1824–1863—Death and burial—Fiction.
    3. Chancellorsville (Va.), Battle of, 1863—Fiction. I. Title.
    II. Series: Lacy, Al. Battles of destiny; bk. 8.
    PS3562.A256T87 1998
    813'.54—dc21   97-48890
                                                                  CIP

98 99 00 01 02 03 04 — 10 9 8 7 6 5 4 3 2 1

For Mike O'Donell—
Christian brother, loyal fan, dear friend,
and insurance agent supreme.

God bless you, Mike.

1 THESSALONIANS 5:16

PROLOGUE

For more than a century and a quarter, in the minds of Civil War buffs like myself, the Battle of Chancellorsville—May 1–4, 1863—has remained the ultimate campaign of General Robert E. Lee's Army of Northern Virginia.

I have never picked a side to favor in the Civil War. I see gallantry and heroism on both sides. I understand the cause of both sides. President Abraham Lincoln was against slavery. I am against slavery. As a Bible-believing, born-again child of God, I do not believe that my heavenly Father wants one human being to own as chattel another human being, regardless of the color of his skin.

But the issue that sparked the flame for the War between the States was not slavery, it was states' rights. The Southern states resisted the intent of the Northern states to force the abolition of slavery upon them. They felt they had the right to make their own decision in the matter. And I generally agree with that principle too.

People have asked me if I have a favorite character on each side of the War. I do. Though many soldiers on both sides have caught my attention as I've studied the War, two stand out in my mind. Both of them were Christian men with positive testimonies of having trusted the Lord Jesus Christ and His shed blood, death, burial, and glorious resurrection for their salvation.

Those men are Major General Joshua L. Chamberlain, the shining hero of the Battle of Gettysburg, and Lieutenant General Thomas J. "Stonewall" Jackson, the hero of numerous battles, and certainly the shining star in the Battle of Chancellorsville.

My faithful readers know that I have already written a novel on the Gettysburg battle, *Season of Valor.*

Though in the Battles of Destiny series I have not written the novels in chronological order, I am following the previous novel, *Wings of the Wind,* with the book you now hold in your hands. I want to pick up the story where *Wings of the Wind* left off after the Battle of Antietam, where much of the spotlight was on Thomas "Stonewall" Jackson. I not only want to proceed with Jackson's part in the War, but with the life of his longtime friend and personal physician, Dr. Hunter McGuire. This, of course, will also throw the spotlight on McGuire's lovely fiancée, Jodie Lockwood, who ultimately becomes his wife.

Also, in chapter 5 you will meet Chaplain B. Tucker Lacy, who is not a fictional character. Although his last name is the same as mine, I did not create Chaplain Lacy for the story; I have simply followed history. Lacy was a close friend of General Stonewall Jackson and was appointed Chaplain General to II Corps by Jackson himself.

Several years ago, after casually reading a brief historical sketch about the Chancellorsville campaign, I picked up a modern road atlas and tried to find the city of Chancellorsville on the Virginia map. When I couldn't locate it, and it was not listed in the directory of Virginia cities, towns, and villages, I figured the city of Chancellorsville must have either had a name change since the Civil War or died out.

Further study showed me that Chancellorsville never was a

city, town, or village, but simply a mansion two and a half stories high, built in 1816 by wealthy George Chancellor. It stood at the intersection of the newly built Orange Turnpike and Ely's Ford Road. Chancellor built it large enough to provide a sufficient home for his large family, plus bed-and-breakfast rooms to provide accommodations for turnpike travelers. He gave the place its name—Chancellorsville.

The famous battle took place around the huge estate, and the mansion itself was severely damaged by cannonade.

General Lee's army was outnumbered more than two to one. They faced a foe better equipped and better supplied and lacked the presence of one of their two corps commanders, yet they were able to crush and demoralize the federal Army of the Potomac in one of the most daring engagements in military history.

The Chancellorsville battle forever solidified the lasting fame of the wise and gallant General Thomas J. "Stonewall" Jackson.

This fact, however, belongs at the end of the story. Let's go back to September 17, 1862, at the Battle of Antietam, where our story really began....

ONE

On the winding banks of Antietam Creek, near Sharpsburg, Maryland, a raging titanic combat had begun just after the break of dawn. It was now midafternoon, and the heat was almost unbearable as powder smoke hung densely above the valley. The sun's rays shone through only when a gust of wind parted the veil of smoke.

Men went down by the dozens as the hostile battle lines of both Union and Confederate armies unleashed fire without letup. In spite of the carnage, there was an air of excitement. Both sides eagerly pressed the battle to the enemy—an almost reckless disregard for life in a wild quest for victory.

Dead men sprawled over the ground from the Potomac River to Antietam Creek, and to the east for a mile. Some were crumpled in hollows, and a few lay draped over waist-high stone walls and split-rail fences.

The acrid odor of gunpowder, hot metal, and blood filled the hot September air. The smell of burnt and splintered trees and blasted earth only intensified the stench of death.

Unmerciful artillery had wreaked havoc—fences torn apart, farm buildings destroyed, cornfields trampled, trees reduced to naked stumps. Human limbs were heaped beside hospital tents, and army horses and domestic animals lay lifeless among thousands of dead and dying soldiers.

The Confederate II Corps's commander, Major General Thomas J. "Stonewall" Jackson, stood on a brush-covered knoll in the west woods with one of his aides, Private Henry Kyd Douglas. Jackson's artillery troops were situated in the woods along the edge of the trees, and infantry were spaced intermittently among the cannons.

Major General George B. McClellan's Union infantry came across the open fields in seemingly interminable columns of blue, flanked by artillery batteries. Jackson's artillery cut loose, and the infantry followed suit, ejecting the wild, bloodcurdling Rebel yell. Cannon and musket belched their volleys with telling accuracy.

Casualties in the Union ranks were appalling, but on they came with a flash of bayonets and flutter of flags, halting the lines only long enough to readjust for their fallen comrades.

Stonewall Jackson stood fearlessly on the very edge of the terrible battle, observing it through binoculars. The enemy was showing itself indomitable. No matter how many Yankees the Confederate guns cut down, there were always more to take their place. Not so with the men in gray. They had started short in number and were becoming even fewer.

Suddenly a fierce battle opened up in a cornfield owned by a farmer named Miller. Jackson swung his binoculars there and focused on the action.

Major General Joseph Hooker's Union infantry swept into the cornfield with the crushing weight of a landslide. The Rebels were grossly outnumbered but fought back valiantly.

Even as Jackson watched the battle from his position on the knoll, great patches of corn were blasted by artillery, and most of the field looked as if it had been struck by a hailstorm.

At the north end of the cornfield, in the heat of the action, was the Eighteenth North Carolina Infantry Regiment commanded by

Major Rance Dayton. The Eighteenth was part of Jackson's II Corps.

Jackson caught a glimpse of Major Dayton and briefly thought of their time together at the Virginia Military Institute, where Jackson had been a professor. Each time Jackson had talked with Dayton about the Lord Jesus, the young cadet had listened politely, but that was all. Then, a few days ago, the general had talked with Dayton again about his need to know the Lord. But all Rance would say was that he would think about it. Jackson's last words to him had been: "Just don't die while you're thinking about it."

Now Jackson prayed silently, *Dear God, don't let Rance get killed down there. Please don't let him die lost.*

Major Rance Dayton hunkered down with his regiment amongst the cornstalks. Most of the field was flattened, but some of it still stood almost seven feet high. They had met a fierce onslaught from the enemy infantry and repulsed it with musket fire so rapid and well aimed that the Yankees had backed off to regroup.

Flanking Major Dayton were Privates Chad Lynch and Bo Gentry. Lynch peered through the thick stand of corn toward the ravine where the Yankees had retreated and said, "How long you think it'll take 'em to regroup, Major?"

Dayton removed his campaign hat and paused to sleeve sweat from his brow before saying, "Not long. Ten minutes, maybe."

"Sir," said Gentry, "aren't those Yankees gonna run out of men pretty soon? How many do we have to kill before they decide that taking this cornfield isn't worth it?"

Dayton grinned. "I think they grow new Yankees instantly when they pull back to regroup. I declare, I'm sure I've shot some of the same Yankees every time they've come at us."

Both privates chuckled nervously.

Major Dayton ran his gaze over the men he could see. They looked weary and hollow-eyed as they crouched among the cornstalks. They had already fought for over nine hours. Since their meager breakfast of dried beef, two-day-old biscuits, and water from the creek, they'd had nothing to eat but the corn they were munching on now, while their dead and wounded comrades lay around them. Some were helping the wounded drink from canteens.

A sergeant appeared from the rear and knelt beside Dayton. "Major, we're runnin' mighty low on ammunition."

"Get to General Branch and tell him we need more."

"That's where I just came from, sir. He said there isn't much more left in the caissons."

"Then we'll have to throw rocks till they close in. Then we'll go to bayonets, fists, and teeth. Has General Branch sent word to General Jackson that we're low?"

"I don't know, sir."

"Go find out."

When the sergeant had disappeared, Dayton let his eyes move over the dirty faces of his men. "We're low on ammunition, boys," he said. "Pass the word to gather the cartridge boxes off the dead and wounded. We'll need all we can get!"

"Major!" shouted one of the lieutenants. "Here they come!"

Every eye fastened on the heavy lines of men in blue who came out of the ravine like a swarm of insects.

"All right, men, listen to me!" Dayton called loudly so that all could hear. "Hold your fire until I give the word! We're hard to see in this corn! I want them so close you can tell the color of their eyes before you fire!"

The men's nerves were strung tight, and sweat poured down their faces as they watched the blue lines coming toward them. Soon the first line of Federals drew dangerously close. Suddenly Dayton shouted, "Fire!"

Muskets roared and flamed in the Federals' faces like a blaze of lightning. The entire front line, with few exceptions, went down in a virtual wall of hot lead. Those who were not hit wheeled and ran back toward the next wave, which halted under their stunned commander's orders.

While the Federals regrouped, Dayton shouted, "Take the guns and ammunition off those dead Yankees, boys!"

As the men of the Eighteenth North Carolina Regiment scurried to gather the guns and ammunition, Dayton saw a fresh horde of Yankees swarm out of the ravine.

"Get ready, men!" shouted the major. "This'll be a big one! Don't fire till I say so!"

The Federals were closing in. Rance could hear them shouting curses. He waited until they were almost upon the Eighteenth, then gave the order: "Fire!"

Suddenly the whole world seemed to explode as guns on both sides belched flame. The air filled with dust and smoke and the cries of wounded men. Dayton saw the Yankee leader—a young major—go down.

The volley of fire by the Confederates and the heaps of blue-uniformed bodies on the ground had the Yankees in disarray. They pulled back, looking for their leader. When they couldn't find him amidst the dust and smoke, they pivoted and headed back across the field.

"After 'em, men!" Dayton shouted, and led the charge.

They were some two hundred yards out from the cornfield, firing at the retreating Federals, when Dayton saw more Yankee reinforcements forming at the far end of the field.

"Back!" Dayton shouted. "Back to the cornfield! Re-form the lines!"

The Eighteenth North Carolina wheeled at their leader's command and ran for the cornfield. As the space between blue and gray widened, Union artillery opened fire.

Cannon shells shrieked their high-pitched song of death, striking the ground and exploding in orange and yellow flame.

The roar was deafening as shell after shell rained down on the Eighteenth. Suddenly the double shriek of a pair of Union shells sounded in a deadly arc close behind them.

"Get down!" Dayton shouted at the top of his lungs.

Every man in the regiment dropped, hugging the ground as tightly as he could. The earth shook as the cannonballs struck and exploded. As soon as shrapnel stopped hissing through the air, Dayton looked up and saw that some of his men up front had taken a direct hit. They were sprawled and crumpled like broken dolls.

"Get up and run!" shouted the major, scrambling to his feet. "The cornfield is out of their range!"

It was every man for himself. Dayton bolted with them, but when he drew near the men who had been hit, he saw movement. Sergeant Buster Camden was still alive!

Dayton halted and knelt by the wounded man while the Union artillery continued to bombard the fleeing Rebels. "I'll carry you, Buster," he said.

"No, Major. Go on. I'm done for anyway."

"No way I'm leaving you here."

Dayton heard the whine of another shell, sensed the concussion as it struck and exploded to his left. He felt something tug at his pant leg but paid it no mind. "Okay," he said, his hands running under Camden's body, "here we go."

When Dayton stood, his leg gave way. He cushioned Buster from the fall and looked down to see torn flesh and a piece of jagged black metal embedded in his thigh.

"Major!" gasped Camden. "Go on! The Yankees…"

Dayton looked over his shoulder. The Union infantry was coming like a deluge. "Can't leave you, Buster." He gritted his teeth against the pain and struggled to lift Camden.

✳✳✳✳✳

The men of the Eighteenth staggered to a halt at the edge of the cornfield and looked back for the first time. Private Billy Dean Baxter's eyes bulged when he saw Dayton's predicament.

"It's the major," Baxter said. "I can't tell who the other man is.… The major's been hit too!"

"I'm going after them!" Everett Nichols shouted as he broke into a run. "Cover me!"

Four other men ran after him—Billy Dean Baxter, Buford Hall, Hank Upchurch, and Chuck Carney. "Cover us!" Upchurch shouted as they bent low, darting toward Dayton and the man he was trying vainly to lift.

The five running men now had the attention of Captain Jack Fleming, who was next in command. "Load up, men!" Fleming shouted. "Shoot around them and over their heads! They'll stay low!"

Rance Dayton saw his men running toward him and glanced back at the oncoming horde of blue uniforms.

"Go back! Go back!" he shouted. "There's no chance!"

The fearless five came on, bent low and zigzagging their way across the field. Billy Dean and Everett lifted the major as the other three hoisted Camden and took off running as fast as they could go. The Federals were now within range, and bullets began to zip and whistle around the rescuers.

Billy Dean grunted and went down, causing Everett to stumble and drop Dayton, who grimaced as his body struck the ground.

The men who were carrying Buster Camden paused.

"Go on!" shouted Dayton, gritting his teeth in pain.

"Billy Dean's dead, Major," Everett said.

"So's Buster," called Hank Upchurch.

"You guys carry the major; I'll be a shield," Carney said.

The other three men quickly had Dayton off the ground and were running toward their regiment, who were cheering them on.

"Look over there!" Carney shouted with a whoop.

A horde of Rebels were charging the Federals from the side, guns blazing. The Yankees left off their pursuit of Dayton and his gallant men and braced themselves for the fresh onslaught.

While the sounds of Union and Confederate guns thundered across the valley, Nurse Jodie Lockwood stood in a hospital tent on the edge of the battlefield and watched Dr. Hunter McGuire lift a patient off the operating table. Dr. McGuire, who was a childhood friend of Stonewall Jackson's, was also his personal physician, as well as head physician of Jackson's II Corps.

What few hospital tents there were, on either side of the battle, didn't have sufficient doctors and nurses to keep up with the number of wounded men. Many died before they could be attended to.

Jodie cleaned the operating table quickly. As soon as the doctor laid the latest surgery patient on the ground outside, he would return with another wounded soldier. She glanced through the tent opening and could see bodies strewn so thickly on the field that there was hardly a place for the stretcher bearers to walk. Moans and cries could be heard above the nearby sounds of battle.

Jodie watched Dr. McGuire as he walked back to the tent, carrying his next patient as tenderly as he would a child. In spite of the tension in the air and the smell of blood, Jodie felt her heart grow warm at the sight of the handsome man she loved. His wavy, thick sand-colored hair fell across his forehead as he walked, and she longed to brush it back and smooth the furrow from between his eyes.

He entered the tent and gently laid the wounded man on the table. When Jodie moved up beside him, Hunter glanced at her and felt the warmth in her eyes and silently mouthed, *I love you.*

A slight smile curved her lips as she held his gaze.

Hunter McGuire had fallen in love with Jodie while doing

intern work at a clinic in Lexington, Virginia, where Jodie worked as a nurse. Though Hunter didn't know it, Jodie had fallen in love with him, too, but circumstances separated them before they could tell one another how they felt.

Seven long years passed as Hunter searched for Jodie, praying earnestly that the Lord wouldn't let her marry another man before he found her.

It had taken the War for them to find each other. Both were working in the medical corps and had been assigned to Antietam. As grounds were being laid for battle along Antietam Creek, Hunter and Jodie had stumbled onto each other. They professed their love for each other, and Hunter had wasted no time proposing marriage. Now they were engaged.

Hunter and Jodie had just finished working on a patient when they heard shuffling footsteps outside the tent. They turned to see two exhausted, panting men carry Major Rance Dayton through the tent opening. Hunter focused on Dayton's pale features and the makeshift tourniquet on the major's leg. "Looks like you took a bullet, my friend," he said.

"Shrapnel," Dayton replied through clenched teeth.

"He asked us to bring him to you, Dr. McGuire," Chuck Carney said.

"All right," McGuire said, nodding. Then to Dayton, "I've got some other men in worse shape, Major, but I'll get to you as quickly as I can."

"That's fine, Doctor. I can wait."

Hunter turned toward Jodie and said, "This is Nurse Jodie Lockwood, Major. She'll check the tourniquet and give you some laudanum to ease the pain."

"Take good care of him, Doctor," Nichols said, as he and Carney headed for the tent flap. "We need him back to lead our regiment as soon as possible."

"Jodie and I will do our best," said McGuire. "You can bank on that."

✤✤✤✤✤

It was almost sunset before doctor and nurse were able to put their full attention on Major Rance Dayton.

McGuire eased him onto the table, and Jodie removed the tourniquet. While the doctor scrutinized the chunk of shrapnel embedded in the major's leg, Dayton said, "Doc, you know the five men in my regiment from Fayetteville?"

McGuire nodded, noting how much flesh he would have to cut to get the shrapnel out.

"Those wonderful men risked their lives to rescue me."

"God bless them," said Jodie.

"Those boys are heroes, Doc. I've never seen such courage on a battlefield."

Jodie placed a flat tin plate that bore medical instruments beside Dayton's head. "Major," she said softly, "such love as those men showed you is a wonderful thing."

Tears welled up in Dayton's eyes, and he managed a slight smile as he said, "And don't I know it, ma'am. If ever I was called upon to hazard my life to save theirs, I'd do it without batting an eye."

"I'm sure you would," she said.

The tears spilled down Dayton's cheeks. "I…I only wish there was some way I could thank Billy Dean for giving his life to save mine."

It was a few minutes to midnight, and weary medical personnel on both sides of the Antietam battle were still working on wounded soldiers, doing all they could to save lives.

On the Confederate side, nurses dashed from tent to tent, seeking supplies their doctors had exhausted. Jodie had just given a portion of her laudanum to a nurse when she saw the tall, broad-shouldered form of General Jackson pass through the tent opening. He smiled and spoke to her.

Hunter McGuire, who was bent over a patient, looked over his shoulder and said, "Hello, Tom. I inquired about you earlier and the stretcher bearers told me you were all right. Thank the Lord for that."

Jackson smiled. "Hunter, I was told that Rance Dayton was brought to you with a hunk of shrapnel in his leg. They said you got it out without any trouble. He doing all right?"

"Yes. He's on the south side of the tent. There's a lantern in the corner not being used. Light it and go see if he's awake."

"I'm glad you didn't have to take the leg," Jackson said quietly.

"So am I. He'll be fine in a few weeks…won't even walk with a limp once it's completely healed."

Minutes later, Stonewall Jackson made his way among the wounded men. Most were asleep. He spotted Dayton and knelt beside him. The major turned his head, blinked at the lantern light, then focused his gaze on the face of the man who had taught him so well at V.M.I.

"Hello, General. I sure am glad to see you."

"Same here, Rance. I saw what you did out there today, risking yourself for Sergeant Camden. You're a brave man."

Dayton batted his eyelids. "How'd you see that?"

"Binoculars."

"So that's how you got two regiments of General Jubal Early's Brigade to intervene just in time!"

"Yes. And I also saw what those five men in your regiment did."

"Yes, sir. I was going to talk to you about them, sir. I sure would like to see them get some kind of commendation from General Lee."

Jackson grinned, rubbing his bearded chin. "I've already got that in mind," he said, pulling a slip of paper out of his shirt pocket. "Got it down right here, with all their names. I talked to some of the men in the regiment."

"Thank you, sir. They deserve to be honored."

"I've got a meeting with General Lee and General Longstreet in a few minutes, Rance. But one thing before I go…"

"I took care of it, sir."

Jackson's eyebrows arched in surprise. "You did? When?"

"When I came to, lying right here. I've been such a fool to put it off, General. When my mind came clear, it hit me that if I'd been killed out there today, I'd be in hell right now. The Lord was so good to me. Men dying all around. Even—even Billy Dean. I called on Jesus to save me, just like you've told me I should. I'm saved now, General. Thanks to you. If you hadn't pressed the gospel to me over and over—well…I know you've prayed for me all this time too."

"You're right about that," Jackson said, brushing tears from his eyes. "I'm so glad you opened your heart to Jesus."

"Best thing I ever did, sir. There's nothing like the peace I have in my heart right now. But then, you know about that, don't you?"

"There's a deep settled peace in my heart, put there by the Lord Himself the day He saved me as a boy. If in God's plan there should be an enemy bullet or cannonball out there with my name on it, I can die in peace, knowing that all is well between Tom Jackson and the One who died for him on Calvary's cross. I'm glad you know it now too."

"Yes, sir. I sure do."

"I have to get going," said the general, patting Dayton's shoulder as he rose to his feet. "I'll check on you again tomorrow."

TWO

★

During the night of September 18, 1862, General Robert E. Lee led his battered Army of Northern Virginia to the banks of the moon-dappled Potomac River at Shepardstown, Maryland. Heavy of heart, the silver-haired Confederate leader guided Traveler, his horse, into the river and halted in the four-foot water midway. From there he watched his troops move past him and touch ground on the opposite bank in the Old Dominion.

Soon Major General Stonewall Jackson appeared in front of his II Corps, rode to the middle of the river, and drew up beside Lee. The general's shadowed face beneath the brim of his hat showed the deep distress he was feeling. He was only fifty-five years old, but tonight he looked twenty years older.

Jackson was trying to think of something to say when Lee spoke in a broken voice. "Well, so ends our Maryland campaign."

"Yes, sir," said the younger man, who would be thirty-nine in four months. "I know you're feeling the weight of our losses, but please don't punish yourself."

Lee sighed. "This battle will go down in history as the bloodiest day in this War, Thomas J." He paused, then added, "That is, unless we have a worse one later. I figure we lost over three thousand men today. We've got better than seven thousand wounded…and a great many of *them* will die."

"I realize that, sir, but—"

"Don't use a soft cushion on me, General Jackson. If a military leader is willing to accept the glory when he's been victorious, he must be willing to take the blame when he's not."

"But we probably killed and wounded just as many Yankees, sir. It was more like a draw than a victory for either side."

"It isn't a draw when one army turns tail and runs back home," Lee said.

"But you're leading us back into Virginia because we're nearly out of ammunition, sir. You have no choice."

"I know, Thomas J., but it was yours truly who made the choice to invade Yankee territory. There was no decided victory in this campaign for the Confederacy. The blame lies with the man who walks under Robert Edward Lee's hat." He choked and swallowed hard. "So many men dead. So many wounded…"

Jackson hipped around in the saddle and watched the troops as they forded the river. They were coming through slowly: caissons, howitzers, cavalrymen on horseback, infantry. At the end of the line were the ambulances and wagons carrying the wounded.

Some of the Confederate medical staff rode along to care for them. The rest of the medical staff had stayed behind to care for the vast number of wounded men who were in no condition to travel. Lee had left enough men, mules, ambulances, and wagons behind to transport the wounded back to Virginia when they were well enough to withstand the long hours on rough roads. Many of those left behind would have to be buried before the last wagons and ambulances headed south.

Jackson thought of his medical chief of staff, Dr. Hunter McGuire. Hunter and Jodie had asked to remain behind where they could do the most good. "Bless 'em, Lord," he said aloud.

Lee turned and looked at his right-hand man. "What say, General?"

"Oh, just something between me and the Lord, sir."

Lee nodded and turned his tired eyes to the lines of men and equipment making their way onto friendly soil.

When the last wagon had crossed the river, Lee left General William Pendleton and his artillery on a bluff above the Potomac in case the Yankees decided to follow. Lee and Jackson then trotted ahead of the lines and called for them to haul up deep in the Virginia woods about five miles south of the Potomac.

"We'll make camp here, men," said Lee, riding amongst them with Jackson at his side. "We'll rest here tonight and hope Little Mac doesn't decide to come after us first thing in the morning."

"Do you think he will, General Lee?" called out a young sergeant.

"He might. Abe Lincoln's going to chew him up and spit him out if he doesn't."

"But what will we fight them with, General?" came another voice. "Aren't we out of ammunition?"

"Almost," said Lee. "But we've reserved enough for rifles and howitzers to give them a fight if they come after us. If we run out, we'll do as General Jackson has taught II Corps—we'll throw rocks, use our fists, and gnash on them with our teeth!"

A rousing cheer went up.

Jackson leaned close to Lee and said, "They don't sound like defeated men, General. I still say you're too hard on yourself."

Lee nodded and managed a tight grin.

When the battered army had eaten their rations, what few military band members there were among them took their instruments out of the wagons. They huddled close beneath the trees, and one of them said, "We've got some Marylanders among us who fought the Yankees with everything they had—on their own soil. How about we show them our appreciation by playing a little of 'Maryland, My Maryland'?"

The others agreed and struck up the band with the familiar song. They weren't more than five or six bars into it when there were loud boos and hisses while angry voices shouted for them to stop.

"All we want to hear is 'Dixie'!" came a loud voice.

When the band played "Dixie," the boos and hisses turned to shouts, cheers, and whistles of approval.

General Lee quietly made his way to a solitary spot in the shadows and sat down on a fallen tree, then bent his head and wept. Over and over he half-whispered, "So many men…so many dead. So many wounded…so many more will die…"

Stonewall Jackson's aide, Private Henry Kyd Douglas, had stayed behind to help bring the wounded along when they were able to travel. Another aide, Private Jim Lewis, drew up to Jackson as he was removing Little Sorrel's bridle and said, "Let me do that, sir. I'll take care of your horse. You go get some rest."

At the same moment, Jackson saw Major Rance Dayton hobbling toward him on the two broken tree branches he was using for crutches.

"Sir," Dayton said, "could we go talk to General Lee? He's sitting alone over there behind those trees."

"Sure," said Jackson, handing the bridle to Lewis. "Thanks, Jim."

"It's my job, sir. And my pleasure."

General Lee heard the snap of twigs on the forest floor. He lifted his head as the two officers drew up, and started to rise.

"Oh, no, sir," said Jackson. "Don't get up. We'll sit down with you."

Jackson helped the major ease onto another fallen log and then sat down beside him.

In the moonlight, Lee's drawn features showed the strain he

was under as he said, "I'm sorry about your wound, Major Dayton."

"I'll be fine, sir, thanks to the skilled hands of Dr. Hunter McGuire. He says I'll not even limp once the wound heals."

"There's none better than Dr. McGuire, that's for sure," said Lee. "What can I do for you gentlemen?"

"We wanted to tell you about the young men of the Eighteenth North Carolina who rescued Major Dayton, sir," said Jackson.

"Ah, yes. General Jackson told me about the incident while we were making preparations to pull out awhile ago, Major Dayton. Four young heroes rescued you from certain death, at the risk of their own lives. And he told me about—" Lee pulled a crumpled slip of paper from his shirt pocket and held it toward a patch of moonlight "—Private Billy Dean Baxter being killed in the rescue attempt."

"Yes, sir," Dayton said quietly, adjusting his position to make his wounded leg more comfortable.

Lee cleared his throat and said, "I was deeply touched by the story when General Jackson related it to me. I agree with him that the men who rescued you are to be commended."

Rance's face brightened.

Lee rubbed his chin thoughtfully. "Major Dayton, General Jackson also told me these were the same men, along with yourself, that I commended in person for going above and beyond the call of duty at Harper's Ferry."

"Yes, sir."

"Well, I'd like those men brought to me immediately."

Dayton's eyes lit up. "Yes, *sir!*"

"Stay where you are, Major," said Jackson, rising to his feet. "I'll bring them."

When Jackson returned in less than five minutes, General Lee and Major Dayton were standing.

Lee smiled as he watched the eager young faces draw near.

When the men were shoulder to shoulder in front of the Confederate leader, they saluted and stood at attention.

"General Lee, sir," Chuck Carney said, "General Jackson informed us you wanted to see us immediately. Privates Everett Nichols, Buford Hall, Hank Upchurch, and Chuck Carney at your service, sir. You met us after the Harper's Ferry incident, sir, but I wasn't sure if you would remember our names."

Lee smiled. "To be honest, Private Carney, I wouldn't have recalled your names. Thank you for giving them to me."

"Yes, sir."

Lee took a deep breath. "Let me say first, gentlemen, that I am deeply sorry about the loss of your friend, Billy Dean Baxter."

"Thank you, sir," the four said nearly in unison.

"You young men went much further today than your gallantry at Harper's Ferry. General Jackson has told me what *he* saw, and filled me in on what Major Dayton told him. What you men—and your friend Baxter—did on that battlefield today is of the utmost valor. To risk your lives to save the life of Major Dayton without the least reservation tells me you men are the backbone and fiber of what the Confederate army is all about. My only regret is that I come up short for words. I cannot express myself fully as I say that I commend you from the depths of this soldier's heart. You are fine, brave young men. I am proud to be in the same army with you, and I salute you!"

The privates flushed with mixed pleasure and embarrassment as the commander of the Army of Northern Virginia snapped them a salute.

"And furthermore, gentlemen," said Lee, "I am making plans to have you honored by President Jefferson Davis and myself at a public ceremony held for this singular purpose at the Confederate capitol in Richmond. This is the kind of heroism that needs to be instilled in all the men of the Confederacy who wear the gray uniform."

Everett Nichols cleared his throat and said, "May I say something, General Lee?"

"Of course."

Nichols licked his lips nervously. "Sir, I'm sure I speak for my comrades here. We're pleasantly stunned that what we did on the battlefield today has gained such recognition from you, but we don't really deserve the public recognition you have planned. We…we're honored, but we're just plain Southern boys who simply did what we could to keep our major from getting killed."

Buford Hall and Chuck Carney nodded their agreement as Hank Upchurch said, "That's right, General. We're really not worthy. We—"

"Nonsense," cut in Lee. "You gentlemen are perfect examples of what Confederate soldiers ought to be. You *will* be honored with public recognition. You've earned it. When President Davis and I present you to the crowd of soldiers and civilians, you are going to have your moment of glory. I appreciate your humility, and I know it's genuine, but my mind is made up. And General Jackson knows that when I make up my mind to do something, there's no deterring me. Right, General?"

"Right, sir," said Jackson, smiling.

"I will set the date for the ceremony when I arrive in Richmond," said Lee. "I'll get in touch with you through Major Dayton. Now, you gentlemen go get yourselves some much needed and deserved rest."

The six men bade Lee good night and walked away slowly to accommodate Rance Dayton, who hobbled on his makeshift crutches. As they moved through camp, weaving around the men, animals, and equipment, Buford Hall said, "Major Dayton, we appreciate your bringing about this commendation."

"Fellas," Dayton said, "it would never have been done without General Jackson telling General Lee about it."

"General, sir," said Chuck Carney, "as Everett has already

stated, we really don't deserve this public commendation. But it will mean more to us than anything that has ever happened in our lives."

It was after midnight, and Stonewall Jackson was inside his tent, on his knees in prayer, when he heard the sounds of pounding horse's hooves and voices. Seconds later, a sentry stood outside his tent and said, "General Jackson, sir…"

"Yes," called the commander of II Corps, opening the flap.

"It's General Pendleton, sir," said the sentry. "He needs to see you."

Jackson looked past him and saw Pendleton's vague form in the shadows. "Come in, General."

When Pendleton stepped inside, he was out of breath. His words came in fits and starts.

"McClellan…the river…blue-clads got over…"

Not only had Major General McClellan crossed the Potomac to pursue the battered Confederates, he had been successful in capturing all of Pendleton's big guns. And he was heading toward the very spot where the Rebels had camped for the night.

Jackson's first thought was for General A. P. Hill and the Light Division. He hurried to find Hill, and within twenty minutes the Light Division was on its way to confront the Union soldiers.

Hill's rugged troops raced into withering, shattering artillery fire, but they kept moving forward, blasting away with their guns, determined to stop McClellan.

Before the sun appeared on the horizon, Hill's division had the Federals in the Potomac, scrambling for the other bank. The Confederates fired their muskets without mercy, downing one

Yankee after another, and soon the Potomac was clogged with blue-clad bodies.

The Confederates recaptured all but four cannons, lost 261 men, but saved their army. It was near total disaster for the Yankees.

McClellan didn't try it again.

Abraham Lincoln's private secretary, John Hay, entered his White House office early on Monday morning, September 22. He was at his desk at 7:50 when the door to the Oval Office opened, and the tall, gangly Lincoln appeared.

"Good morning, John," said the president, looking very tired. "Bring your note pad and come in."

Hay followed the president toward his desk and sat down in his usual chair. "Are you all right, Mr. President?" he asked. "You look as if you haven't slept."

"I didn't get much sleep last night, John, but I'm ready for you to make the announcement to the press."

"All right, sir," said the secretary, poising his pencil above the pad. "Which newspapers?"

"Both Washington papers, Baltimore's, New York's, Chicago's, and Boston's. Once they have it, the rest will pick it up, and the Southern newspapers will have it by Wednesday."

"All right, sir," Hay said with a nod, writing fast.

"And John, make sure they all understand that the Emancipation Proclamation comes on the heels of our Union victory on the banks of Antietam Creek last Wednesday, and that it's to take effect January 1."

"Yes, sir."

"And be sure the newspapers understand that the Proclamation is a fit and necessary war measure designed to suppress the Southern rebellion. My purpose is to deplete the

Southern manpower reserve in slaves. And you can add that I believe it will enhance the Union cause abroad. Especially in Great Britain."

"I'll get it right on the wire, Mr. President," said Hay, rising.

"Good. September 23 will be the big day for the newspapers to announce it all over the North." Lincoln glanced at the grandfather clock in the corner. "Now, General Halleck ought to be out there in your office waiting to see me."

Hay hastened to open the door and peer into the outer office. "Yes, sir. General Halleck is here."

Henry W. Halleck was Lincoln's general-in-chief of all the Union forces. Tough as harness leather and bullheaded, he was a short, stout man in his mid-fifties, with a built-in scowl. His coarse gray hair was always tousled. As soon as the door opened, he rushed through it and said, "Good morning, Mr. President. I appreciate your giving me a few minutes on this busy Monday."

Lincoln was already on his feet behind the desk. "Good morning to *you*, General. My time is your time when it comes to war matters. And I assume it is a war matter this morning."

Halleck took the chair John Hay had vacated and said, "I hope, sir, you have decided to put the Emancipation Proclamation on hold until you replace McClellan with a good man and we win us a decided victory."

Lincoln's lips pulled into a thin line as he sat down, resting his bony elbows on top of the desk. "As a matter of fact, General, I have Mr. Hay contacting the major Northern newspapers right now to let them know that as of tomorrow, I am announcing that the Proclamation will take effect January 1."

Halleck's face darkened. "Pardon me, Mr. President, but I think the announcement that you're going to free all the slaves would give a much stronger moral weight to the Union war effort if it came on the heels of a victorious battle. It would show we have the power to back it up."

"We *did* just have a victorious battle, General," said the president. "A week ago today."

Halleck snorted, running his hand over his mouth and nose. "Sir, I don't know how you can call what happened at Sharpsburg a victory. Tactically, at best, it was a stalemate."

"Not so in my estimation, General Halleck. Lee's withdrawal across the Potomac into Virginia transformed your tactical stalemate into a strategic victory for our side."

Halleck, who had been trying to talk the president into replacing McClellan for months, spoke bluntly. "You say that, even if that pint-sized would-be Napoleon couldn't so much as hold on to Pendleton's big guns, and he let Ambrose Hill's little handful drive him back into the river like a whipped dog with his tail between his legs?"

Lincoln eased back in his chair and rubbed his deep-set eyelids. "It was still a decided victory for the Union, because Robert E. Lee invaded Northern territory and was driven back to where he came from. Now, I didn't say I was happy with General ·McClellan's performance. As far as I'm concerned, he could've repelled Lee had he arrived at Sharpsburg earlier, before Lee had fortified his troops on the banks of the Antietam. General McClellan has once again demonstrated his lack of aggressiveness toward the enemy. If he hadn't been so slow getting his army to Sharpsburg, Lee's forces could have been vanquished once and for all right there."

"Well, sir," said the general-in-chief, "you've accused General McClellan of the 'slows' numerous times already. In my position, I have to know if you're going to keep putting up with it or are you going to do something about it?"

"You are aware, my friend," said Lincoln, "as are other men in high places in the United States government, that I'm having serious thoughts about relieving General McClellan of his command. I haven't been hasty to do so because I must choose wisely the man to replace him. The wrong choice could make things worse than they already are. At least General McClellan has the love and respect of his men, in spite of his 'slows.'"

Halleck ran stubby fingers through his tousled gray hair. "Yes, sir. I understand. But may I say with all due respect to you...while General McClellan is in command of the Army of the Potomac, we're wasting valuable time. If we don't hurry up and wipe the Rebel armies out, they'll wipe *us* out. I'm in no position to tell you what to do, but I certainly hope you make a decision soon."

On the same day the Emancipation Proclamation hit the headlines of the Northern newspapers, Dr. Hunter McGuire and Nurse Jodie Lockwood left Sharpsburg, Maryland, and went to Frederick, where Jodie had been working. There, they agreed on a December wedding.

Since General Stonewall Jackson had told McGuire to go to Richmond and meet him there, or learn where to find him, Jodie quit her job and went with Hunter. She would probably have lost her job anyway when it came out that she'd aided a Confederate doctor at the Antietam battle.

Hunter and Jodie made some visits south of the Mason-Dixon line, including a quick stop at the Jackson home in Lexington. They found the general at home and enjoyed meeting Mary Anna, who was expecting their first baby. General Jackson said he would be home a little while longer, then would go to Richmond. Hunter should wait for him at the army camp outside the city. If for some reason General Lee sent him elsewhere, he would wire Hunter at the camp and tell him where to join him.

Hunter and Jodie arrived in Richmond on September 29. Using his medical influence as chief physician of Stonewall Jackson's II Corps, Hunter was able to get Jodie a job at the large hospital in Richmond.

With this settled, he took her to a boardinghouse a block from the hospital, where many of the single nurses resided. She obtained a room, and Hunter carried up her little bit of luggage.

As he placed the luggage on the sofa, he said, "I've got to get myself to the army camp outside of town."

"You'll come and see me every opportunity you get, won't you?" she asked, walking him toward the door.

"I'll even *make* opportunities." Hunter took Jodie in his arms and kissed her tenderly. "I love you, Jodie."

"I love you too."

They kissed again, then Hunter stepped into the hallway. "I'll have to stick pretty close to the camp until Tom either shows up or I receive a wire telling me where to meet him. I'll visit you as much as I can, but I may have to go in a hurry. But before I leave Richmond, I'll let you know where I'm going."

Tears misted Jodie's eyes. "Oh, Hunter, I'll be so glad when this horrible war is over. When we get married I want us to be able to live a normal life."

He grinned. "I know what you mean, but a doctor who has his own practice doesn't exactly live a normal life."

Jodie stood on tiptoe, kissed him again, and said, "At least when you've got your own practice, we won't have to worry about cannonballs crashing through the roof."

THREE

On Wednesday evening, October 1, Pastor John Griffin of Richmond's First Baptist Church smiled as he looked across his desk at Hunter McGuire and Jodie Lockwood.

"Because of your positive testimonies as believers," he said, "it will be my pleasure to perform your marriage ceremony."

Hunter clasped Jodie's hand as he said, "This church comes highly recommended by many of the men at the army camp outside of town, Pastor. And if the kind of preaching we heard in the service tonight is any indication of what the folks hear around here on Sundays, we're going to feel right at home."

Griffin's smiled broadened. "Well, I preach the same truth whether it's the midweek service, Sunday morning, or Sunday night. I hope the Lord will lead you to put your membership here. I know that with this war going on, and your lives being so chaotic, it's hard to settle on anything. But we sure would love to have you be a part of us."

"Thank you, Pastor," said Hunter. "You're our kind of preacher, I'll tell you that." He glanced at Jodie and she nodded.

"We were both brought up on old-fashioned straight-from-the-shoulder Bible preaching, Pastor Griffin," said Jodie. "And I really liked what I heard tonight too. I love the way you exalted the Lord Jesus Christ."

"He deserves all the glory we can give Him, and a whole lot more, Miss Lockwood," said Griffin.

"Amen," said Hunter, rising from his chair and gently tugging Jodie's hand.

The preacher stood up with them and said, "I'll be willing to work with you on whatever date you set for the wedding. I realize your plans could be interrupted, no matter what date you set. But if that happens, we'll just make the necessary adjustments."

As he walked them to the door, the pastor said, "You might think about a date sometime near Christmas. Maybe both sides will decide not to fight at Christmastime."

"Thank you, Pastor," said Hunter. "We'll see you Sunday morning, Lord willing."

Late on Friday afternoon, Jodie walked past the receptionist's desk at Richmond's hospital after a hard day's work and told the girl at the desk that she would see her the next day. She was almost to the front door when it opened and the man she loved appeared.

"Hello, gorgeous," said Hunter with a big smile. "Busy day?"

Jodie let out a sigh. "Yes...but I feel refreshed now just seeing you."

"Aren't you sweet," he said, taking her hand and leading her toward the army wagon he'd borrowed at the camp.

"Is this visit an indication that you're about to leave Richmond?" Jodie asked. "Did you get a wire from General Jackson?"

"Yes. About an hour ago."

"Oh? Where will you meet him?"

"A place that will surprise you."

"Well, smarty, out with it. When are you leaving?"

"Depends on you."

Jodie looked perplexed. "Me? I don't understand."

"It all depends on whether you want to go with me or not. Because I'm not going unless you go with me."

They had reached the wagon, and as Hunter helped Jodie board, she said, "But you have to go wherever the general orders you to go. You've got me confused, Dr. McGuire."

"It's quite simple, really. You and I have received an invitation to the Jackson home."

"Really? Right away?"

"Yes," Hunter said, rounding the back side of the wagon. As he climbed aboard and took the reins, he said, "Tom's going to be home until a week from Monday, as far as he knows at this time. He and Mary Anna want us to come for whatever time we can between now and then. You start the midnight shift this Sunday night, if I remember correctly."

"Yes…"

"And you have Tuesday and Wednesday off?"

"Well, I don't actually go to work till midnight on Thursday."

Hunter put the horses in motion. "So, would you like to go stay with the Jacksons a couple of days?"

"Oh, I'd love it, Hunter! I really fell in love with Mary Anna when we were there before. Did the general say anything in the wire about how she's feeling?"

"No, but I'm sure that if she was having any trouble with her pregnancy, he wouldn't have invited us. He said in the wire that *they* wanted us to come."

"Wonderful! So what do we do next?"

"We'll go right now to the railroad station and get our tickets. Then I'll wire Tom and let him know the arrival time, and how long we can stay."

Jodie chuckled. "You know, I still have a hard time adjusting to you calling him Tom."

Hunter grinned as he guided the team around a corner and

headed for the depot. "Well, honey, even though I address him as General when we're in the presence of anyone other than Mary Anna or you, he's been Tom to me ever since I can remember. Though he's a few years older than I, we were the best of friends as boys. We did a lot of growing up together until the McGuires adopted me and took me to Boston."

"Yes. But he's such a great man, Hunter, and a magnificent soldier. I understand about you, but I could never call him by his first name."

Hunter chuckled. "Want to hear something?"

"What?"

"He told me outside the hospital tent at Sharpsburg that he hoped you would call him Tom whenever we were alone with him."

"He did?"

"Yes'm. He sure did."

Jodie blushed. "Hunter, I could never do it."

"Why not? We hadn't been at their house ten minutes the other time when Mary Anna told you not to call her Mrs. Jackson. You started calling her Mary Anna immediately."

"I know, but it's different with him. His position as major general, and the…well, the dignity he carries. I couldn't do it."

"It'll make him happy."

"And it'll make me uncomfortable."

Hunter purchased their tickets at the depot then drove her to the army camp, where he sent a wire to Stonewall Jackson to advise him they would arrive in Lexington at midafternoon on Tuesday and leave on Thursday morning.

Then they went for supper at the Capitol Café. They hadn't been seated long before they began to talk again about the Jacksons.

"Let's see now…Mary Anna's baby is due in December, isn't it?" Hunter asked.

"Yes. Unless her doctor has changed his mind about the due

date, it's to be the first week of December."

"Well, then, if we took Pastor Griffin's advice and set the wedding close to Christmas, she would no doubt be up to being your matron of honor."

"Mm-hmm. I was thinking the same thing. What about December 20? We agreed we should get married on a Saturday, and the twentieth is the last Saturday before Christmas."

"Strange how great minds run on the same track," he said, chuckling. "I was going to suggest the same thing to you. I was studying a calendar just this morning at the camp."

"Then December 20 it is," said Jodie, her eyes glistening with joy.

The waitress came and took their order and filled two cups with steaming coffee.

"On Sunday we'll talk to Pastor Griffin and tell him the date," Hunter said.

Jodie's smile reflected the joy she felt as she said, "The Lord has been so good to me, Hunter. All those years we were apart I kept praying that in His own way and in His own time He would let us find each other. Of course, I had to pray that He wouldn't let you fall in love with someone else, since you didn't even know how I felt about you."

"It was the same with me," Hunter said. "The Lord made you for me as sure as he made Eve for Adam. He already had it worked out. How would either of us have guessed He would use this awful war to bring us together?"

"We couldn't have guessed that, darling. But isn't it wonderful to serve the great God of the universe? He not only loved us enough to send His Son, but He also loves His children so much that He plans out their lives."

Hunter nodded. "That's why it behooves us to walk close to Him so we don't mess up His plans with some of our own. No Christian will ever go wrong if they walk close to Him."

Just then the waitress came with their food. As she was placing it on the table, Hunter said, "I'm so hungry I could eat a bear!"

"Sorry to disappoint you, sir," said the waitress, "but all you get in this place is the fried chicken you ordered. We don't cook bears here."

Hunter and Jodie laughed out of all proportion to the waitress's quip. It felt so good to let go after all the pain, misery, and death they had seen on the Antietam battlefield.

A storm was rolling in from the west, and it was beginning to rain in Richmond as Hunter and Jodie boarded the train for Lexington. Masses of inky clouds boiled overhead, driven by high winds, and a fork of white lightning flashed. Thunder followed like the booming of cannons.

Far to the east the sky was still clear, with shafts of orange light shooting up from the rising sun to touch the dark, encroaching clouds.

Inside their coach, Hunter guided his fiancée to a seat near the front and said, "There you go, sweetheart. You sit next to the window."

"I won't argue about that," said Jodie. "I want to get a good look at the Blue Ridge Mountains in this storm."

Hunter placed their hand luggage in the rack overhead and was just sitting down beside her when she pointed out the window at the Rebel soldiers boarding the train. Some were climbing on top of the cars. "I'm glad they always have soldiers on these trains, Hunter."

"Me too."

"But those poor men riding on top are going to get soaked."

"I guess that's part of the Jefferson Davis Protection Program," Hunter said, chuckling. "If these trains are going to be safe for civilians to ride, the army has to guard them, no matter what the weather."

Jodie nodded. Then, after a moment, she said, "I just wish the Yankees would all go back north where they belong and leave the Southerners alone. This war isn't accomplishing anything but getting a lot of good men on both sides killed or maimed. I don't believe the Southern plantation owners should be into slavery...not for a minute. But getting thousands and thousands of men killed over it isn't the answer. War is such a horrible thing."

"Can't argue with that," said Hunter. "War has been a blight on the human race ever since Cain declared war on Abel."

"Thank the Lord the day is coming when Jesus will return to earth and set up His kingdom and put an end to war," said Jodie.

"Won't that be wonderful! When the Prince of Peace reigns on earth, this battle-scarred old world will finally know real peace."

Jodie and Hunter noticed an elderly man being helped into the coach by the conductor and another man. The two men guided him to the seat across the aisle from them.

The old gentleman thanked the conductor, then the man with him said, "Now Grandpa, when you arrive in Amherst, Paul and Della will be there to meet you. Don't try to get off the train by yourself. Let Paul and this nice conductor help you, okay?"

"All right, Ronald," said the old man, whom Hunter guessed was somewhere in his late eighties.

"I'll look after him, sir," the conductor said.

Ronald thanked the conductor and left the coach. After a few seconds, the conductor exited the coach at the opposite end. The engine whistle blew.

Hunter crossed the aisle and leaned over the old gentleman. "Hello, sir," he said. "My name is Hunter McGuire. I'm a medical doctor."

The elderly man smiled and raised a shaky hand. As Hunter shook his hand, the old man said with quavering voice, "Are you the Dr. Hunter McGuire who heads up the medical staff for Stonewall Jackson's II Corps?"

Hunter nodded.

"Well, I'm proud to make your acquaintance, young man. My name is Grover Maddox. You know my grandson, Dr. Wayne Maddox."

"I sure do! He's one of my staff physicians in II Corps."

"Well, let me tell you, Wayne thinks the world of you. He's written home about you several times. In fact, I got a letter from him just a few days ago. He was telling me about the horror of that battle near Sharpsburg, Maryland. Pretty bloody, eh?"

"Yes, sir," said Hunter. "Well, I just wanted to let you know who I am, so that if you should need me on the trip, I'm right here to help."

"Thank you, Doctor." Grover Maddox glanced past Hunter. "This lovely lady your wife?"

"Not yet, sir. Her name is Jodie Lockwood. She's a certified medical nurse. We're getting married in December."

"Well, congratulations to both of you!"

"Thank you, sir," said Jodie, smiling at him warmly.

The train lurched, and Hunter grabbed the edge of the old man's seat. "So you're going to Amherst, Mr. Maddox?"

"Going to visit one of my granddaughters and her husband. I'll stay about a month. My wife, Sadie, died two years ago. Since I'm getting up in years, some of my family members take me into their homes for a month or so to spend some time with me."

"That's nice of them."

The train was rolling out of the station now, and as the conductor came through the front door, ready to punch tickets, two Confederate soldiers could be seen, rifles in hand, standing on the platform between cars.

Hunter sat down beside Jodie just as stark white lightning cracked through the black clouds. A roar of thunder vibrated the coach, and rain splattered the window, sending tiny rivulets down the panes.

The conductor walked to the rear of the coach, wheeled about, and worked his way forward. "Tickets, please!" he said. "Have your tickets ready!"

The train was at full speed by the time the conductor reached Grover Maddox. The old gentleman handed him his ticket with shaky fingers and then replaced it in his coat pocket after it was punched.

Jodie peered through the window, trying to see the beautiful Virginia countryside through the rain. Hunter watched her and then took her hand and leaned close, saying, "I love you."

She turned and met his gaze and whispered a response.

When Hunter glanced across the aisle toward Grover Maddox, then looked back to Jodie, she said, "Go ahead, darling. If you weren't here to do it, I would."

"The Holy Spirit's really running wild in my heart," he said.

"I'll be praying."

Hunter squeezed her hand and slipped across the aisle to sit next to Grover Maddox.

The old man turned to Hunter with a smile. "Some storm, eh?"

Hunter nodded. "Sure is. Mr. Maddox...you mentioned a few minutes ago that your wife died."

"That's right."

"I'd like to ask you a question, if I may?"

"Certainly."

"Mr. Maddox, when your time comes to die, do you know that you'll go to heaven?"

"Can't say that I do, son. Nobody can know for certain."

"Oh, but they can, sir. God says so in His Word."

Maddox licked his wrinkled lips. "You sound just like Sadie and some of my relatives, Doctor. Sadie was always telling me about Jesus being in her heart, and begging me to believe on Him. I believe in Jesus Christ, Doctor, but not like Sadie did. She was consumed with Him. Just like some of the other relatives...even the two I'm going to visit in Amherst—my granddaughter, Della, and her husband, Paul."

"What do you mean by *consumed*, Mr. Maddox?"

"Well, always going to church, and having friends in from the church for a hymn sing...talking about how wonderful it is to be saved and know you're going to heaven. That's just a crutch, Doctor. A shaky crutch. I say nobody can know whether they're going to heaven or hell until they die and stand before God at the judgment and find out if their good deeds outweigh the bad."

Hunter nodded. "Well, when you say you believe in Jesus, but not like your wife and some family members...what do you mean?"

"I believe He was a good man and did a lot of good for people when He was here on earth...and He looks down on us from heaven right now. But every person has to prove to Him that they deserve heaven in order to get in."

"So you do believe that Jesus rose from the dead after He was crucified, and He's in heaven right now?"

"Oh, sure."

"And you believe that He's more than just a good man. You believe that He's the virgin-born Son of God?"

"Sure. That's what the Bible says, doesn't it?"

"Yes, sir, it does. And it also says that Jesus came into the world for one purpose: to save sinners from hell. In order to do that He had to pay the price that God's holiness and justice demanded—a blood-shedding death as the sacrificial Lamb of God. Do you believe that?"

"Well-l-l...yes."

"And the same Bible says that you can know you're going to heaven when you die. You don't have to guess or wonder about it."

"Sadie did show me something about that, Doctor, but it just didn't fit with the way I believe it."

"Well, sir, what your wife believed is based on God's Word. On what do you base your belief?"

"On what I feel in my heart."

"Just a minute," Hunter said and stepped across the aisle to get his Bible out of a small overnight bag. He sat back down beside the older man and flipped some pages as he said, "Let me show you what God says about the human heart, Mr. Maddox, including yours."

Hunter turned to Jeremiah 17 and placed the Bible in the old gentleman's hands. "Can you read the print, sir?"

"Hold on," said Maddox, reaching in his shirt pocket. He took out a pair of half-moon spectacles, placed them on his nose, and hooked the wires behind his ears. "Now I can."

"All right. Read me verse 9, right there. This is what God says about the human heart."

Grover read the verse silently at first, then aloud, "'The heart is deceitful above all things, and desperately wicked: who can know it?'"

"All right, sir. According to the next verse, who does search the heart and know it?"

"God does."

"Since your heart, like mine, is deceitful above all things, is it capable of deceiving you?"

Maddox thought on it briefly, then said, "I suppose so."

"Will God deceive you, Mr. Maddox?"

"Well, of course not."

"Then, rather than listen to your heart, you ought to listen to God's Word. Shouldn't you?"

Another pause. "Ah…well, yes."

"That's what Sadie did, sir. Am I right?"

"Yes, she did."

"Then she did the right thing, didn't she?"

"Yes. I see that now."

"And I know for a fact that your grandson, Wayne, does the

same thing, sir. He and I have talked about it. He's a fine Christian man."

"That he is, Doctor."

Hunter flipped back to the book of 1 John, chapter 5. "I want you to see what God says about those who have believed on the name of His Son. Read me verse 13, Mr. Maddox. When God speaks of these things that have been written, He's talking about the Scriptures."

The old man read aloud: "'These things have I written unto you that believe on the name of the Son of God; that ye may know that ye have eternal life, and that ye may believe on the name of the Son of God.'"

"Do you understand, sir?" Hunter asked. "God says that He gave us the Scriptures so that we could learn of salvation in His Son and believe on His name. If we believe on His name the Bible way, He saves us, and we can know—not hope or think or wish—but *know* that we have eternal life while we're right here on earth."

The old man shook his head. "Why have I been so blind, Doctor? Sadie and many of my family tried to tell me this, but I just couldn't see it."

Hunter nodded encouragingly and said, "The Lord has to open our eyes to see the truth, Mr. Maddox. The psalmist wrote in Psalm 119, 'The entrance of thy words giveth light; it giveth understanding unto the simple.'"

Grover Maddox looked at Hunter with a new light in his eyes as he said, "Well, I see the light, and I've sure been simple. Now it comes back to me what Sadie and the others told me. To believe on the name of Jesus Christ is to believe that He is the one and only Saviour who does all the saving all by Himself, without human works or religious deeds, and to turn in repentance of my sin and unbelief and call on Him to save me."

"They've taught you well, sir. That's it!"

"I'm ready, Doctor. Will you help me?"

Jodie had been watching the scene as she prayed. Now she was wiping tears and thanking the Holy Spirit for working in Grover Maddox's heart.

When the old gentleman had finished calling on Jesus, Hunter prayed and asked the Lord to help him grow in his new Christian life.

Maddox, wiping tears from his cheeks, said, "What a fool I've been all these years, Dr. McGuire. If I had died as a fool, I would have gone to hell…and I would never have seen my precious Sadie again."

"That's right."

"But now that I'm saved, when I die I'll go to be with her in heaven! I'll see her and hold her again, Doctor!"

"That you will, sir," said Hunter, patting his arm.

"Thank you for talking to me, Dr. McGuire. Thank you!"

"It was my honor and pleasure, sir."

"I'm so happy for you, Mr. Maddox," came Jodie's voice nearby.

Both men looked up to see her standing beside them.

The train rolled westward, making a few stops along the way. Each depot had its share of gray-clad Rebel soldiers who stood sharp-eyed and alert.

The storm moved further eastward, and soon the rain stopped and the clouds broke up, letting the sun's rays shine through.

Jodie pressed her cheek to the window, trying to see if the rugged line of the Blue Ridge was in view yet.

"You should be able to see them pretty soon," Hunter said, "but instead of the storm, you'll see those mountains in sunshine."

"Either way is fine," she replied, glancing past him to Grover

Maddox, whose head was cushioned by a pillow as he leaned against the window with eyes closed. "Mr. Grover's had quite a nap."

Hunter glanced at the older man and nodded.

"Where is Amherst, Hunter? Will Mr. Maddox be getting off soon?"

"It's about ten miles this side of the Blue Ridge. Last depot before we enter the mountains and come out at Lexington on the other side. We should be in Amherst in about an hour and a half."

Jodie nodded and laid her head on his shoulder. "Wake me when we can see the mountains, will you, darling?"

"Sure."

Jodie was dreaming about their wedding when she felt Hunter's shoulder move and heard his voice. "Honey, I'm sorry to disturb you, but—"

"Oh, can we see the mountains now?" she asked, straightening on the seat and brushing stray locks of hair from her forehead. She pressed her cheek to the window.

"You'll be able to in a few minutes, but that's not why I woke you. I'm concerned about Mr. Maddox." Hunter stood up as he spoke. "His color doesn't look right."

Some of the passengers watched as Hunter eased onto the seat next to Grover Maddox and studied the elderly gentleman. He pressed his fingertips against the side of Maddox's neck. Jodie got up to stand beside him.

"Hunter, is he…?"

"Yes," Hunter said in a low tone. "He's dead."

FOUR

A few passengers heard Hunter McGuire's words. Some gasped, while others stared silently in shock.

"It appears to be heart failure," said Hunter, reaching for one of the blankets in the overhead rack. He quickly covered Maddox's head and face.

Jodie's eyes misted as she said, "I understand now why the Holy Spirit was pressing you so strongly, Hunter. He knew it was almost time for this dear old man to die, and He wanted you to talk with him before it was too late."

"Yes," said Hunter, fighting his own tears. "The message was clear to me to get to him right away." He drew a deep breath. "Well, bless his heart, he and Sadie are in each other's arms now and looking into the face of Jesus."

"Oh, yes. Thank the Lord!"

"Looks like we'll be the bearers of good news along with the bad," Hunter said. "Mr. Maddox said his granddaughter and her husband in Amherst are Christians. They tried to lead him to the Lord. At least we can tell them that before he took his last breath he called on Jesus to save him."

Someone had gone after the conductor, who drew up beside

Grover Maddox's seat, his eyes wide. He looked at Hunter and said, "I'm told Mr. Maddox just died, sir."

Hunter smiled as he replied, "Not really…he's just begun to live."

Mary Anna Jackson looked up at her tall, broad-shouldered husband as the train from Richmond chugged into the Lexington station. Her dark eyes flashed as she said, "It will be so good to see Hunter and Jodie again!"

"Yes. I'm glad for this respite in the fighting so that we could have them come."

The engine bell clanged as the big locomotive rolled to a halt and ejected a blast of steam. A moment later, passengers began to alight from the three cars. While the Jacksons watched for Hunter and Jodie to appear, the soldiers atop the cars stood up. One of them spotted the general and called out, "Hey, look! It's General Stonewall Jackson! Hello, General!"

Passengers who had stepped onto the platform smiled at the sight of the famous general waving at the soldiers.

"There they are, Tom!" exclaimed Mary Anna.

Stonewall saw Hunter and Jodie at the same time and took Mary Anna's hand, leading her toward them.

Hunter had jumped off the train and turned to help Jodie down the steps when Jodie spotted the Jacksons. The instant her feet touched the platform, she hurried to meet Mary Anna, whose arms were open wide. The two women embraced for a long moment, then Mary Anna embraced Hunter.

General Jackson grinned down at Jodie and said, "Well, if that quack doctor can hug my wife, I guess I can hug his wife-to-be!"

The four got into the Jacksons' buggy, and as they rode across town Jodie told them of Hunter leading Grover Maddox to the

Lord and of Maddox's death shortly thereafter. Both of the Jacksons marveled at the way God had orchestrated the event and praised the Lord that the old man became a Christian before going into eternity.

"Maddox..." said Jackson thoughtfully, as he held the reins. "Hunter, do you suppose he was any kin to Dr. Wayne Maddox?"

"He sure was, Tom. He was Wayne's grandfather."

"Well, what do you know! Wayne'll be plenty glad to learn that his granddaddy got saved, won't he."

Thomas and Mary Anna Jackson lived in a large two-story white frame house in Lexington near the Virginia Military Institute. Hunter was assigned a bedroom on the second floor, and Jodie's room was on the ground floor at the rear of the house.

After Hunter and Jodie had been given time to unpack their luggage, Mary Anna served coffee in the parlor. The couples sat on love seats that faced each other over a large oak coffee table.

"Does your doctor still say the baby is due the first week of December, Mary Anna?" asked Hunter.

"Yes, and I can hardly wait!"

"And I'm praying hard there will be no complications," said the general.

Mary Anna smiled at her husband and took his hand. To Hunter, she said, "I imagine Tom told you about Ellie."

"Yes," Hunter said, nodding, "but Jodie doesn't know."

"What's that?" asked Jodie. "Who's Ellie?"

"Tom's first wife," said Mary Anna.

"Oh. I wasn't aware..."

"Ellie died in childbirth," said Mary Anna. "And the baby—a boy—was stillborn. That's why Tom's a bit on edge with me having a baby."

"I can understand that," said Jodie.

"I've been taking it to the Lord in prayer," Jackson said.

"There's another similarity in the story, Jodie," said Mary Anna. "Ellie was the daughter of a Presbyterian preacher, as I am. I think in the back of Tom's mind he fears that the loss of his preacher's-daughter wife and their baby will be repeated with this preacher's-daughter wife and *our* baby."

Hunter looked at his lifelong friend. "What are you hoping for, Tom? A boy or a girl?"

"It really doesn't matter. I just want Mary Anna and the baby to come through the birth with no complications."

Jodie sipped her coffee, then said, "Have you picked out names?"

Mary Anna glanced at her husband and smiled. "Yes, we have. We've agreed that if it's a boy, we'll name him after Tom's father, whose name was Jonathan."

"I know that Jonathan is your middle name, General," said Jodie. "So, of course, you were named after your father."

"Not in the usual sense," said Jackson. "Actually, my parents didn't give me a middle name. I gave it to myself a few years ago in honor of my father. He died back in 1836."

"Oh. That was a beautiful thing to do, General."

"He was a great man, Jodie. And while I'm thinking of it, I told Hunter to tell you to call me Tom."

Jodie's features tinted as she flicked a sidelong glance at Hunter and saw him grin. She cleared her throat. "Umm…General Jackson, sir, I really don't think I can do that. I hold you in the highest esteem. And…you being a major general and all, I'd feel that I was being audacious to call you by your first name."

Jackson studied her for a moment. "Even if I say I would *like* for you to call me Tom? That since you're engaged to marry the best friend I have in this world, it gives you a special place in my life, and I *want* us to be on a first-name basis?"

Jodie glanced at her fiancé again. Hunter appeared to be enjoying the moment.

"I know, sir. But…well, you've been called General Robert E. Lee's right arm. By the general himself. Such dignity behooves me to call you *General.*" After a few seconds' pause, she said, "I know! How about when I become your best friend's wife, and my name is Jodie McGuire? I'll start calling you by your first name then."

"Promise?" said Jackson, grinning broadly.

Jodie smiled and said, "Let's just say it's a pending possibility."

The general shrugged. "Well, I guess that's better than a flat no."

Mary Anna and Hunter laughed, then Mary Anna said, "Anyway…if our baby should be a girl, Tom and I have agreed to name her after his mother—Julia—who died in 1831."

"I like that name," said Jodie. "It's beautiful, and so feminine."

The general rose and poured more coffee around. Mary Anna watched him for a moment then said, "Have you two set a date for the wedding?"

"Indeed, we have," replied Hunter. "Saturday, December 20, unless the war interferes."

"Will it be in Richmond?"

"Yes, ma'am. At First Baptist Church."

"First Baptist?" said Jackson. "I knew Hunter's adoptive parents were Baptists and they would raise him to be Baptist. Is that your case too, Jodie?"

"Yes, sir," said Jodie, catching the impish gleam in the general's eye. "The people who raised me were also Baptists."

The general shook his head. "What a shame. You two ought to straighten up and become Presbyterians. At the very least you should get married in a Presbyterian church."

Jodie flipped her hair back with a toss of her head and said, "But General, our new pastor's name is John Griffin. Hunter and I will be married by John the Baptist."

Mary Anna giggled, and Jackson laughed heartily and came back with, "Well, *our* pastor's name is John—John Brooks."

Jodie crinkled her nose and said, "But where in the Bible did you ever read of John the Presbyterian?"

Hunter guffawed as Jackson's smile disappeared.

Mary Anna laughed and clapped her hands together. "Tom, you may be the Presbyterian deacon here, and you may be the Army of Northern Virginia's general most famous for maneuvering forces in combat, but this little Baptist nurse just outmaneuvered you!"

"Jodie, I could use you at my side on the battlefield!" the general said.

"If they'd let women do that, Tom," said Mary Anna, "we'd whip the socks off those Yankees in no time and end the war!"

When the laughter subsided, Hunter said, "Tom, I have an important question to ask you."

"Sure," said the general, draining his coffee cup and setting it back in the saucer.

Hunter scooted to the edge of his seat and rested his elbows on his knees. With a gleam in his eyes, he said, "I want you to be best man in the wedding."

"I'm deeply honored, my friend," Tom said. "I...I'm at a loss for words."

"How about, 'Yes, Hunter, I'll be best man in your wedding'?"

The general got an impish look in his eyes again and said, "I'll be happy to be your best man, Hunter *if* they'll allow a Presbyterian deacon inside a Baptist church!"

"I hadn't thought of that, Tom. Guess I'll have to check with John the Baptist Griffin and see if he'll let Thomas the Presbyterian Jackson stand on his platform!"

"Well, he'd better!" Jodie said. "Because the lady I want to be my matron of honor is not only a Presbyterian preacher's daughter, but she's married to a Presbyterian deacon named Stonewall Jackson!"

Mary Anna blinked hard. "Jodie! Really? You want *me* to be your matron of honor?"

Jodie rose from the love seat and leaned over to hug Mary Anna. "I sure do! *Will* you?"

"Oh, yes! I'm thrilled and honored! The baby's due at least two weeks before the wedding date. I should be back to full strength by then."

Jodie gave her another squeeze. "Thank you," she said softly, and kissed Mary Anna's temple.

Hunter watched Jodie return to sit beside him, and said to the Jacksons, "Of course, like I said, it'll be December 20 unless the war interferes."

"Never know about the Yankees," said Jackson, "but if they're willing to ease off fighting at Christmastime, we certainly will too. Even if you have to postpone it until we have another break in fighting, like we're enjoying right now, Mary Anna and I will very happily take part in your wedding."

"It's all in the Lord's hands," said Jodie. "We'll leave it there and trust Him to work it according to His plan."

"Amen," said the general.

"I've written my adoptive parents in Boston," Hunter said. "I told them I finally found Jodie and that we're getting married on December 20, the Lord willing. There hasn't been time enough to hear back from them—*if* the letter even got through—but I'm sure if it did, they'll come unless travel into the South is restricted from Northern civilians."

"That changes on both sides quite often," said Jackson. "Just like getting the mail through. Depends on how things are going for either side at the time. I sure would enjoy seeing the McGuires again."

"And I'd love to meet them," said Mary Anna.

"Me too," Jodie said with a chuckle, "since they're going to be my in-laws!"

Tom Jackson leaned back and looked up at the ceiling. "I'll never forget the day Dr. Jason McGuire and his wife showed up in our little town," he said.

"Nor will I," said Hunter. "They were willing to take this poor little orphan boy, raise him, educate him, and give him a happy life. They're wonderful people."

"So you became a medical doctor because your adoptive father was one, is that it?" asked Mary Anna.

"Yes, ma'am. He's the best. I had the greatest example to follow."

"And I'm sure he's proud of you."

"Yes, ma'am. That he is. And so's Mom."

"We had some marvelous times as boys," said Tom. "Even though I was a few years older than Hunter, we were great friends."

Hunter laughed. "Except when I sneaked up on you a couple times when you thought you were alone with your girlfriend. What was that one girl's name?"

"Cancel that memory," Tom said, chuckling.

Mary Anna gave a mock scowl, and Jodie laughed.

"Okay. New subject," said Hunter. "Tom...any ideas on what the Yankees are going to do next? Now that they've driven us out of Northern territory?"

"General Lee wired me yesterday. Word from Confederate spies in Washington is that Lincoln's about to send McClellan's army on a march toward Richmond. General Lee has beefed up security around the city, and he has scouts on alert. I was already scheduled to go there on Friday, but General Lee especially wants me there with my Corps in case McClellan shows his face on the Virginia border. He also wants me there because on Saturday he and President Davis are having that special public meeting at the army camp to honor the four young heroes of the Eighteenth North Carolina."

Jodie nodded her approval as Hunter said, "Ah, yes. The men

from Major Rance Dayton's hometown who so gallantly saved his life at Sharpsburg."

"Tell me about it," said Mary Anna.

Some of the liveliness went out of Mary Anna's face as she listened to her husband tell of the young men from North Carolina who saved their wounded major. Her voice quavered slightly as she said, "And President Davis and General Lee are going to have a special public meeting to honor them?"

"That's right, honey. Of course there will be a posthumous commendation for Billy Dean Baxter."

"I think that's wonderful. Those have to be very brave young men."

"That they are. President Davis and General Lee want to honor them in front of as many military personnel and civilians as they can muster for the occasion…to let our men in uniform know what kind of soldiers they should strive to be."

"I'll be working the midnight shift," said Jodie to Hunter, "so I'll be free to attend the ceremony. I really would like to see it."

"Me too," said Hunter. "This should bolster the morale of the entire Army of Northern Virginia. I expect President Davis and General Lee hope it will instill a greater desire in the hearts of all our men to redouble their efforts to win this war."

Tom let out a huge sigh, then said, "The Lord knows we need something to help us overcome the horrible losses we suffered at Sharpsburg. I don't know where the next big battle will take place, but we'd better win it decisively. Even the morale building can't carry us if we have the kind of losses we experienced in Maryland."

Mary Anna gave her shoulders a small shake, as if shrugging off a weight, then said, "Won't it be wonderful when Jesus comes back to earth to establish His kingdom? Just think of it. No more war!"

Jodie glanced at Hunter and then back at the Jacksons and said, "We were saying the same thing on the trip over here."

"Well, amen," the general said. "I'll say it with the apostle John at Patmos…'even so, come, Lord Jesus!'"

*****

General McClellan's diminutive form was highly recognizable as he rode up Pennsylvania Avenue toward the White House, flanked by eight cavalrymen. One of the riders was Brigadier General Alfred Pleasonton, commander of the Cavalry Division of the Union Army of the Potomac.

At the entrance to the White House grounds, the guards saluted and swung open the gate. The guard in charge said, "Welcome, General McClellan, sir! President Lincoln advised us through his personal secretary that you would be arriving at 9:45 this morning." He smiled as he said, "You are precisely on time, sir. Welcome to the White House."

"Thank you, Corporal," said McClellan.

"I'll lead you to the front door, sir. Mr. Hay didn't tell me these other men would be seeing the president."

"No...and they won't. General Pleasonton and his men have come along as my escorts. Never know when some Confederate spy might decide to do a little sniping."

"You can't be too careful, sir," responded the guard. "If you'll follow me..."

McClellan and the others stayed in their saddles until they reached the front portico of the White House. When two stern-faced guards stepped forward from their posts at the door, the gate guard said to them, "Only General McClellan is to see Mr. Lincoln. General Pleasonton and his men will be seated in the reception room to await the general's return."

As McClellan and the others dismounted, the guard who had escorted them said, "Your horses will wait in the barn across the street, General McClellan. It will only take a few minutes for us to return them to you when you're finished."

McClellan thanked the man, and one of the door guards opened the front door to allow them inside. The other door guard stepped in behind the group and pointed out presidential secretary John Hay, who was coming across the vestibule.

"Mr. Hay is here to escort you to the president's office, General McClellan," he said. "General Pleasonton, sir, if you and your men will follow me…"

John Hay drew up to General McClellan and shook his hand. "Mr. Lincoln appreciates promptness, General. He'll be glad to see you even a few minutes before ten o'clock."

Moments later, Secretary Hay ushered General McClellan into the Oval Office.

Lincoln rose from behind his desk, his gaunt figure reminding the general of some of the Union men he'd seen who had spent time in Southern prison camps. The president's deep-set eyes seemed even deeper than before, and his cheeks a little more sunken.

McClellan held his campaign hat under his left arm and saluted. "Good morning, Mr. President."

"Good morning, General. Please sit down."

When both men were seated, Lincoln said, "General McClellan, I won't spend a lot of time rehashing my disappointment when you didn't pursue General Lee and his army as they ran back to Virginia."

"Yes, sir," said Little Mac, his features stoic.

"I sent for you because I believe—as does General Halleck— that we need to strike hard and fast at Lee's army before they can rebuild their forces. My spies below the Mason-Dixon line tell me that Lee is running low on ammunition as well as morale. We must hit them full force before they replenish their ammunition supply, and before they get over the losses they incurred at Antietam."

"I agree, sir," said McClellan.

"Good. Then this meeting will be quite brief. To put it succinctly, General, I want you to take your army across the Potomac as soon as possible and give battle to the enemy. I want Richmond captured. That will end the war. Let's get it done. We outnumber

Johnny Reb almost two to one. We have more horses, mules, wagons, guns, ammunition, and experienced army officers. Win the war for the North, General."

At the tone of finality in Lincoln's voice, McClellan rose from his chair, saluted the president, and said, "It's been nice to see you, sir."

Lincoln rounded the desk, towering over the general by twelve inches. As they walked toward the door, he laid a hand on McClellan's shoulder and said, "Now, General, this time I want action. No more slows. Understood?"

As the president opened the door for him, McClellan nodded his assent, passed through the outer office, and disappeared into the hallway.

Abraham Lincoln drew in a deep breath and let it out slowly through his nostrils. As John Hay stepped up beside him, he said, "I don't know, John. Somehow I don't think I've gotten the message across to him yet."

FIVE

★

Southern newspapers had announced the commendation ceremonies several days in advance, and loyal Southerners came from miles around to honor the five young privates of the Eighteenth North Carolina Regiment.

The Virginia countryside looked golden beneath the sun's bright rays as thousands of people gathered at the army camp a mile north of the Confederacy's capital city. White cottony clouds, rambunctious in a light westerly wind, made a drifting patchwork of light and shadow over the land.

Near the grassy spot where a portable wooden platform was set up, a creek meandered among towering oaks, elms, and evergreens, its dappled surface sparkling in the bright sunlight.

The ceremony was scheduled to begin at 2:00 P.M. sharp. At 1:50, a military band next to the platform began playing rousing Southern songs while soldiers and civilians gathered, most of them sitting on the grass.

The newly designed Confederate flag—one flag at each corner of the platform—flapped in the wind.

Most of the high-ranking officers of the Confederate Army of Northern Virginia were in attendance. On the platform with

President Jefferson Davis were Generals Robert E. Lee, Thomas J. Jackson, James Lane (commander of the North Carolina Brigade within II Corps), and James Longstreet (commander of I Corps), along with Major Rance Dayton and the four young privates to be honored.

Also on the platform—at Stonewall Jackson's request—was his close friend, Presbyterian evangelist B. Tucker Lacy, whom Jackson had appointed Chaplain General of II Corps.

A delegation from Fayetteville, North Carolina, including family members of the honorees, was seated on the ground directly in front of the platform.

At precisely 2:00 P.M., under the eyes of some twenty thousand spectators, President Davis stepped to the center of the platform. The band was just finishing a snappy song, and when the music faded, Davis raised his hands to quiet the crowd and gave a few opening remarks.

This was followed by cheers and applause, but when the band struck up Daniel D. Emmett's "Dixie," the crowd came to its feet. When the song ended, everyone cheered, prodding the band to play the song again. They remained on their feet as the band played out the last notes, and President Davis called Chaplain Lacy forward to open the meeting in prayer.

Lacy's voice carried strongly as he thanked God for the reason they were assembled. He asked the Lord to give special comfort to the Baxter family, who had lost their loved one during the gallant rescue.

After the amen, Lacy returned to his seat, and President Davis introduced Major General Thomas J. "Stonewall" Jackson, who gave testimony of what he had seen on September 17 on the battlefield near Sharpsburg, Maryland. When Jackson was finished, he called Rance Dayton to address the crowd. The soldiers and civilians applauded and cheered as Dayton limped to the center of the platform.

"Mr. President, General Robert E. Lee, honored military leaders…I thank you for making this day possible. And ladies and gentleman, I thank you for honoring, by your presence, five of the bravest young men you will ever meet. In a moment, we'll introduce them to you. But first let me say that I would not be here today if it weren't for these men who put their lives on the line…and one of those men gave up his life. I count it an honor to command these men in battle, and I count it the highest honor to also call them friends."

Dayton proceeded to tell in graphic detail the story, holding the crowd spellbound. When he came to the part about Private Billy Dean Baxter's death, his composure faltered. As he spoke in a broken voice of the fine young soldier Baxter had been, and that he would never forget Billy Dean's willing sacrifice, all eyes went to the Baxter family. They wept openly, flooded by pride and sorrow.

When Dayton finished the story, he turned to the four young heroes and said, "Ladies and gentlemen, it is now my privilege to introduce to you Privates Everett Nichols, Hank Upchurch, Buford Hall, and Chuck Carney. Come forward, gentlemen!"

The young men, somewhat embarrassed by all the attention, made their way to the center of the platform and stood with their commander.

The crowd rose to its feet as one, and the roar of voices and applause, along with the blaring horns of the band, grew deafening. The "fearless four," as they had been dubbed by their fellow soldiers, humbly accepted the glory showered on them.

Then Dayton introduced Brigadier General James Lane, who eloquently praised the courage of the five young privates. "The gallantry of these men is a supreme example to all the soldiers in the Confederate armies. I am proud to wear the same gray as Privates Everett Nichols, Hank Upchurch, Buford Hall, Chuck Carney, and Billy Dean Baxter."

As soon as Lane sat down, General Robert E. Lee gave a speech about heroism, explaining that what the five young soldiers had done, in his estimation, was the epitome of courage and self-sacrifice.

President Davis joined Lee as the general called for Billy Dean's father to come to the platform. Together, Davis and Lee presented Baxter a written posthumous commendation for Billy Dean.

Jodie clung to Hunter's arm as tears rolled down her cheeks, and the sound of weeping could be heard all through the crowd.

As soon as President Davis and General Lee presented written commendations to the four other young men, General Stonewall Jackson came forward again. The crowd grew momentarily quiet as Jackson told the honorees that each was being promoted to corporal. Then turning to the crowd, he said, "Ladies and gentlemen, I present to you the South's four 'lions of notability'!"

When Jackson started to follow the newly promoted corporals to their seats, General Lee said, "Wait a moment, General Jackson. While these other gentlemen take their seats, I want you to remain." He then called for President Davis and General Longstreet to join them.

"Ladies and gentlemen," said President Davis, "as you are about to see, this meeting actually has a double purpose. I have asked General Robert E. Lee to explain."

Lee smiled at his two generals, then turned to the crowd and said, "As all of you know, Major General James Longstreet and Major General Thomas Jackson are two of the finest men who ever wore a Confederate uniform. They are heroes themselves, in every sense of the word. What I'm about to say will take these two fine gentlemen by surprise. President Davis and I have created a new rank for these two generals. They have both been major generals for some time, but they're now being promoted to the rank of lieutenant general.

"The word *lieutenant* has several meanings. One of those meanings is 'representative' or 'aide-de-camp.' In this sense, President Davis and I are promoting these fine soldiers to lieutenant general as aide-de-camps to myself and as my personal representatives before the Confederate states and the Confederate armies."

As the zealous throng lifted its loudest ovation yet, the band once again played "Dixie." This time it could hardly be heard for the tumult of the crowd.

When the crowd began to disperse, General Lee slipped up to Longstreet and Jackson and told them to come meet with him immediately.

Minutes later, when they were seated in his tent, Lee said, "Gentlemen, just before noon I received word from our leading spy in the capitol in Washington. He tells me that Lincoln has given McClellan strict orders to begin a move on Richmond."

"Do you suppose the move will actually begin immediately, sir?" asked Longstreet.

Lee chuckled. "Well, not unless old Abe has somehow been able to change Little Mac's philosophy of warfare. However, since there's no way to know that, we will proceed with maneuvers to block the attempt to move on our capitol. I jotted down a few notes right after receiving the message. Here's what we'll do...."

On Wednesday morning, October 15, John Hay was at his desk in the White House, writing letters for the president, when General-in-Chief Henry Halleck came through the doorway from the hall.

"Good morning, General Halleck," said Hay.

Halleck's scowl showed that it was anything but a good morning as far as he was concerned. "Unh," he grunted. "Mr. Lincoln is expecting me."

"Yes, sir," said Hay, rising from his chair.

Halleck followed Hay to the Oval Office door and waited for the secretary to announce his presence.

Lincoln stood up behind his desk as Halleck entered, took one look at his face and said, "General, you look like I feel."

"Good," said Halleck. "Maybe if both of us get angry at the same time, we'll get something done about little molasses-blood McClellan. Sir, I have never known a man to be so slow."

Lincoln shook his head and sat down. "I haven't either, General. It was a week ago today that I told him to move his army toward Richmond *immediately.* Instead of offering battle, he's offering excuses."

"Such as?"

"I sent him a message on Monday, asking what was delaying him moving across the Potomac." Lincoln picked up a wrinkled sheet of paper and scooted it across the desk to Halleck. "Look at his reply."

Halleck read the message, raised his bushy eyebrows, and met Lincoln's gaze. "His horses are fatigued and must rest before crossing the Potomac to move on Richmond? Mr. President, this is absurd."

Lincoln nodded and handed him a slip of paper. "This is my reply, General. It's going to him by messenger in about thirty minutes."

Halleck smiled as he read the president's words:

Major General George B. McClellan, Field Commander
Camp Headquarters, Union Army of the Potomac

My dear sir, will you pardon me for asking what the horses of your army have done since the Battle of Antietam that fatigues anything?

A. Lincoln

Halleck chuckled. "I'd like to see the general's reply, sir."
"You shall. That is, if I get one."

At the federal camp on the north bank of the Potomac River, a few miles outside of Washington, Major General McClellan was standing outside his tent in conversation with Major Generals John Sedgwick and George G. Meade when a messenger galloped in and slid from his saddle.

"General McClellan, sir," the messenger said as he saluted, "I'm sorry to disturb you, but I have a message for you from President Lincoln."

"Excuse me, gentlemen," said McClellan, turning slightly to look the messenger in the eye. "No disturbance, Corporal. You're just doing your duty."

"Yes, sir." He handed McClellan a sealed envelope. "I've been instructed to await your reply in writing, sir."

"Of course," said McClellan with a smile, ripping open the envelope. "You wait right here."

McClellan turned to Sedgwick and Meade. "We'll take up the subject at another time, gentlemen. Right now, I must attend to the president's message."

McClellan entered his tent and scanned the piece of paper. As he read, his face paled. Then he quickly turned to his crude, portable desk, took out a sheet of paper, and dipped a pen in the inkwell to write:

President Abraham Lincoln
White House
Washington D.C.

My dear Mr. President,
Our horses are doing better, and I am now beginning preparations to make a sustained march on Richmond. We should have an unconditional surrender from the enemy within a few weeks.

Respectfully,
Maj. Gen. George B. McClellan
Field Commander, Union Army of the Potomac

President Lincoln and General Halleck waited in Washington for news of McClellan's move across the Potomac River into Virginia. Finally, at dawn on Sunday morning, October 26, the Army of the Potomac began the crossing.

By nightfall, all the troops, guns, and wagons were across, and they camped on the south bank.

McClellan was eating breakfast in his tent at dawn when his aide, Corporal Leonard Smith, called from outside, "General McClellan, sir. I have Lieutenant Roger Malloy from General Alfred Pleasonton's First Cavalry Division out here. General Pleasonton asked that you see the lieutenant immediately upon his arrival."

The previous night, just after midnight, McClellan had sent Pleasonton's division of the cavalry corps farther south as scouts.

McClellan greeted Malloy and said, "I assume no campfires were seen, or I would have heard last night."

Malloy saluted. "We saw no campfire, General, but at first light we caught sight of a massive force of Rebels spread across what would be our path to Richmond. General Pleasonton asked that you ride down immediately and take a look for yourself."

An hour later, McClellan returned to the Union camp and called all of his Corps commanders together. Standing before them, he said, "Gentlemen, south of here, about four miles, is a massive force of Rebels ready to greet us with heavy artillery and a well-fortified infantry. I saw it with my own eyes."

Major General Oliver Howard, commander of XI Corps, voiced the question that was in everyone's mind. "We *are* going to meet them head-on, whip them, and go on to Richmond, aren't we, sir?"

McClellan rubbed his jaw nervously. "No, we're not, General Howard. Bobby Lee has quite strongly interposed his army between us and Richmond, and I'm fearful that our men are still so low in morale from our devastating losses at Antietam that they're not ready to attack such a well-situated bastion. It is my decision that at this time we must pull back across the Potomac."

"What?" Abraham Lincoln gasped as he read a message handed to him by John Hay. "This is preposterous! Get General Halleck over here right away!"

In less than twenty minutes, General Halleck stood in Lincoln's office reading the message from General McClellan.

"So Little Napoleon figures his men are too low in morale, eh?" Halleck said. "Maybe. Or is it, Mr. President, that General McClellan is too low in courage to charge into the jaws of enemy artillery?"

Lincoln ran splayed fingers through his hair. "I don't understand it, General. When General McClellan has a mind to fight, he is unequaled in leading an army into battle. But this— I'm at a loss for words."

"Well, sir," said Halleck, "since I'm being paid to serve as your number-one military advisor, my advice is: Get rid of McClellan. If you don't, we're going to lose this war."

On November 5, 1862, Abraham Lincoln issued orders for Major General George Brinson McClellan to be relieved of his command. Much to the surprise of General-in-Chief Henry Halleck and the men of the Union Army of the Potomac, Lincoln appointed Major General Ambrose E. Burnside in his place.

Two days later, Halleck appeared in John Hay's office, asking for a meeting with the president.

"I'm sorry, General Halleck," said Hay, "but the president isn't in his office at this time."

"I see. All right, when will he be in so I can see him?"

"Probably not until tomorrow morning, sir. Mrs. Lincoln is quite ill with influenza, and the president is at her bedside."

"Oh. Well, I'm sorry to hear that," said Halleck.

"I will let Mr. Lincoln know you want to see him, General, and unless you hear differently, you will have the first appointment tomorrow morning."

The next morning, Halleck was ushered into the Oval Office by Hay, and a weary Abraham Lincoln said, "Sorry I couldn't see you yesterday, General, but Mary really needed me. I consider myself a husband and a father before I am president of the United States."

Halleck managed a tight smile. "I can appreciate that, sir. Is Mrs. Lincoln doing better?"

"Yes. Her fever has come down, and she's much better today."

"I'm glad to hear it."

Lincoln leaned forward, placed his elbows on the desk, and asked, "What did you need to see me about?"

"We've got a real problem, sir—your appointment of General Burnside in McClellan's stead. There is an undercurrent of dissatisfaction among our military leaders over it. As you well know, Mr. President, none will dare openly question your wisdom in this, but the man is a known loser. Our military leaders feel that we're worse off now than with McClellan. And I have to be honest, sir. I agree with them."

Lincoln eased back in his chair but didn't reply.

Taking advantage of the silence, Halleck said, "Word is, sir, that General Burnside told you he's incapable of leading an army the size of ours. Is this true?"

Lincoln nodded. "Yes, it's true."

"And you still made him field commander?"

"Yes. General Burnside is a good man, General Halleck…and a bit humble."

"But sir, if he doesn't even have confidence in himself to command the Army of the Potomac, how can *you* have confidence in him?"

"Like I said, he's a good man. And you must admit that everybody likes him."

"Yes, General Burnside is a kindly, unselfish man with a gentle nature, and he definitely is liked amongst his peers. But his fellow officers cringe at the thought of him in charge of their army. Are you aware, Mr. President, that when traveling to the war in Mexico, General Burnside lost his traveling money to a Mississippi riverboat gambler? Do you know that after the Mexican War, he lost his entire fortune in a financial venture, which to any thinking man had the marks of failure from the beginning?"

"No. I had not heard these things," said Lincoln.

Halleck inched closer to the edge of his chair. "The crowning embarrassment was his wedding ceremony. When the minister asked the bride, 'Do you take this man to be your lawfully wedded husband,' she said 'No' and walked out of the church, leaving him standing there in front of hundreds of people. Mr. President, the man is a born loser. And you know that while serving under McClellan at South Mountain and Antietam, he made some inexcusable blunders."

Lincoln sighed. "Yes, I know that. But he's the best man I have to replace McClellan."

"But sir, what about General Porter? Or General Sumner? Or General Meade?"

"I considered them…along with Generals Franklin and Hooker."

"General Franklin would be good, sir…or Sumner, Meade, or Porter. I would suggest you consider one of them."

Lincoln shook his head. "No, General. My decision has been made, and I am sticking to it unless and until General Burnside actually proves himself incapable. I can't change horses in midstream, as they say. General Burnside has already begun preparing his army to launch an offensive that both he and I believe will ultimately take us to victory at Richmond."

SIX

At the camp near the Rappahannock River, where General Lee had established his bastion against encroachment by the Federal troops, revival spirit was in progress. Dr. Joseph C. Stiles, chaplain of I Corps, had been invited by Lieutenant General "Stonewall" Jackson and Chaplain Lacy to preach an old-fashioned camp meeting to the entire Army of Northern Virginia. Though attendance at the preaching services was not mandated by General Lee, most of the men attended faithfully.

Jackson, Lacy, and Dr. Hunter McGuire served as counselors at the close of the sermon each night and had the joy of leading a great number of soldiers to Jesus Christ.

After one such service, Stonewall Jackson was sitting on a chair near the altar. He had his Bible open, and by the light of a nearby campfire he was writing notes from Stiles's sermon in the margins.

Nearby, a cluster of infantrymen stood around a young sergeant named Ryan Colston, who was known to be a blatant unbeliever.

Something Colston had just said caught Stonewall's attention, and he rose from the chair, Bible in hand, and headed toward the group.

With a sneering laugh, Colston said, "What kind of a God would put people in hell? Huh? Can you guys tell me that?"

The others saw Jackson's approach but didn't let on.

Suddenly, from behind the mocker, came the general's strong, deep voice: "The kind who hates sin and will not have it in His presence in heaven, Sergeant."

Colston whirled around at the sound of the familiar voice. He had the grace to blush as he stammered, "Wh-what's that, sir?"

"You just asked a question—what kind of a God would put people in hell. I answered your question. The kind of God who hates sin and will not let it into heaven."

Colston felt a trickle of sweat start to roll down his forehead. "Well, no offense, General," he said, "but I don't believe in hell. Nobody can convince me that such a place exists."

"God will convince you."

"What's that, sir?"

"I said God will convince you. The choice of how He does it is up to you. You can allow Him to convince you by His Word…or when you die and wake up in the flames of hell. Problem with the latter is it's too late to do anything about it."

"Again, no offense intended toward you personally, General," said Colston, "but it's my belief that God is going to take everybody into heaven."

"Based on what?"

Colston thought on it, then replied, "Based on my belief that God is good, kind, and loving."

"Mm-hmm. What would you think about a judge who has a convicted murderer standing before him. The judge's duty is to pass sentence on the man for his vile crime. But the judge smiles sweetly and says, 'Mr. Jones, I know you've been convicted of murdering your neighbor's three children, but I'm going to release you. You see, Mr. Jones, I am a good, kind, and loving judge, and

I just couldn't be so unkind as to send you to the gallows for your crimes. When you go back out there in society, you try to be a better man.' What about that judge, Sergeant? What would you think of him, turning the killer loose so he could snuff out more innocent lives?"

Colston licked his lips. "I…uh…well—"

"Would the judge be right to endanger other lives by turning the cold-blooded killer loose on them, just because he's a good, kind, and loving judge?"

Colston cleared his throat. "Well, uh…no, sir. No, that wouldn't be right."

"But you think God—the righteous Judge—is going to let wicked, unregenerate sinners into heaven. What kind of heaven would that be?"

"Well, they'll be good after they die. They won't be bad anymore."

"Your theory won't hold scriptural water, son," said Jackson. "God points to eternity in Revelation 22:11 and says, 'He that is unjust, let him be unjust still: and he which is filthy, let him be filthy still.' Dying doesn't change a sinner's nature. Only being born again by the Spirit of God can do that."

Colston shook his head. "I still don't believe in hell."

"But you do believe in heaven?"

"That's right."

"Why?"

"Well, we have to go somewhere when we die. So I believe we all go to heaven."

The general's voice remained quiet as he said, "Are you aware, Sergeant Colston, that you wouldn't know there was a heaven except that you learned it from the Bible? That's our only source for the knowledge that there's a place called heaven."

Colston shrugged. "That's good enough for me."

"I see. So you're willing to take the Bible's word for the fact that heaven exists."

"Sure."

"Well, son, the same Bible says hell exists. What about that?"

There were snickers among the small group when Sergeant Colston found himself without a sensible reply.

Jackson opened his Bible, flipped to Matthew 23, and said, "Look at what Jesus Christ said to unbelievers, Sergeant—here in verse 33: 'Ye serpents, ye generation of vipers, how can ye escape the damnation of hell?'"

Flipping back a few pages to Matthew 13, Jackson said, "In this chapter, Jesus twice calls hell a furnace of fire. Look at verse 42: 'And shall cast them into a furnace of fire: there shall be wailing and gnashing of teeth.' Verse 50: 'And shall cast them into the furnace of fire: there shall be wailing and gnashing of teeth.' Sergeant, are you so bold as to call Jesus Christ a liar?"

While Colston was trying to come up with a reply, Jackson flipped forward to Luke 16. Look, here, Sergeant. This is a true story told by Jesus about a man who went to hell. See? In verse 23 Jesus says the man lifted up his eyes in hell, being in torments. What was causing the torments? Next verse. The man in hell says he is tormented in 'this flame.' Hell is real fire. The man in hell said so. Jesus said so."

Colston licked his lips nervously.

"I'll ask you again, Sergeant," said Jackson, "are you going to call Jesus Christ a liar?"

"Well, I—"

"Do you think Jesus came from heaven, shed His blood on the cross, and died to save you from nothing, Sergeant? If there was no hell to save you from...why did He go to the cross? And if there was no hell to save you from, why did He lie and say there was?"

Sergeant Ryan Colston's eyes filmed with moisture, and his lower lip quivered slightly. "General, sir, I...I've been wrong. I'm lost. Would you help me? I want to be saved."

Jackson quickly showed Colston that Jesus demanded repen-

tance of sin, and faith in Him alone, before He would save a sinner from hell. He then showed him Romans 10:13: "Whosoever
shall call upon the name of the Lord shall be saved."

The Spirit of God had done His supernatural work. Where
previously a cynical scoffer had stood, now a humbled and convicted young man called on the Lord Jesus Christ to save him.

While General Lee and his army waited on the banks of the
Rappahannock for news from Confederate intelligence, Jodie
Lockwood climbed aboard a train in Richmond and headed for
Lexington, early on Tuesday morning, December 2.

It was midafternoon when Jodie alighted from the hired
buggy with her small overnight bag in hand, paid the driver, and
stepped onto the front porch of the Jackson house.

Before she could knock, the door opened, and a middle-aged
woman greeted her with a warm smile, saying, "Miss Lockwood?"

Jodie smiled back and said, "Yes…and you're Mrs. Zimmer."

"Come in, child," said the chubby woman. "And you can call
me Gertie. Short for Gertrude May."

"All right, Gertie." Jodie followed her inside. "And you can
call me Jodie. Short for Joan Elizabeth. How's Mary Anna?"

"She's doing fine. Taking her nap right now."

"No, I'm not," came a voice from down the hall. Mary Anna
suddenly appeared, waddling uncomfortably toward them in a
bulging robe and slippers. "Jodie! I'm so glad you're here!"

"You look like you could blossom any time," Jodie said as the
two women embraced.

"Oh, I'd love to have the baby while you're here, Jodie. I guess
you met Gertie. She's a member of our church, and she's been
such a good friend to me."

Jodie nodded. "Yes, we met, and I like her very much
already."

"Same here, Jodie," said Gertie.

"Gertie has been with me day and night for over a week. She won't leave me for a minute."

"That's awfully sweet of you, Gertie," said Jodie. "Since I'll be here tonight, would you like to go home and sleep in your own bed?"

"No need. I'm a widow, so there's nobody at home to take care of. And the bed I've been sleeping in is very comfortable. Besides…I want to be here when that baby comes."

"Well, I can tell you right now," said Mary Anna, smoothing some loose strands of hair from her forehead, "it's mighty close to time."

Jodie took Mary Anna by the arm and said, "All right, little lady, as your visiting nurse I want you to go back to bed and lie down. You look very tired."

"I am a little fatigued. Didn't sleep well last night. Backache."

"Well, the cause of the backache will soon keep you awake in another way," giggled Jodie. "You know…wa-a-ah, wa-a-ah, wa-a-ah!"

Mary Anna rolled her eyes and Gertie burst into laughter.

As Jodie started to guide Mary Anna down the hall, Gertie took the expectant mother's other arm. "Come on, honey," she said. "Do like your nurse has told you…back to bed."

When Jodie and Gertie had tucked the covers around Mary Anna, Jodie said, "You close your eyes, now. Sleep if you can. We'll be right here."

Mary Anna pulled the covers up under her chin. "What do you hear from Hunter, Jodie?"

"Same thing you hear from the general. Everybody's waiting for the Yankees to make their move."

"Oh, I'll be so glad when this war is over! It will be wonderful to have Tom home for good. I'd love to have him teaching at the institute and home with the baby and me every night."

"Maybe that isn't so far off," spoke up Gertie. "The kind of trouble Abe Lincoln is having with his army…he just might decide to call the war off and let us all settle down to a normal life again."

"I'd love to believe that," said Jodie.

Mary Anna fell asleep while both women sat by the bed, chatting quietly.

Gertie finally stood up and whispered, "I need to go to the market and buy some groceries, Jodie. Usually I have to call in a neighbor to stay with Mary Anna while I shop, but since you're here, I'll leave you in charge. I'll be back in an hour."

Jodie nodded. "How far away is her doctor…just in case she should start labor?"

"He's about four blocks from here. Name's Dr. Harvey Roberts. If that should happen, the neighbors next door to the west will fetch him for you. Their name is Nelson. Just give them a holler, and stay close to Mary Anna."

When Gertie left, Jodie stood over her sleeping friend for a few moments, smiling down at her, then adjusted the covers and eased back onto the chair.

Gertie had been gone just over an hour when she arrived back at the Jackson home and pushed the little cart up the walk and alongside the house to the back porch. As she picked up a grocery bag, she heard a sharp cry from inside the house.

"Mary Anna!" she gasped, dropping the bag into the cart and bounding up the steps and through the kitchen door. She heard another cry and hurried toward Mary Anna's bedroom.

She could hear Jodie speaking in low tones. When she entered the room, Jodie was bent over Mary Anna with her hands on Mary Anna's knees, saying, "Take a deep breath, honey, and push!"

Mary Anna's face was shiny with perspiration, and her eyes were closed.

When Jodie sensed movement behind her, she turned in relief and said, "Her water broke right after you left! The baby's head is showing! I ran over to the neighbors like you said, but they aren't home. I tried two other houses. They're not home either. Would you go bring the doctor?"

Gertie nodded and dashed out the door.

When Gertie Zimmer arrived at Dr. Harvey Roberts's office, his nurse informed Gertie that he had been called to a farm outside of town to deliver a baby, and she had no idea when he might return.

Gertie had been gone about an hour and a half when she returned to the Jackson house. Puffing from exertion, she mounted the steps, bustled through the door, and forced her weary legs to hurry down the hall.

When she stepped into the bedroom, Mary Anna was sitting up in bed, holding a small bundle in a blanket, a smile of contented joy on her face. Jodie, who was seated next to her on a wooden chair, looked exultant from the miracle she had just witnessed. Gertie just stood there like a statue, eyes wide, mouth gaping.

"Come, Gertie," said Mary Anna. "I want you to meet Julia."

On Saturday morning, December 6, Dr. Hunter McGuire had already attended to several minor medical problems inside the hospital tent on the east bank of the Rappahannock. As he applied salve to a soldier's back, the tent flap parted.

"Hello, General," said Hunter, looking up to see his lifelong friend.

"Hello, yourself," said Stonewall. "How long you going to be tied up here?"

"Just about done. I think this man is my last patient."

"I'll wait outside...I've got some good news."

Hunter grinned. "The baby?"

Stonewall tried to cover a smile as he said, "I'll see you outside when you're finished."

"It's a girl, isn't it?"

Jackson gave him a mock scowl. "I said I'll see you outside when you're finished."

Five minutes later the soldier Hunter had been treating emerged from the tent, slipping on his coat. The December air was quite nippy. "General Jackson...?"

"Yes, Private?"

"Did your wife just give birth?"

The general took him by the arm and led him a safe distance from the hospital tent. "Yes!" he said in a low voice. "I just wanted to tell Dr. McGuire first."

"Is Dr. McGuire right, sir?" asked the private in a whisper. "Is it a girl?"

"Yes! But I don't want him to know it yet."

"Could I spread the word? We've all been waiting for your baby to be born, sir."

Jackson laid a hand on his shoulder. "Give it a few minutes, will you, Private? Then you can spread the word."

"Sure, General. Is Mrs. Jackson all right?"

"Yes. Mother and baby came through it just fine."

"Oh, that's good, sir." The private started to walk away, then turned back. "Oh! What's the baby's name, General?"

"Julia. After my mother."

The private nodded, and hurried away. Jackson returned to the tent and waited near the opening.

Seconds later, Hunter came out, smiling from ear to ear. "Okay, General Jackson," he said, looking the man in the eye, "Was I right? Is it a girl?"

Jackson smiled broadly. "How'd you know?"

"By the way Mary Anna was carrying the baby. I'm a medical doctor, remember?"

"Oh, yeah! I almost forgot!"

Hunter laughed. "Sometimes I can be fooled...but most of the time, I'm right. So when was little Julia Jackson born?"

"Tuesday. Mary Anna wrote me a long letter about it."

"Mama and baby all right?"

"Fine."

"Praise the Lord!"

"Amen. But there's something else, Hu—" The general looked around to see if anyone was within earshot then continued. "There's something else I want to tell you."

"Yes?"

"It was Jodie who delivered Julia."

"Jodie! How did that happen?"

"She used her two days off this week to visit Mary Anna, and the baby decided to come while she was there. Our doctor was out in the country delivering another baby, so Jodie did it all by herself."

"Well, what do you know!" said Hunter. "I knew from her last letter that she was planning to visit Mary Anna, but she hadn't settled on when." Hunter scratched his chin. "Tom, since Jodie delivered your daughter, and Jodie's going to be my wife...doesn't that make you and me some kind of relatives or something?"

Jackson chuckled. "I guess we're in-laws of some kind!"

"Did Mary Anna say if Julia looks like either of you?"

"She has lots of dark hair, like I used to have before it started thinning, but she strongly resembles her mother."

Hunter chuckled. "Well, little Julia can be thankful for that!"

Suddenly the general and the doctor were surrounded by soldiers who had come to congratulate the new father. After a few minutes, when most of men had gone, Rance Dayton and the four Antietam heroes walked up.

They congratulated Jackson on the birth of his baby girl, then Dayton said, "General, sir, these men and I took up a little collection among us. We'd like you to send it to Mrs. Jackson to buy your little girl something she might need."

As he spoke, Dayton handed the general a wad of Confederate bills. "It's ah…twenty-three dollars, sir. Actually, it was Corporal Carney's idea."

"Aw, Major, it wasn't either," said Carney. "It was Buford's idea. I'm just the one who brought it up to you."

Jackson was touched by the gesture and said, "Thank you…all of you. I'm sure Mary Anna will find something real nice for Julia with all this money. Your kindness means a lot to me."

"General Jackson," said Hank Upchurch, "we just wanted you to know how much we look up to you and respect you, sir."

"And we mean it from the bottom of our hearts, sir," said Everett Nichols. "We're proud to serve in II Corps, because you're our commander."

"Thank you," said Jackson. "You men are very kind."

"Just truthful, sir," said Carney.

Jackson ran his gaze over their fresh young faces. "I've not had the opportunity to ask you gentlemen about your spiritual state. Are you Christians? Do you know the Lord?"

Everett Nichols cleared his throat lightly and said, "We…ah…we're not like you and the major, General. We have our own ideas about religion, but we appreciate your concern for us."

"Major Dayton has talked to us about his newfound faith, General," said Chuck Carney. "But we're just not ready to get that involved with religion."

"It isn't religion, men," Dayton said. "I've told you before, there's a difference between religion and salvation—"

"Excuse me, gentlemen," said Lieutenant General James Longstreet, drawing near the small group. "General Lee asked to meet with us, General Jackson. He just received news from intelligence."

Rance Dayton and the young heroes excused themselves, and Jackson headed toward Lee's tent with Longstreet.

"Do you know what it's about?" asked Jackson.

"No. I just happened to be passing by his tent when a messenger handed him an envelope. He saw me and asked me to find you. Said the message was from intelligence, and he needed to talk to both of us."

Lee was standing in the opening of his tent as the two lieutenant generals drew up. "Come in, gentlemen," he said, gesturing them inside.

Lee waited until the two men had sat down, then said, "It's been a month since Lincoln replaced McClellan with Ambrose Burnside."

Longstreet and Jackson nodded.

"I figured things would begin to move," said Lee. "The message I just received from Confederate intelligence is that Burnside is gathering his troops in preparation to cross the Potomac and head for Fredericksburg on a planned march to capture Richmond. Burnside wants to capture Fredericksburg first, which would serve as a stronghold for his rear flank as he marches to Richmond."

"So he'll be coming down the Rappahannock, right at us," said Longstreet.

"That's it. So, gentlemen...we're going to move on down to Fredericksburg and be there to meet Ambrose and his boys."

That night, before retiring, General Stonewall Jackson sat at his portable desk and took out pen, ink, and paper.

December 6, 1862
My sweet Mary Anna,

Oh, how thankful I am to our kind heavenly Father for having spared my precious wife and given us a little daughter! I cannot tell you how gratified I am, nor how much I wish I could be with you and see my two darlings!

You will be happy to hear that we have had revival here in the camp. Dr. Stiles did the preaching, and several hundred men have come to the Saviour! We are now about to engage the enemy once again. Thank you for praying for your husband.

Tell my little Julia that Papa loves her. And never forget that I love her mother with all my heart!

I will see you both when God wills.

Your loving Tom

On December 10, General Burnside began laying pontoons across the Rappahannock River just north of Fredericksburg, Virginia. His plan to take Fredericksburg would leave him a direct, unhindered route to march his army fifty-seven miles due south to the Confederate capital.

General Lee was ready for him, having devised a plan using the ingenuity of his "right arm," Stonewall Jackson.

While the pontoon project was under way, Lee had the town evacuated on December 11. Once the people were out of Fredericksburg, Lee's Confederate sharpshooters were stationed in the trees along the river's banks and started picking off Union soldiers who were assembling the pontoon bridge. Dozens of bluecoats dropped dead in the water.

Angered at the Rebel guns, Burnside commanded his artillery to bombard the town. By December 12, the battle was in full array. Stonewall Jackson's II Corps distinguished itself in the battle along the river while I Corps, under General Longstreet's command, unleashed a bloody horror on the Yankees from atop a hill called Marye's Heights. General Lee was on the hill with Longstreet, looking on.

By darkness on December 13, the Union forces—though outnumbering the Confederate forces nearly two to one—had been soundly whipped by Lee, with losses mounting to over six thousand.

The discouraged and beaten Yankees pulled back to Falmouth, taking as many wounded with them as possible. Burnside's tactical blunder had cost the Union Army of the Potomac dearly.

On December 14, presidential secretary Hay knocked on the door of the Oval Office.

"Yes, John?" came the president's voice.

"A wire just came for you, sir."

Lincoln extended his bony hand to receive a white envelope. Hay waited while Lincoln read the message, and saw his countenance fall.

"Bad news, sir?"

Lincoln crumpled the paper in his hand. The permanent furrows in his brow deepened. "Yes. General Burnside has been defeated at Fredericksburg. Six thousand casualties. They've retreated back to Falmouth."

Hay bit his lower lip. "General Halleck will say he told you so, sir...as will many others."

Lincoln nodded. "I'm going to try to give General Burnside the benefit of the doubt, John. Some other general might not have done any better, given the same circumstances and an already discouraged army to lead."

"Yes, sir."

"Send for General Halleck, now, so I can talk to him."

When Hay was gone, Lincoln pressed stiff fingertips to his temples. He was close to letting down, but he couldn't let on to anyone how he really felt about having chosen Burnside to follow McClellan. In spite of everything, he still couldn't come up with another man he would have picked instead.

SEVEN

On Monday, December 15, Jodie Lockwood was back on the day shift at the Richmond hospital. As she washed up after assisting in surgery, Nurse Nan Fenton joined her and plunged her hands into the bowl of lye soap.

"I haven't talked to you in a couple of days, Jodie," she said. "Is Dr. McGuire still at Fredericksburg?"

"Yes," said Jodie, scrubbing her hands with vigor. "His wire yesterday said it's going to take quite some time to do the surgeries and patch up all the men who were wounded in the battle. General Lee is trying to get some more doctors there to help. Besides Hunter, there are only three other doctors. He says some of the wounded have died because they can't get to the men soon enough. They're working day and night as it is."

"Hmm. What about your wedding plans for Saturday?"

"I'm doing a lot of praying about it, I'll tell you that much."

"I sure hope you don't have to postpone the wedding."

"It's in the Lord's hands, Nan. Pastor Griffin says if Hunter can't get loose to come home, we'll have the wedding within a few days after he does get here. We have to give everybody who's invited a little bit of notice so they can attend."

"Well, I'll be there with bells on," said Nan, scrubbing her hands vigorously. "One thing about being a child of God...we know He has His powerful hand on our lives, and He cares about what's important to us. If next Saturday is His choice for your wedding day, Dr. McGuire will be back in time."

Jodie gave her friend a sunny smile and picked up a towel. "That's right, Nan. And Hunter and I only want His will in our lives. So...I'm praying that Hunter will be here in time, since the Lord says for us to pray; but whatever our heavenly Father chooses for us, we're willing to accept it."

On Wednesday morning, Jodie had her time of prayer and Bible reading, then went to breakfast in the dining room of her boardinghouse. She had just returned to her room when someone knocked at the door.

Outside was a young corporal, who grinned at her and said, "Another wire for you, Miss Lockwood. It came to the camp from Fredericksburg about fifteen minutes ago."

"Thank you, Corporal."

As soon as Jodie closed the door, she ripped open the envelope and quickly read the message. "Oh, thank You, Lord Jesus!" she said. "Thank You!"

The wire from Hunter told her that extra help had come, and he and the other doctors were wrapping things up at Fredericksburg. He would be home late tomorrow afternoon.

When Jodie arrived at the hospital to begin her shift, Nan Fenton met her in the hall. One glance at Jodie's face and Nan said, "Did you get some good news?"

"Hunter will be home tomorrow! I stopped by the parsonage on the way to work and told Pastor Griffin."

"Oh, Jodie, that's wonderful! Guess I'd better get my bells ready!"

Jodie sighed. "I wish bells were all I had to get ready! Hunter and I will have only one day to wrap up what we don't already have done."

"Is there anything I can do?"

"No, but thank you. What's left are things that only Hunter and I can do. We've already paid a month on our new apartment, so it stands ready. Looks like everything's going to go as planned."

"Miss Lockwood!" came the voice of the corporal who had delivered the wire at the boardinghouse.

Jodie turned and saw an envelope in his hand and giggled. "More?" she said.

"Yes, ma'am. This one's from Mrs. Stonewall Jackson."

"Oh, yes. Probably advising me of her and baby Julia's arrival on Friday."

Moments later, Jodie stepped into the ladies' powder room and opened the envelope. Her smile faded as she read the message.

At the same time Jodie was reading the wire from Mary Anna, Stonewall Jackson stood inside General Lee's tent at the army camp near Richmond.

As soon as they finished the meeting, Lee said, "Are Mary Anna and the baby still due to arrive Friday?"

Jackson smiled broadly. "Yes, sir! I can hardly wait to see both of them, but it will be especially sweet to see my little Julia for the first time."

"I assume, then, that Dr. McGuire's wedding is still on for Saturday?"

"It must be, sir. I'm sure that either Hunter or Jodie would have let me know by now if it wasn't. Last word I had from Hunter was, the doctors you sent had been such a big help that everything was under control."

"Good!" said Lee. "I'm looking forward to attending the doctor's wedding myself."

"Doc and Jodie make a beautiful couple."

When Longstreet and Jackson stepped outside the tent, the same corporal who had delivered the wire to Jodie Lockwood stood before them. He saluted and said, "General Jackson, I have a wire here from Mrs. Jackson. I would have had it in your hands sooner, but I didn't want to intrude on your meeting."

"That's all right, Corporal. Thank you."

The corporal and Longstreet walked away together, and Jackson opened the envelope. As he began reading the message, a deep frown penciled itself across his brow, and his shoulders slumped.

"General," came Lee's voice from behind him. "Something wrong?"

Jackson turned slowly, lifting his eyes from the paper. "Yes. Mary Anna's having some complications from the birth…some slight hemorrhaging. The doctor says she'll be all right, but she can't travel. I won't get to see her and my little Julia this weekend after all. She says she wired Jodie to let her know she can't be in the wedding."

When Hunter McGuire arrived in Richmond, late in the afternoon on Thursday, Jodie told him about Mary Anna and that she had chosen Nan Fenton to be her matron of honor. Hunter knew Nan and liked her. If Mary Anna couldn't be there, Nan was a fine replacement. Nan's husband was in the Confederate navy and was somewhere on the Gulf of Mexico.

The wedding practice on Friday night went well, though Stonewall Jackson couldn't hide his sadness at Mary Anna and baby Julia's absence.

Hunter and Jodie were also saddened to learn that Hunter's

adoptive parents would not be able to attend. All passenger trains heading south out of Union territory had been halted for the time being.

Saturday evening came, and the wedding moved with precision.

The newlyweds had only two days for a honeymoon, which they spent in a small cabin in the Blue Ridge Mountains.

On Monday, December 22, Gertie Zimmer thanked the messenger who had brought a telegram and then headed for the parlor. Mary Anna, looking a bit pale, had just finished feeding little Julia. She looked up quickly as Gertie entered the room.

"Is it a wire from Tom?"

"Yes," said Gertie. "Let me take the baby so you can read it."

As Mary Anna read the message, a distressed expression captured her wan features and her lower lip began to tremble.

"He won't be coming home for Christmas, will he?" Gertie said levelly.

"No. General Lee is keeping his entire army right where they are. Tom says General Lee fears the Yankees might try to take them off guard because it's holiday time. They must be prepared."

"Well, even though I was going to go home in another day or two," said Gertie, "I'll just stay right here. I don't want you alone on Christmas."

Mary Anna pressed fingertips to her lips and blinked against the tears that had surfaced. "I was alone last Christmas, too, because of the War. Maybe…maybe by next Christmas, this will all be over and Tom can be here with us."

"I sure hope so, honey."

Mary Anna looked up at her loyal friend and said, "You can come and spend Christmas with us, Gertie. I don't want you alone on Christmas either."

"I'll take you up on it," Gertie said, kissing little Julia's chubby cheek. "I'll look forward to it."

On Christmas day, General Burnside's army was still camped at Falmouth, Virginia.

Late in the afternoon on the following Monday, December 29, word came to President Lincoln and military officials in Washington that General Burnside was preparing to lead his troops south. The message contained no details, but Lincoln and the officials with him realized this would mean another crossing of the Rappahannock, and another battle at or near Fredericksburg.

Shortly after the president had learned of Burnside's intentions, presidential secretary John Hay looked up from his desk to see a crimson-faced General Halleck stomp through the door.

"I want to see the president...now!" Halleck said.

Hay laid down his writing instrument and spoke quietly as he said, "President Lincoln anticipated your arrival, General, and is also expecting Mr. Stanton. He told me to tell both of you gentlemen that he's trying to make contact with General Burnside, and that it would be better if he met with the two of you after he learns some details from him."

Halleck's face grew darker, and his breathing sounded ragged.

"The president said I was to tell both you and Mr. Stanton to be here at ten o'clock tomorrow morning. He will discuss the situation with you then."

Halleck exhaled gustily and said, "I want to talk to the president right now!"

Hay let a smile tug at the corners of his mouth and said firmly, "I have given you Mr. Lincoln's message, General. Your meeting with him is tomorrow morning at ten o'clock. Therefore, I will not venture to knock on his door and tell him you demand to see him right now. However, if you wish to barge through the door on your own and make your demand, there it is."

Halleck stood, clenching and unclenching his hands. He stared for a moment at the door that led to the Oval Office, then pivoted and walked away, mumbling curses at Burnside.

On Tuesday morning at 8:30, John Hay was filing papers in the cabinet behind his desk when Secretary of State William Seward entered.

"Good morning, Mr. Seward," Hay said with a smile.

"And good morning to you, John. Is Mr. Lincoln in his office?"

"Yes, sir."

"I have Brigadier Generals John Newton and John Cochrane in the hall. They've just arrived from Falmouth and would like to see the president. They said it's of the utmost importance and has to do with General Burnside's latest announcement."

"Mr. Lincoln has an appointment at ten o'clock with General Halleck and Secretary Stanton, Mr. Seward, but I think he'll have time to see the generals before then. Just a moment."

Hay entered the Oval Office and returned a minute later. "Yes, Mr. Seward, the president will see Generals Newton and Cochrane in a few minutes. Have them come in."

Seward ushered the generals into Hay's office and introduced them, then excused himself. Hay took their hats and coats and invited Newton and Cochrane to sit down, saying that Mr. Lincoln would see them shortly. Then he returned to his work at the filing cabinet.

Some three or four minutes had passed when the hall door opened and a nine-year-old boy entered.

"Hello, Tad," said Hay as the boy approached him.

"Hello, Mr. Hay. I need to see my father."

The generals looked on in bewilderment as Hay preceded the

boy to the office door, knocked, and then stuck his head in to say, "Mr. President, Tad is here to see you."

"Send him in," came the familiar voice.

When Hay closed the door behind Tad, he turned to the generals and said, "I'm sorry, gentlemen, but you'll have to wait until Mr. Tad Lincoln has whatever time he needs with his father."

"I would think the boy could have waited until after we saw the president," Cochrane said.

John Hay smiled. "It doesn't work that way, sir. Mr. Lincoln considers himself a husband and father first, and president and military commander-in-chief second."

The generals exchanged glances again. Then Cochrane's frown disappeared as Newton said, "I'll say this, General Cochrane...the whole world would be in better shape if all husbands and fathers took the same philosophy!"

Cochrane nodded, and after a few seconds, replied, "Can't argue with that."

Almost ten minutes had passed before the door to the Oval Office finally swung open and the president appeared with his son.

"Thank you, Papa," said Tad, smiling up at his father.

"My pleasure, Tad. See you tonight."

"See you tonight, Papa," said Tad, heading toward the hall door. When he reached the door, he looked back and said, "I love you, Papa."

"I love you too, son."

When Tad was gone, Lincoln set his deep-set, tired gaze on Cochrane and Newton, and said, "Come in, gentlemen." He shook their hands, bid them sit down, and lowered himself to his chair with a sigh. "All right, gentlemen," he said, his voice revealing his weariness, "what can you tell me about the situation at Falmouth?"

With concern evident on his face, Brigadier General Newton said, "Mr. President, we've been sent here by Major Generals William B. Franklin and William F. Smith, who would have come themselves, but in their positions of command they don't dare leave Falmouth at this time."

Lincoln nodded. "All right."

"Sir," spoke up Cochrane, "Generals Franklin and Smith have asked us to inform you that all of the generals in the Army of the Potomac have lost faith in General Burnside, as have the other officers, and even the bulk of the troops." Cochrane paused, then said, "And I have to be honest with you, Mr. President. I didn't have faith in General Burnside from day one. He's a good man…but he isn't leadership material for an army the size of ours."

"I agree, sir," said Newton. "As we see it, this is an army scarred by repeated failures under George McClellan, and now a devastating defeat at Fredericksburg under Burnside. No failure under McClellan, however, has seemed so senseless and pointless to the men as the one under Burnside."

Lincoln scrubbed a bony hand across his mouth, blinking slowly to acknowledge that he understood what Newton was saying.

"Sir," said Cochrane, "Generals Franklin and Smith, as well as all the other generals, fear that the men are so demoralized that they might do the unthinkable if they have to enter another battle under Burnside—they might simply refuse to fight, and walk away."

Lincoln's jaw slacked in disbelief.

"Yes, sir," said Cochrane. "The officers have picked up an undercurrent of talk in that direction."

"I have a meeting at ten o'clock with General Halleck and Secretary Stanton," Lincoln said. "I will relay this information to them." He rose from his chair and shook their hands. "I want to thank you gentlemen for coming. And please express my appreciation to Generals Franklin and Smith for sending you. Tell them I was not aware things had gotten this bad."

"We'll do that, sir," said Newton. "And thank you for giving us of your time."

"My pleasure. I assure you, gentlemen, that good will come from this interview. And please make sure Generals Franklin and Smith know that I said so."

"We will do that, sir," said Newton.

Lincoln followed them into the outer office, where John Hay gave them their hats and coats.

As soon as they had passed through the door, the president turned to Hay and said, "John, when General Halleck and Mr. Stanton arrive, bring them into my office without delay."

On Saturday afternoon, January 3, 1863, Confederate unit leaders were gathering their men at the campsite on the Rappahannock, some in the forest and others by the river.

Major Rance Dayton stood before the four hundred men of the Eighteenth North Carolina Regiment, who were seated on the riverbank. The air had a bite to it, and the men could see their breath as they huddled together and pulled up the collars of their overcoats.

The closest unit to them was some thirty yards downstream.

"Men," said Dayton, "as you know, all unit leaders had a meeting with Generals Lee, Jackson, and Longstreet a little while ago. Word has come from our Washington spies that there's serious trouble in the ranks of the Army of the Potomac."

There was a low murmur as the men smiled at each other. They listened closely as Dayton explained that General Burnside had been about to move his troops out of Falmouth and begin another offensive on Fredericksburg as a minor pause on his way to Richmond. However, the big brass put a stop to it.

A hoot of laughter went up.

"We understand," Dayton said, "that last Tuesday Abe Lincoln had a meeting with General Halleck, his general-in-chief, and Secretary of War Edwin Stanton. Lincoln had received word there was talk amongst the men of rebellion if they had to fight another battle under Ambrose Burnside."

More laughter.

"This rebellion, our spies tell us, is actually being led by some of the Yankee generals. They have no confidence in Burnside as a military leader. Word is that after Lincoln met with Halleck and Stanton, he sent a message to Burnside to scrap the idea of moving on Fredericksburg again, and to stay put, pending further orders. Lincoln now has the proverbial tiger by the tail. He's afraid to hang on and afraid to let go. General Lee believes Lincoln is probably losing sleep while he tries to come up with another general to take Burnside's place. No doubt this will give us a respite in fighting until he's got a new leader for his Army of the Potomac."

The men of the Eighteenth raised a cheer. Other cheers went up around the camp as the other groups of soldiers heard the news.

When Dayton had dismissed the men of the Eighteenth, he and the four corporals from his hometown huddled around a fire and talked about old times in Fayetteville. Dayton had no family there anymore, but the corporals shared news from letters they had received from family members.

Soon the conversation went to the War.

Buford Hall said, "Maybe ol' Abe Lincoln will just get so fed up tryin' to find a general who can lead his Army of the Potomac that he'll call the whole war off."

"Wouldn't that be wonderful?" said Dayton. "Then we could all go back home and try to put our lives together."

Chuck Carney held his cold hands over the fire as he glanced at Dayton and said, "Major, do you think you can get elected sheriff of Cumberland County again?"

"I'm not even going to try, Chuck."

"Why not? You've said plenty of times that you want to get back into law enforcement."

"I'll definitely do that, but not in Fayetteville. I guess a moment ago I should have said *you* can all go home and try to put your lives back together. Since my family has died off, Fayetteville isn't really home to me anymore."

"Where will you go, sir?" asked Hank Upchurch.

"When the War's over, I plan to go out West and start a new life on the frontier. I want to become marshal of one of those cattle towns, find the right woman, get married, and enjoy life."

Buford Hall grinned at the major and said, "A lot of women out there in the wild and woolly West don't want to marry a man who wears a badge, sir. I've read about it in some magazines. The women are afraid of becomin' widows too quick."

Dayton chuckled. "That's why I said I'd find the right woman, Buford. The Lord will cross my path with the one He has chosen for me. She'll be the right one, and she'll marry me in spite of my badge."

Everett Nichols went to the nearby pile of firewood and threw some more logs on the fire. As he sat down again, he said, "Major, you sure won't have any problem findin' a job as a lawman out there in the West. Not if those folks know about your fantastic record as a deputy sheriff and then as sheriff of Cumberland County."

"That's for sure," put in Chuck Carney. "I remember reading about that when you were running for sheriff. And you got a big write-up in newspapers all over the South when you resigned as sheriff to join the Confederate army."

"Yeah!" said Nichols. "Rance Dayton hunted down and brought to justice more criminals than any peace officer on record in the entire South!"

"How many murderers did you put on the gallows, Major?" asked Hall.

Dayton chuckled. "I really don't recall. I didn't keep a record book."

"I'd be safe in sayin' he put at least thirty coldblooded killers' necks in the noose," said Upchurch. "And probably sent better'n a hundred and fifty to prison for lesser crimes."

"Well, one thing's for sure," said Carney, "once people out West know his record, they'll be standing in line to pin a badge on him."

Hank Upchurch got misty-eyed as he realized that even if they all survived the War, life would never be the same. Maybe more of his boyhood friends would strike out for parts unknown. He felt sadness wash over him, but all he said was, "Major, Fayetteville sure won't be the same without you livin' there. We'll really miss you."

The others murmured agreement, and then a somber quiet settled over the small group.

It was Dayton who seemed to speak for everyone when he said, "Well, there are five marvelous men I'll never forget, I'll tell you that much. I wish Billy Dean were alive to hear me say it…but I want to thank you men one more time from the bottom of my heart for laying your lives on the line to save mine. You'll always be very special men in my memories, and in my life."

"The same goes for us, Major," said Hank.

Dayton smiled. "Fellas, if there's ever anything I can do for any of you…consider it done."

Chuck guffawed and said, "Who knows! Maybe someday we'll all need a favor!"

EIGHT

O n Sunday morning, January 25, 1863, General-in-Chief Henry Halleck and Secretary of War Edwin Stanton walked down a long hall of the White House, greeting maids and janitors as they went. When they reached the east wing, they started up the winding staircase to the second floor.

"I sure hope he's going to tell us Burnside is out and General Meade is in," said Halleck. "And if not Meade…then Porter, Sumner, or Franklin."

"You're aware that he's also considered Hooker?" asked Stanton.

"Yes, and I've already expressed my opinion of Hooker to the president. I can't believe Mr. Lincoln would consider putting that man at the head of the Army of the Potomac."

At the top of the stairs they turned toward the open door of John Hay's office.

Hay stood and greeted them with a smile, saying, "Good morning, General Halleck, Secretary Stanton. Mr. Lincoln said to bring you in as soon as you arrived." He walked them to the door of the Oval Office and without knocking ushered them in.

Lincoln greeted the men and gestured for them to sit down

before he eased into his own chair with a sigh. He looked at them with a steady gaze and said, "My decision has been made, gentlemen. As of today, I am relieving General Burnside of his command."

"This is good news, sir," said Stanton. "I was hoping the purpose of this meeting was to let General Halleck and me know that you had decided to replace him."

"Indeed it is good news, Mr. President," said Halleck almost boisterously. "And I trust you're appointing one of the generals we discussed earlier."

Lincoln nodded. "I'm appointing Major General Hooker in General Burnside's stead."

Both men looked as if they'd been slapped in the face.

Lincoln watched their expressions closely as he said, "General Hooker is the best qualified of any general I have."

"But, Mr. President," said Halleck, "what about General Meade?"

"He hasn't the combat experience of General Hooker," Lincoln said flatly. "Neither do Generals Sumner, Porter, or Franklin. Hooker has more experience than all of them."

"But, sir," said Stanton, "Hooker is a hard drinker. What if he gets drunk when it's time to lead his army?"

"He won't. He knows better than to do that."

Stanton frowned. "But he's also foul-mouthed, sir. I've heard many men who have served under him say they feel like they need to wash their ears out after having a conversation with him. I realize we can't change a man's speech habits, but as a leader of men, he should be an example as an officer and a gentleman. No gentleman uses his kind of language... especially in front of others."

Stanton looked toward General Halleck, silently urging him to support his comments.

"Mr. President," Halleck said, "the man's morals are corrupt. On many occasions when he's been camped somewhere between battles, he's brought prostitutes to his men."

"That's right," said Stanton. "The man is vulgar."

Lincoln bent his head and rubbed his tired eyes, then said, "Gentlemen, I know General Hooker's character is far from what it ought to be. I abhor the prostitute thing and his foul mouth…but I've got a bloody war on my hands, and General Hooker's record as a leader of men in combat is extraordinary. That's why he's been dubbed Fighting Joe. Right now he's stronger in his military prowess than any other general in the eastern theater. And as I've already stated, he's the most experienced in battle leadership of all the leaders I have to pick from."

"But, sir," said Halleck, "I wish you would consider one of the other generals in spite of the experience element."

"He is the man I must appoint to lead the Army of the Potomac, General Halleck," said the president, "for he's the best choice there is. I'm convinced he's the right general to command this shaken army, which desperately needs its confidence restored."

Halleck and Stanton exchanged glances but could think of nothing more to say.

Lincoln leaned his bony elbows on the desktop and said, "If either of you gentlemen can suggest another man who has as much experience as General Hooker in combat leadership and the willingness to engage the enemy in battle, I'm ready to listen."

Halleck and Stanton were silent for a long moment, then Halleck chuckled. "There is one man, Mr. President. He has much more experience in combat leadership than Hooker, and he's never hesitated to lead his men into battle, no matter how fierce. And he's been the victor in battle after battle."

Stanton stared at Halleck, trying to think of whom he spoke.

Lincoln's heavy eyebrows arched. "Well, who is he?"

Halleck chuckled again. "That's the one hitch, sir. He isn't one of our generals. But if we could persuade Stonewall Jackson to switch sides and take over the Army of the Potomac, we'd see this war finished in a hurry."

Stanton chortled. "That's for sure! Think what that man has done with a much smaller number of troops than he would have if he was on our side. A shortage of guns, ammunition, and supplies, yet he's brought off victory after victory."

"Well, only in our dreams will we ever persuade General Jackson to become a Yankee," said Lincoln.

"How well I know," said Halleck. "But you can't fault me for wishing."

Lincoln managed a slight smile. "But since we must face reality, and between us we can't come up with a man from our army to match General Hooker's military experience...my decision to appoint him as field commander of the Union Army of the Potomac will stand."

On Monday afternoon, at his field tent on the Rappahannock, General Lee received a wire from Confederate intelligence and immediately called for his corps leaders. While he was waiting for them to arrive, the mail came, and in it a letter from Confederate Secretary of War James A. Seddon.

Lee had finished reading the wire and the letter by the time Lieutenant Generals Longstreet and Jackson entered his tent.

As soon as they were seated Lee said, "Gentlemen, I have a wire from intelligence and a letter from Mr. Seddon. The wire informs me that Mr. Lincoln has appointed Major General Joseph Hooker as new commander of the Union Army of the Potomac."

"Hmm," said Longstreet. "Ol' Fighting Joe, eh?"

Jackson rubbed the back of his neck. "Well, if they can keep Joe off the whiskey, he'll be leading his army this way once he can get it reorganized. We'll have some real war on our hands with him at the head of it."

"We will act accordingly," said Lee. "Now, for Secretary Seddon's letter. He says there is unusual activity at the southern tip of the Virginia Peninsula, which as you gentlemen know has long been held by the Yankees. Seddon fears they may be planning to launch an attack against Richmond from that direction, or they may even be preparing to open a new front in North Carolina."

"Either way, we need to get some manpower headed in that direction, sir," said Longstreet, tugging at his long beard.

"Correct," said Lee. "I was thinking about it while waiting for you gentlemen. We must not delay. I'm going to send two crack divisions out of your I Corps, General Longstreet—George Pickett's and John Bell Hood's."

"Yes, sir."

"And I'm going to send you with them, General," said Lee. "I'll feel better if you are leading them."

"If you say so, sir, it's all right with me."

"Good. I'll command I Corps here in northern Virginia myself."

Longstreet chuckled. "Once the men serve directly under you, sir, they'll see what a great soldier you are, and they won't want me back."

Lee grinned and said to Jackson, "The man's a flatterer."

"Yes, sir. But my mother used to say that flattery is only soft soap, and soap is 99 percent lye!"

The three men had a good laugh.

On February 2, Mary Anna Jackson was washing diapers in the kitchen when she heard a knock at the front door. She let the scrub board slide back into the tub of water and quickly dried her hands as she hurried to the door.

"Jodie!" she exclaimed when she opened the door, spreading her arms wide.

Jodie dropped her overnight bag on the porch and gave her

friend a big hug. Mary Anna quickly pulled Jodie inside as she felt the cold air rushing past her into the parlor.

"Oh! It's so wonderful to see you, Jodie! To what do I owe this pleasant surprise?"

Smiling broadly, Jodie said, "To the fact that this is little Julia's two-month birthday!"

Mary Anna laughed and hugged her friend again. "Does this mean you'll come and see us every two months?"

"Can't guarantee that, but I just couldn't wait any longer to see both of you!"

"Julia's asleep in her crib right now, but we can go into my bedroom and sneak a look at her if you want to. I only put her down about twenty minutes ago. She usually sleeps a couple of hours."

"Let's go," Jodie whispered. "I can't wait to see how much she's grown!"

The women tiptoed into the bedroom, and tears came quickly to Jodie's eyes as she studied the chubby little face and marveled over how much the baby had changed already.

Mary Anna quietly placed another log on the fire, then led the way to the kitchen.

While Jodie pitched in to help with the washing, Mary Anna asked for all the details of the wedding. By the time the washing was done, they were talking about how the War was going in the western theater, and discussing the new developments to the east.

"With the way things are shaping up on the peninsula, and the threat of Hooker coming down the Rappahannock, I know Hunter has been tied to the camp," said Mary Anna. "Tom's letters keep me up on news of him."

"Yes," said Jodie. "I haven't seen much of him since we returned from the honeymoon. And according to Hunter's letters, General Jackson hasn't yet been home."

"You mean Tom, don't you?" said Mary Anna. "You did say

you would consider calling him Tom after you and Hunter were married."

Jodie laughed. "Oh, I did, didn't I? Well, while I'm considering it, I'll still speak of him as the general."

Mary Anna shook her head in mock exasperation, then her expression sobered. "It's so sad that the baby is two months old and her papa has yet to lay eyes on her."

"It sure is," agreed Jodie. She paused for a moment and then asked, "In his letters, has the general described the winter quarters he and Hunter are sharing?"

"Oh, yes. Sounds pretty nice, doesn't it?"

Soon they were comparing notes on the way their husbands had described the English-style manor house on an estate called Moss Neck, which overlooked the Rappahannock River some eleven miles below Fredericksburg.

By the time they had the kitchen cleaned up, baby Julia's cry could be heard from down the hall, and Jodie rushed to pick her up. Mary Anna watched as Jodie lifted the baby out of the crib. Immediately Julia stopped crying.

Jodie kissed her soft little face and said, "I think we've got another dirty diaper to deal with."

After the infant had been changed and powdered, Jodie carried her into the parlor and Mary Anna followed. When they sat down, facing each other over the coffee table, Jodie cooed to Julia, and the baby smiled as Jodie jiggled her little fat cheeks.

From a small end table next to where she sat, Mary Anna lifted a magazine. "Have you seen this, Jodie?"

Focusing on the cover, Jodie saw that it was the January issue of the *Southern Literary Messenger*. She shook her head no.

"Well, you've heard of the well-known Rebel correspondent, Peter Alexander, haven't you?"

"Oh, yes. Quite a writer. I've seen his articles in other magazines and newspapers. Has he written something in that issue?"

"Yes, and it's about Tom!"

"Oh, really? Tell me about it! What does he say?"

Jodie kissed Julia's chubby cheeks again as Mary Anna opened the magazine and flashed the two-page article with a small photograph of the general. The headline read:

HERO OF THE WAR: LIEUTENANT GENERAL

STONEWALL JACKSON

Mary Anna began reading the article aloud, which described Jackson's reputation as an outstanding military officer. The article also identified the many distinguished foreign visitors who had visited Stonewall at Moss Neck. He was greatly admired abroad as well as at home.

Jodie was touched by the article and smiled from ear to ear. "You must be very proud of your husband, Mary Anna," she said.

Mary Anna swiped at tears rolling down her cheeks and said, "Oh, I am very proud of him, Jodie, and I miss him so terribly!"

"Too bad nothing was said about the general's strong Christian character, his love for the Bible, and his love for the Lord."

Mary Anna nodded. "I guess Mr. Alexander wasn't interested in that side of my husband."

"Apparently not. He can't help but know that the general is a Christian, though. Too many people talk about his clear testimony of faith in Christ, and his eagerness to bring others to Him."

"Oh, Mr. Alexander knows what my husband is, all right, but this article was just to show him as the soldier. Plenty could be written of him as a Christian husband and his dedication to the Lord. And once he has a chance to be with his daughter, I know he'll shine as a father." Mary Anna suddenly looked stricken. "I just hope he can see little Julia soon."

Jodie stood up with the baby in her arms and said, "Honey, let's just talk to the Lord about that right now."

Jodie lay Julia on the sofa, and the two women knelt beside her and prayed together, asking the Lord to allow Tom to be able to see his little daughter soon. They also prayed that God would protect their husbands in the War.

As the weeks passed after his appointment as commander of the Union Army of the Potomac, Major General Joseph Hooker gained popularity in the North in spite of his dissolute character.

Given to arrogant pretension, Hooker was quoted in the Northern newspapers as saying, "My battle plans are perfect. May God have mercy on Bobby Lee, for I will have none."

Such a positive note, though edged with self-boasting, was enough to give hope to the people of the North that they could yet be victorious in the War between the States.

Songs were written about 'Fighting Joe' Hooker, and balladeers sang them in theaters, drinking establishments, and even on street corners. One song, which became popular quickly, had a line that proclaimed: "Joe Hooker is our leader; he takes his whiskey strong!"

Spirits rose in the Union camps along the Rappahannock as Hooker continued to form his battle plans. With his blessing, a number of officers sent for their wives and children to join them in their quarters, lightening everyone's mood.

As far as many of the men in his army were concerned, Fighting Joe's stock was rising fast. And by early April, the Union Army of the Potomac, in Hooker's words, was "in condition to inspire the highest expectations."

Those expectations, however, were diminished by two things—relentless rain, and the fact that nearly a third of Hooker's infantrymen were scheduled to leave the army in the next three months. They had signed up for two years early in the War and would be discharged by the end of June.

Hooker announced that he would do all in his power to convince them to reenlist. But they were tired of fighting, and many were still not convinced that the Union could be victorious over the Confederacy and its doggedly stubborn leaders and fighting men. Unsure of his success in getting them to reenlist, Hooker planned to move his campaign ahead as soon as the rains let up.

During the rainy season in Virginia, even the best-equipped and best-prepared army would be hostage to the inclement weather. This was the case as one hard rain after another turned Virginia roads to bottomless mud, transformed small creeks and brooks into raging rivers, and made rivers like the Rappahannock too deep and swift for even cavalry to ford safely.

At the Confederate capitol in Richmond, on a rainy day during the first week of April, General Robert E. Lee and President Jefferson Davis stood together, looking through a rain-splattered window at the storm. With lightning flashing, thunder rolling, and trees limbs cracking in the wind, Lee said, "Hooker offers me no more to worry about than any of his predecessors, sir."

"Well, I'm glad to hear that, General," said Davis.

"I hold very little respect for the man."

"Are you referring to his low morals?"

"Well, I didn't have that in mind, although it certainly disgusts me. What I meant was, as a soldier I hold very little respect for him. His arrogance and constant bragging about what he's going to do to me is a bunch of hot air as far as I'm concerned."

"He does blow hard, doesn't he?"

"Yes. Now, George McClellan is one Yankee leader I did respect—both as an officer and a gentleman. His timidity, however, made him relatively easy to predict. I have only contempt for General John Pope. He blundered the Union's chances of victory in the second battle at Bull Run, and certainly General Burnside's floundering at Fredericksburg drew him no respect from this Southern boy."

Davis had to raise his voice above the rumble of thunder as he said, "So what do you think of all this talk by Hooker of a master battle plan?"

"Hot air, sir. I don't expect any surprises from him. If the commander of an army really has something big to spring on his enemy, he doesn't blow off about it. He implements it quietly. All this loud talk doesn't impress me, even though Hooker will command an army twice the size of mine when we go to battle."

"What about that latest quote of his that he commands the finest army on planet earth?"

"More of the same old stuff. His army is untested under his command. Such a statement is meant to intimidate us. Well, Mr. President, we will not be intimidated, but we *will* meet Mr. Hooker on the field of battle and let him see what a small army of determined, courageous men can do." Lee paused, then said, "Only don't tell him I said so. I don't want to sound like a braggart."

Davis uttered an appreciative laugh.

The heavy rains continued almost daily, keeping the land soft and the roads virtually impassable.

On April 17, Stonewall Jackson met with General Lee at Lee's headquarters in an old farmhouse near the raging Rappahannock.

"Well, of course I don't mind, General," said Lee. "It's past time for you to see your little daughter and to be with Mary Anna. Exactly where is William Yerby's farm?"

"Only three miles due north of the Moss Neck place,

sir...but it would give us some privacy that we wouldn't enjoy at Moss Neck. Too many other officers and medical personnel have moved in there."

"Will Dr. McGuire remain at Moss Neck?"

"He feels it best to let me have all the privacy I can get when my family comes."

"You know this Yerby family well, do you?"

"Not real well, but they are admirers of mine and made the offer so I could have a place to spend time with Mary Anna and the baby."

"You had better move fast on it, then," said Lee. "The rains will begin letting up as we get closer to May, and when those roads start drying out, ol' Joe Hooker will be moving this way."

"I'll send Mary Anna a wire and get her here with the baby as soon as possible," said Jackson. "Thank you for understanding, sir."

"I'm a family man too," said Lee with a smile. "It's just that my children are all grown. I miss my Mary like you miss your Mary Anna, but it's got to be eating your heart out that you haven't held that baby in your arms."

"Yes, sir, it is."

"Well, keep me posted as to when you're going to move to the Yerby place, and be sure to greet Mary Anna for me."

"I'll do that, sir." Jackson headed toward the door.

"Oh, and General...give little Julia a hug from Robert E. Lee, would you?"

"As soon as I give her a hundred from her father, sir."

Lee was still grinning as Jackson left him.

On April 18, Stonewall Jackson was in the room he shared with Hunter McGuire at the Moss Neck estate when there was a knock at the door. McGuire was cleaning his medical instruments at a table, and Jackson was sitting in a chair in a far corner, polishing his boots.

"I'll get it, Tom," said Hunter, heading toward the door.

"Wire for General Jackson, Doctor," said a corporal as he handed an envelope to Hunter. "It's from Mrs. Jackson."

"Thanks, Corporal!" called Jackson, waving at him.

Hunter closed the door and turned to face his friend. "Want me to read it to you, Tom?"

"Sure," Jackson said, rubbing a boot with a soft cloth to bring out the shine. "Since it's a wire, there won't be any mushy stuff, which would be none of your business!"

Hunter laughed and tore open the envelope. After reading the brief message, he said, "Well, it's going to happen, Tom. Mary Anna is bringing your daughter on the train from Lexington on Tuesday. They will arrive at Guiney's Station at ten-thirty that morning."

"Hallelujah!" Jackson shouted.

The rain had fallen all day on Monday and was still falling on Tuesday morning, April 21, when Stonewall Jackson's aide, Corporal Jim Lewis, drove him in a borrowed carriage to the depot.

"Since this carriage has a roof on it, sir," said Lewis, "I'll wait here for you and your family."

"Fine, Jim," said Jackson, picking up an umbrella at his feet. "See you in a few minutes."

Even as the general spoke, the sound of the train whistle filled the air, and he jumped down from the carriage and dashed to the depot.

A few people waited inside for the arrival of passengers. The general recognized two lieutenants from Longstreet's I Corps and nodded at them.

As the train chugged in and stopped, Jackson scanned the three coaches, trying to see inside, but the windows were covered with rain and filmed with moisture on the inside.

Suddenly Stonewall's eyes locked on the small dark-haired woman who was stepping off the rear platform of the second car. She was cradling a small bundle in her arms.

When Mary Anna's eyes found Tom's, his heart leaped in his chest.

NINE

In no more than a few seconds, Tom had enfolded Mary Anna, with the baby between them, in his arms.

His face and hat brim dripped rainwater as he bent his head to kiss her. "I hope you don't mind getting a little wet."

Mary Anna let him know how little the rain mattered as her tears mingled with the raindrops and she returned his kiss.

Easing back after a prolonged kiss, Jackson eagerly reached toward the covering blanket and said, "Let me see her!"

"Excuse me, Mrs. Jackson," came the voice of the conductor beside them. "Here's your luggage."

"Oh, yes," said Mary Anna. "Thank you, Mr. Compton."

"I'll take it, sir," said Jackson. "Thank you."

"You are most welcome, General," said the conductor, admiration showing in his eyes. "God bless you, sir."

"And may the Lord bless you too, Mr. Compton," Jackson said with feeling. As the conductor walked away, Stonewall turned back for the first look at his baby daughter.

Mary Anna lifted the blanket from Julia's face, and Jackson smiled broadly as he said, "Oh, sweetheart, she's beautiful! I...I want to hold her, but this slicker is sopping. I don't want to get her wet."

The sound of his strong, deep voice drew little Julia's attention. She set her eyes on him and released a toothless grin.

"Look, Mary Anna, she's smiling at me! She knows me! Hello, precious darling. You know I'm your papa, don't you?"

Julia made a cooing sound.

"Did you hear that, Mary Anna? She said yes!"

By this time, a small crowd had collected to take in the rare scene of the rugged military leader reduced to mush.

A middle-aged woman said to her husband, "That's the way you acted the first time you saw your little Harriet, Ralph."

"Hey, General Jackson!" came the voice of a Confederate soldier with sergeant's stripes on his arm. "Congratulations, sir! We heard you'd had a baby. I...I mean that your wife had a baby."

The other soldiers with him laughed.

Stonewall looked up and smiled, then said, "Let's go, sweetheart. Jim Lewis is waiting in the carriage. I'll hold my little darling when I can get out of this slicker."

Rain was still pouring down as Stonewall Jackson picked up Mary Anna's small piece of luggage and held the umbrella over her and the baby as they hurried to the carriage.

Jackson quickly introduced Mary Anna to Jim Lewis and helped her into the carriage, then placed the suitcase and umbrella on the floor behind the second seat and peeled out of his slicker. He laid it on the third seat and tossed his hat on top of it, then jumped in beside Mary Anna and closed the door.

He held his arms open, and Mary Anna gently laid the baby in her husband's hands.

"Jim," said the general, "this is absolutely the most beautiful baby girl the Lord ever made!"

Lewis twisted on the seat and glanced at the dark-haired infant. "Well, I declare, sir, you're right! She sure is!"

"And what if Jim had not agreed with you?" said Mary Anna.

Stonewall chuckled. "He'd be lying out there in the road with a broken neck!"

Lewis laughed. "Sure am glad I have good eyesight, sir!"

The general took hold of Mary Anna's graceful chin and kissed her softly, then said, "Thank you for giving me such a precious little daughter!"

Stonewall caressed little Julia's tiny cheeks, speaking words of love to her, and every few seconds he kissed her face. Mary Anna felt a warmth flood her heart at the sight of how much her husband loved and delighted in the baby.

The drive to the Yerby farm was less than four miles. When they arrived, Corporal Lewis drove them to the front porch, and General Jackson thanked his aide for driving the carriage and all that entailed—taking the carriage to the barn and unhitching the horses, then riding his own horse back to the Moss Neck estate, where he had a room.

Inside, Jackson introduced Mary Anna to William and Frances Yerby. Though Jackson had already been occupying the large guest room at the rear of the house, the Yerbys led them upstairs and down the hall to the room. Frances Yerby wanted to explain to Mary Anna where everything was kept.

The room was beautifully furnished, and Frances had made sure Mary Anna had everything she needed to care for the baby. Little Julia even had her own crib, which stood near the large canopied bed.

When they were finally alone, Tom Jackson laid the baby on the bed, kissed her cheeks some more, then took Mary Anna in his arms. When they had held each other for some time, the baby began to fuss.

"She's just jealous," said the general.

Mary Anna put her hands on her hips and laughed. "Oh, so that's it. I almost forgot I was married to quite a ladies' man."

"Wasn't that why you fell for me? Because I'm so handsome and irresistible?"

"Why, of course. I just couldn't help myself."

"Well, neither can Julia. She's crazy about me and jealous when I hold another woman." He stooped over to pick up the baby. As soon as he did, she stopped fussing. "See? What did I tell you? She was jealous."

"My eyes tell me you're right," said Mary Anna contentedly as she sat down in an overstuffed chair.

Jackson carried little Julia to a large full-length mirror that stood near the door. Placing her tiny face next to his own, he studied their images in the glass. "You know what, Mary Anna?"

"What?"

"Julia really does look a lot like you."

"That's what most people say."

"Of course, as I look closely, I can see that she does have my nose."

"I've noticed that myself. But I'm sure her nose will get prettier as she grows older."

Jackson laughed. "How could something so perfect get prettier?"

Julia began to fuss again and Mary Anna got up from the chair and held out her arms. "She's hungry and no doubt needs a diaper change." Grinning slyly, she added, "Tell you what. Why don't you change her diaper while I get ready to feed her?"

II Corps's brave and dauntless commander turned pale. "Me? Change her diaper? But, honey, I...well, I've never changed a diaper in my whole life! I—"

Mary Anna burst into laughter. "I was just kidding! You sit down and rest your bones, O fearless Stonewall. I'll take care of it."

Later, when little Julia was in her crib asleep, the Jacksons sat down together on a love seat and settled comfortably against each other.

As they gazed out the nearby window and watched the storm clouds break up, they talked about Julia's birth. Tom told her how very much he appreciated Jodie's being there to deliver the baby, and that she had shown up at the house for Julia's two-month birthday.

"Jodie's very special, darling," said Mary Anna. "I believe I'd have to say that just as Hunter is your best friend in all the world...Jodie has become mine. I can't wait to see her again."

The general squeezed her hand. "Well, I did a little something toward that."

"What do you mean?"

"Hunter went home to spend some time with Jodie right after I came here. When I moved in, the Yerbys asked about Hunter. They know about him being chief physician of II Corps, and that he and I are close friends. They also were aware of Hunter's marriage to Jodie, so they asked if possibly the McGuires could come and spend some time with us while we're here."

Mary Anna's eyes were dancing as she said, "Are you telling me they're coming here?"

"Yes, ma'am! I wired them...explained that the Yerbys had offered them a nice room to stay in if they could come, and they're coming."

"Oh, when?"

Mary Anna forgot to keep her voice low, and Julia began to stir. Mary Anna covered her mouth and looked toward the crib. The baby made a few grunting sounds and was soon quiet again.

Whispering, Stonewall said, "They'll be here Saturday. The train arrives at Guiney's Station at noon."

"Oh, wonderful!" whispered Mary Anna. "It will be good to see them again. And I'm anxious for Hunter to see our baby!"

The Virginia sky was cloudless, and the sun's single eye watched as the Jacksons met the McGuires at Guiney's Station on Saturday noon. After they had greeted each other, Jodie took the baby from

Mary Anna and held her up so Hunter could see her.

"Look, honey! Isn't she the most beautiful baby girl you've ever seen?"

Hunter took the baby from Jodie and scrutinized her carefully. He shook his head in wonderment, saying, "You're right, she is. I've never seen such a beautiful baby girl."

Stonewall Jackson's chest puffed out, and a wide grin spread over his face. "Now that's the smartest thing I've ever heard you say, Doctor!"

The women just smiled at one other.

"She really is, Tom," Hunter said. "Of course that will all change when Jodie and I have our first girl."

Jackson squared his jaw and narrowed his eyes into slits. "Only if she looks exactly like Jodie and nothing like you!"

The two couples had a good laugh together as they left the depot.

As the Jacksons and McGuires neared the Yerby farm in the carriage, Stonewall turned to Jodie and said, "I want to thank you for delivering our little Julia, and for being such a good friend to my Mary Anna."

"For both, General," she said softly, "the pleasure was and is mine."

"Tom," Mary Anna said, "you haven't told them about the services tomorrow."

"Oh, that's right. We're going to have an open-air meeting tomorrow with probably two thousand soldiers in attendance, plus locals. Chaplain Tucker Lacy is preaching."

"He's Chaplain General of II Corps, isn't he?" Jodie said.

"That's right," Jackson said.

"General…" Jodie said.

"Yes?"

"It is my duty to warn you that Chaplain Lacy is not a Presbyterian. He's a Baptist spy!"

Stonewall Jackson threw back his head and laughed as he pulled the carriage to a stop in front of the Yerby house. "Baptist spy! That's a good one, Jodie!"

Sunday, April 26, was a sunny day, and nearly twenty-five hundred Confederate soldiers, along with well over three hundred local farmers and townsfolk, were gathering for the preaching service, which would begin at ten o'clock.

The site was an open field next to the Confederate camp some five miles south of Fredericksburg, on the west bank of the Rappahannock River. Everyone knew Joe Hooker's Army of the Potomac was camped barely eight miles north on the other side of Fredericksburg, but General Lee's scouts were keeping a sharp eye on the Yankee camp. Any suspicious move would be spotted, and there were some sixty-three thousand Rebel troops in the camp who were not attending the preaching service.

Next to the hastily built speaker's platform, Stonewall Jackson was showing off his new daughter.

Nearby, Hunter McGuire made it a point to introduce Jodie to Chaplain B. Tucker Lacy. She found the preacher warm and delightful.

Before the McGuires walked away to find a place to sit down, Jodie glanced toward Stonewall and said, "Chaplain Lacy, would you do me a favor?"

"Sure," he said. "What is it?"

Stonewall Jackson was on the platform, sitting beside his chaplain general, as a young lieutenant stood before the crowd seated on the grass and led them in several hymns and gospel songs. The final song was John Newton's "Amazing Grace." When the last note faded, the song leader sat down and General Stonewall Jackson stepped forward. He led the crowd in prayer, asking the Lord to shine His gospel light into hearts during the preaching, then introduced Tucker Lacy as his good friend and "one of the greatest Presbyterian evangelists of the nineteenth century." Jackson shook hands with Lacy and returned to his chair beside the song leader.

When Lacy stepped to the crude wooden pulpit and laid his Bible down, he ran his gaze over the crowd and said, "My good friend General Stonewall Jackson just introduced me as a Presbyterian evangelist. Well, folks, I suppose I really ought to make a confession here in front of all of you. Actually, I am a Baptist spy!"

A roar of laughter spread over the crowd. Jackson first covered his face in mock embarrassment, then settled his eyes on Jodie McGuire and shook his fist at her. Jodie turned palms up and shrugged her shoulders.

When the laughter drained away, Lacy said, "We've had a little fun here. Now I want to speak to you from the gospel of Luke, the sixteenth chapter, on a very serious subject."

Tucker Lacy preached his heart out about the rich man and Lazarus, warning those in the crowd who had never been saved that they would spend eternity in hell with the rich man unless they repented of their sin and opened their hearts to Jesus Christ, trusting in Him and Him alone to save them.

As many of the soldiers and some local men and women responded to the invitation, the Christians in attendance were elated, and for a little while the War seemed far away.

✸✸✸✸✸

The next day, there was indication at the Union camp that General Hooker was getting ready to move at least some of his troops from the camp near Falmouth. Confederate scouts reported it to General Lee, and Lee called for a conference with Stonewall Jackson and all brigade and regiment leaders.

When the conference was over, Jackson returned to the Yerby farm and told Mary Anna and the McGuires that the entire Army of Northern Virginia was on alert. Once Hooker had declared his intentions, the Confederates would need to be prepared to meet him. Because fighting could break out on short notice, it was imperative that Hunter stay with the troops.

The general looked at Mary Anna's distressed face and said, "Sweetheart, I wish you and Julia didn't have to be in Lexington, so far away."

"They could stay with me in Richmond…for as long as Mary Anna wants to," said Jodie.

Mary Anna's expression brightened immediately, and the general smiled as Mary Anna clapped her hands and said, "Oh, Jodie! I accept."

The husbands kissed their wives as they put them on a train to Richmond. Thomas J. Jackson shed tears as he hugged and kissed his baby daughter last of all.

Shortly after daybreak on Wednesday, April 29, General Lee was awakened by a knock at his door in the farmhouse near the Rappahannock.

"Just a moment!" he called, rolling out of bed and hurrying into his uniform.

When he opened the door, hair tousled and eyes still fighting sleep, he found Lieutenant James P. Smith of Stonewall Jackson's staff looking at him with solemn eyes.

Smith saluted and said, "Sorry to bother you, General, but General Jackson wants you to know that Joe Hooker is moving part of his army due west across the Rappahannock from Falmouth under cover of fog."

"All right," said Lee, "tell your good general that I will meet him at the front shortly. If Hooker's troops keep moving west, they'll be in the Spotsylvania Wilderness by midmorning. Old Joe just might want to fight us there. Tell General Jackson to keep his scouts alert. I'll grab a little breakfast, and when I get to the front, I'll want to know exactly where those Yankees are."

"Yes, sir," said Smith, hurrying toward the front door where two sentries looked on. "I'll tell him."

The wilderness of Spotsylvania was a distinctive stretch of Virginia woodland of some seventy square miles. North to south it ran from the Rappahannock and Rapidan Rivers to three or four miles south of Chancellorsville, which was simply a rural cross-roads marked by a large red-brick, white-columned mansion that had once been a bed-and-breakfast stopover for travelers, as well as the home of the wealthy George Chancellor family.

Just west of the Rappahannock, a group of investors had financed construction of the Orange Turnpike in 1812. The turn-pike connected Fredericksburg with Orange Courthouse thirty-six miles to the west. In late 1816, George Chancellor opened his "overnight stopover" to cater to traffic on the Orange Turnpike where it intersected the busy Ely's Ford Road.

Chancellorsville, as George had dubbed it, was exactly ten miles due west of Fredericksburg, and sat on seventy acres of open land that edged the dense forest of the wilderness. George's dream was that his roadstop would evolve into a settlement, then a town. Though his dream was never realized, his mansion at the crossroads became the most prominent landmark in Spotsylvania County.

When George Chancellor died in 1836, his widow carried on with the overnight stopover until she died in 1860. At that time, the mansion was inherited by George's brother, Stanford, who died shortly thereafter, leaving it to his widow, Fannie Pound Chancellor, and their nine children.

In 1863, Fannie had seven of her children in the mansion with her—two sons and five daughters, all unmarried. Since the War's beginning, troops had marched along the turnpike, and the Chancellor girls had become the apples of many a Rebel soldier's eye.

For the most part, the Spotsylvania Wilderness was rugged, uneven ground, much of it marshland. A series of boggy water-courses cut ravines across it to empty into the Rapidan and Rappahannock, or the Ny River to the south. The low ridge lines between the watercourses ran generally north and south, and there were scattered marshes and sloughs, one of them extensive enough to be called Big Meadow Swamp. What cleared ground there was in the wilderness was mostly along the turnpike and a road called the Plank Road. The largest clearing was the seventy acres at Chancellorsville.

Fannie Pound Chancellor and her seven children were just finishing breakfast when they heard the sound of horses blowing and the tinkle of harness.

Twenty-year-old Matthew shoved back his chair and moved to a side window. He could see Union soldiers on horseback, in wagons, and on foot drawing up to the front of the house. Sixteen-year-old Malachi was just getting up from the table when Matthew said, "Mama! It's Yankees!"

Fannie Chancellor feared for her daughters. The oldest was nineteen, and the youngest was thirteen. Rising from her chair, she said, "Upstairs, girls! Now! Hide under the beds!"

The girls headed for the front of the house where they would mount the winding staircase, and Fannie called after them, "Don't make a sound, and don't come out until one of the boys or myself tells you it's safe!"

Fannie and her sons moved toward the front door to face the enemy soldiers.

"Should we get our guns, Mama?" asked Matthew.

"No! We cannot fight them, boys. All we can do is try to stay calm and see what they want."

They could hear heavy footsteps on the front porch and could make out men in dark uniforms through the lace curtains that covered the door windows. Suddenly there was a loud knock on the door.

Matthew hurried ahead of his mother to unlatch the door and swing it open.

A tall, husky man with a handlebar mustache speckled with gray stood in the doorway. Four stern-looking men in blue flanked him. His mouth was a thin, grim line as he said, without bothering to touch his hat brim, "Mrs. Chancellor, I presume."

"Yes," Fannie said nervously.

"I am Major General George Meade, commander of V Corps, Union Army of the Potomac."

Fannie's sons kept themselves a half-step ahead of their mother. Their eyes never left Meade's.

"I am here to tell you that Major General Joseph Hooker has chosen your house for his headquarters until the Rebel Army of Northern Virginia and their Bobby Lee have been vanquished."

Fannie's back arched, but before she could speak, Matthew moved closer to Meade and said, "No army can whip General Robert E. Lee's army! And this house is not for rent!"

Meade took a step through the door, and men with bayoneted rifles followed. "We're not asking to rent it, son," Meade said evenly. "We're telling your mother that General Hooker is taking it over until further notice."

Matthew moved up to meet Meade nose to nose, his face set

in rigid lines. "Your General Hooker has no right to move in here, and it's not going to happen, General Meade!"

One of the soldiers swung the butt of his rifle at Matthew's jaw and knocked him to the floor. Fannie's hands trembled as she fell to her knees beside him. He was out cold, and there was a gash on his jaw.

Malachi looked at the Yankee soldier, his eyes glowing with hatred, as Fannie screamed, "Look what you've done!"

The soldier who had hit Matthew nodded and said, "Your son needs to learn some manners, ma'am."

"Now, as I was saying," said Meade, "we're taking over this house as headquarters for General Hooker. Any more arguments?"

TEN

Fannie Chancellor ignored General Meade's question as she cupped Matthew's face in her hands and said, "Malachi, get me a wet towel."

Meade hunkered down beside her and said, "General Hooker wants the largest downstairs bedroom for his office, Mrs. Chancellor."

Fannie continued to caress her son's head. Matthew's eyes began to flutter, and he ejected a moan.

"Did you hear what I said, woman?" Meade said.

"I'm not deaf, General," she said without looking at him. "But right now I'm concerned about my son."

Malachi came running back with a dripping wet towel in his hands. Fannie took it and began dabbing at Matthew's face, then pressed the towel to the cut on his jaw. Holding it there while Matthew's eyes cleared, she looked at Meade with undisguised wrath, then turned her gaze on the soldier who had struck Matthew. "If I were a man, I'd take that gun away from you and put that bayonet through your belly!"

The soldier just smirked at her.

Matthew shook his head, winced, and let his eyes run past his mother to Meade, then to the other Yankee soldiers.

"You're cut, honey," said Fannie. "Let's get you to the kitchen so I can put a bandage on it."

"Mrs. Chancellor," said Meade, as Fannie and Malachi helped Matthew to his feet, "we want the largest bedroom on this floor as an office for General Hooker. Now where is it?"

"That's my room, but you're not welcome to it," Matthew said, blinking.

Meade drew in a deep breath, let it out slowly, and said, "Mrs. Chancellor, I would suggest you explain to your son that we are in control here, and if he gives us any more trouble, he'll get more of what he just got. Cooperate, and no harm will come to you or your children. If any of you refuse to obey us, you will suffer the consequences."

Fannie stared at him icily but nodded her acquiescence.

"Now, where are your daughters?" asked Meade.

Fannie's face paled.

"We won't harm them, ma'am. But we want the whole family together. My men will be stationed throughout the house so we can keep an eye on all of you."

Fannie blinked in bewilderment. "You mean you want us to stay here in the house? I thought—"

"That we'd throw you out? Oh, no, ma'am. We want all of you to stay right here. We can't have you running around out there, now, can we?"

Fannie's pallor became a red flush of anger. "So we're your prisoners, is that it?"

"That's it. But let me say it again, ma'am. None of you will be harmed in any way if you cooperate with us."

"You're telling me that my daughters are safe with Hooker in the house? I know about that lecher, General."

Meade's jaw stiffened. "Ma'am, I assure you…there won't be a hand laid on you or your daughters by General Hooker or anyone else in this army. And I repeat, if all of you cooperate with us, there won't be any more incidents like what just happened to your son."

"All right, General Meade, we'll cooperate because I believe you are a man of your word." Then to her younger son she said, "Malachi, bring your sisters downstairs to the kitchen."

As Malachi headed up the winding staircase, Meade called after him, "Don't get any ideas about trying to escape, son. We've got men surrounding the house."

Malachi looked back over his shoulder but didn't reply.

Fannie was about to guide Matthew toward the kitchen when the soldier who had struck him moved close and said, "How come you're not in a gray uniform, fella? You afraid to leave mama?"

Fannie gave the man a cold, level stare and said, "Matthew was born with a defective heart. He's not supposed to exert himself."

The soldier looked chagrined. "Oh."

General Meade turned to a corporal who was standing on the porch just outside the door and said, "Corporal Wingate, ride to General Hooker and tell him the Chancellor mansion is now secured for his occupancy."

It was midmorning when Major General Joseph Hooker arrived on the seventy-acre clearing that made up the Chancellor estate. He was on horseback and accompanied by some two dozen cavalrymen from First Division, including Brigadier General Alfred Pleasonton.

At forty-nine years of age, Joseph Hooker had puffy sacks under his pale blue eyes from many years of heavy drinking. An 1837 graduate of West Point, he was rawboned and stood three inches under six feet. He was the only officer to be breveted three times during the Mexican War, and this due to the frightening ruthlessness he displayed in battling the enemy. Thus he was dubbed "Fighting Joe" before he entered the Civil War.

Hooker let his gaze take in the tents outside the Chancellor mansion and the men in blue who stood on the wide porch and at each corner of the house. "Looks like we have it secured for sure," he said to Pleasonton.

"I'll be glad when we have the entire South secured as well, sir," said the brigadier general.

"Well, I'm expecting the battle we're about to enter with Bobby Lee will be the beginning of that."

They drew up to the front porch and General Meade came out the door.

"Good job, General," Hooker said to Meade as he dismounted. "Looks like everything is under control here."

"Yes, sir," said Meade. "We've got the largest bedroom on the ground floor set up for you, desk and all. We borrowed the desk from the library."

"Good. Any problems from the widow Chancellor or her offspring?"

"A little at first from the oldest son, but we've got him under control. You'll see a bandage on his face. Corporal Tedderman had to clobber him. Cut his jaw."

"I'm sorry to hear that. I don't want civilians hurt unless they force us to do it."

"Matthew forced us, sir."

"How old is he?"

"I'd say nineteen or twenty."

"Oh? Wonder why he isn't in the Rebel army."

"Has a bad heart, according to Mrs. Chancellor."

"I see. Well, I hope we won't see any more resistance out of him or any of the others. If I recall correctly, there are five teenage girls."

"Yes. And a teenage boy about fifteen or sixteen."

"And you've assured the widow that if they cooperate, no harm will come them?"

"Yes, sir."

Hooker dismissed General Pleasonton and his cavalrymen to return to the Falmouth camp and entered the mansion to find that Meade had Fannie and her children seated in the parlor. Three soldiers stood guard.

Meade led Hooker into the room and said, "General, this is Mrs. Chancellor and her children."

When none of the family stood up, Meade said, "It is customary that when the field commander enters a room, civilians rise to their feet."

"I don't want to sound uncooperative, General Meade," said Fannie, "but that would be true only north of the Mason-Dixon line, wouldn't it?"

Meade's features stiffened. "Now, see here—"

"Well, if you were a civilian up in the North, and General Robert E. Lee or General Stonewall Jackson entered the room…would you stand up to honor him?"

Joe Hooker laughed. "I like this lady, General Meade. She's got spunk." He addressed his next remark to Fannie. "I'm sure he wouldn't stand for either of those men, ma'am…and neither would I. You and your children stay seated."

"Thank you, General," said Fannie, giving Meade a cool glance.

"Well!" said Hooker. "I'd like to see my quarters."

"It's my bedroom, General Hooker," Matthew said. "I would appreciate it if you'd take good care of it."

"I will, son," replied Hooker. "When we've conquered Lee, we'll pull out for Washington with the stars and stripes waving the victory sign, and the South will once again be part of the Union. And your room will be intact, I assure you."

Meade said, "I'll take you to your quarters, sir."

They started toward the hall, then Hooker paused and looked back at Fannie. "Did General Meade tell you we will cook our own food outdoors, the same as we do when camped?"

"I hadn't brought that up, yet, sir," said Meade.

"Is that because you don't wish to impose on me, General?" asked Fannie, who at forty-one was still quite attractive. "Or because you're afraid I might poison you?"

"Definitely the latter, ma'am," said Hooker with a smile.

Fannie smiled cryptically. "And you are right, General."

More Union army personnel arrived during the afternoon, and that evening General Hooker sat down in his new office with Major Generals John Sedgwick, John Reynolds, Daniel Sickles, and John Gibbon.

Fannie and her daughters were on the second floor in a sitting room, and Matthew and Malachi were in Malachi's bedroom, which was next door to Hooker's office.

Upstairs, Fannie told her girls she had learned that the only soldier who would sleep in the house was Hooker, who would use Matthew's bed. There would be night sentries inside and outside the house, but all others would sleep in the tents they had pitched around the house.

In Malachi's bedroom, the Chancellor brothers pressed their ears to a weak spot on the wall, which they had discovered a few months earlier. They could easily hear every word spoken in the next room.

Hooker looked at his generals and said, "I have devised a series of deceptions that, if executed properly, will bring about swift victory over Bobby Lee."

In the next room, Matthew whispered, "Malachi, get me a pencil and some paper. I need to get this down!"

Hooker explained that on Friday, which was May 1, General

Sedgwick would lead his VI Corps, and Reynolds his I Corps, across the Rappahannock below Fredericksburg to feign a major attack on Stonewall Jackson's II Corps. To confuse Lee's scouts even further, two other units—Sickles's III Corps and Gibbon's II Corps—would remain temporarily in the camp at Falmouth, but clearly visible to Confederate pickets.

In the adjoining room, Matthew wrote hurriedly as Malachi whispered, "Are you getting it?"

"I'll have to rewrite it so it's legible," Matthew said, "but I'm getting it."

"These deceptions will give the rest of our massive army a good edge to wipe out Bobby Lee."

"It's ingenious, sir!" said Reynolds. "Even using our units as decoys, you'll still have some ninety thousand men to swarm Lee's mere sixty-five thousand."

"Yes!" Hooker said, banging his fist on the desk. "We'll win this one, gentlemen. Bobby Lee is about to meet his Waterloo! God Almighty Himself couldn't keep me from victory!"

There was a sudden hush in the room as the generals exchanged fearful glances.

"What's the matter?" asked Hooker, frowning.

"Excuse me, General Hooker," John Sedgwick said, "but as God-fearing men, we respectfully request that you not speak in such bold terms concerning almighty God."

Hooker blinked as Daniel Sickles said, "I was named after the great prophet Daniel in the Bible, sir. In the book of Daniel, the story is told of King Belshazzar, who mocked God while banqueting with a thousand of his lords. During the banquet, God's own finger wrote a message on the wall to the brash king, saying he had been weighed in the balances and found wanting. That very night Belshazzar was slain by his enemies. If I were you, General Hooker, I wouldn't tempt God to show me that He could prevent me from a victory…and instead bring me defeat."

Joseph Hooker laughed. "I'll win this battle, General Sickles.

You can bet your last dollar on it!"

In the next room, Matthew Chancellor was copying his hastily written notes to make it readable to other eyes. While the voices of the Union generals continued to come through the wall, he whispered, "It's dark now, Malachi. I wish I could be the one to deliver this, but you know I don't dare put that much strain on my heart."

"I'm glad to deliver it," whispered Malachi. "Should we talk to Mama about it first?"

"We can't. You know she wouldn't want either of us taking the risk. You'll have to do it without her knowing. I'm not sure where General Lee is, but I know General Jackson is just south of Fredericksburg, close to the river. You've got to get this information to him!"

With the folded slip of paper in his shirt pocket, Malachi Chancellor eased through the open window of his bedroom, with Matthew's help, and dropped quietly to the ground.

The night was a shroud of darkness as he pressed his back to the brick wall and inched toward the rear of the house. There was no moon, and the sky was partially covered with clouds, leaving little starlight to guide him.

Malachi hauled up as he reached the back porch. Two sentries were there, talking in low tones. He could barely make them out, but both had their backs to him.

The boy's heart pounded as he veered away from the house, moving from tree to tree, trying not to step on a twig or stumble on a stone and give himself away.

When he reached the last tree before the open stretch to the corral and barn, he paused, looked back, and saw the shadowed forms of the two sentries moving toward the other side of the house. Malachi knew there were at least four other sentries out-side. Two of them were at the front, and he had no idea where the other two might be.

He made his way to the corral gate and cautiously slipped between the rails of the fence and moved toward the barn.

He decided to enter from the rear, rather than on the side where the sentries might be. It took Malachi three or four minutes to reach the back side of the barn by inching his way along the wall. He held his breath as he tripped the latch as quietly as pos-sible and eased the door open. The hinges voiced their objection, but moving the door very slowly kept the sound to a minimum.

Two of the horses nickered at Malachi's presence. He paused to let them get used to his being there, then moved along the wall in the almost pitch-black gloom to where the saddles and bridles hung near the front of the barn. Soon he had the desired bridle in his hand, and peering into the inky blackness, he whispered, "Bucky! Bucky! Where are you?"

A familiar nicker came from a few feet away. Soon, Malachi had a hand on the muzzle of his horse and slipped the bridle on, gently pressing the bit into Bucky's mouth. He buckled the strap and whispered, "Okay, boy. We're going for a little bareback ride. Be real quiet."

Malachi wished the corral had a back gate, but there was only the gate at the front side of the barn. He led the horse out the rear door and walked him slowly along the wall. When they reached the front of the barn, Malachi paused, trying to see the sentries at the rear of the house. They were no doubt somewhere there in the shadows, but he couldn't make them out.

His eyes burned as he scanned the darkness near the gate and strained his ears for any telltale sounds of the enemy. There was nothing.

Holding one hand over Bucky's muzzle, he led him slowly across the corral. Once he was past the area where the tents had been pitched, he would ride to the edge of the woods, then put Bucky to a gallop and head for the Confederate camp on the Rappahannock.

Malachi reached the gate and eased the latch from its place. The latch made a clicking sound, and the boy froze, listening for the sentries. His muscles ached from the sheer fright that gripped him.

He heard only silence, but even that was like some great force squeezing his lungs.

He inched the gate open until there was room enough to lead Bucky through. The horse followed obediently, his hooves making soft muffled sounds on the spongy ground.

When Malachi had Bucky out of the corral, he held the reins at length while closing the gate. The latch dropped in place much quieter than it had come out. He raised the reins over the horse's head and swung up on his back.

Suddenly there was a rustling sound in the direction of the house, and a voice pierced the darkness. "Hey! Who goes there?"

Bucky nickered at the sound, and a cold, icy hand clutched Malachi's heart.

He could hear the sound of pounding footsteps as a soldier called out, "Rex, what's going on out there?"

"Got somebody on a horse, Sergeant!" came the quick reply. The next words came out harshly. "Identify yourself or die, mister!"

Malachi felt the muscular quivering of near panic as his breath came in jerky gasps. "It's...me. Malachi Chancellor."

In the sitting room on the second floor, Fannie Chancellor was playing a word game with her daughters. Suddenly they heard heavy footsteps in the hall, followed by a deafening knock on the door.

"Mrs. Chancellor!" boomed a heavy voice.

Wide-eyed, the girls watched their mother open the door. Two husky soldiers stood before her, their faces rigid.

"Ma'am," said the one who had knocked on the door, "we've got a problem downstairs. General Hooker wants you there immediately."

"Well, what is it?"

"Your sons are in trouble. Come with us."

Fannie looked over her shoulder and said, "Girls, you stay here. I'll be back shortly."

As the soldiers ushered Fannie toward the winding staircase, she said, "What did my boys do?"

"They overheard General Hooker's conversation with some of his generals and wrote down what was said. Your oldest addressed a note to Stonewall Jackson, telling him all about General Hooker's battle plans, and your other boy tried to ride to Jackson and give it to him. We caught him, ma'am. And General Hooker is very upset!"

When Fannie entered Hooker's office she found two pale and frightened boys standing before the commander.

Hooker wheeled as one of the sentries said, "Here's their mother, sir."

Fannie rushed to her sons, throwing an arm around each of them, and held them tight.

Hooker stepped up to her, and said, "Look at this!"

Fannie glanced down at the slip of paper and took it in her hand.

"Your sons were eavesdropping on a meeting I held with some of my unit leaders. We caught the youngest one about to ride to Stonewall Jackson to give him my strategy!"

Fannie nodded. "Your men told me about it, General."

Hooker's face was flushed and his eyes bulged as he said, "You'd better have a good long talk with these boys, lady! I'm not going to punish them this time, but if something like this happens again, you're not going to like what I do to the whole family!"

Fannie held his gaze for a long moment, then said in a low tone, "May we be excused, General?"

"Just make sure you get the message across to them."

"There won't be any more episodes like this one, General," she said, pushing her sons toward the door. When they reached it, Fannie stopped, looked over her shoulder, and said, "You have to admit it was pretty good thinking on their part. That information might have thwarted your battle plans. If you had been in their place, General, what would you have done?"

Hooker wiped a hand over his dissolute features. "I…well, I guess I have to say I'd have done exactly what they did."

Fannie smiled.

"But I'm telling you, lady…if they do anything akin to it again, the whole family's going to be sorry."

"As I've already told you, General, they won't."

Fannie took the boys into Malachi's room, closed the door, and keeping her voice low, said, "I'm proud of both of you! I'm glad you were willing to risk getting caught in order to get the message to General Jackson. But please, don't do anything like that again. Hooker means what he says. He'll punish all of us."

"We won't, Mama," said Matthew. "But I can't help wishing Malachi had been able to get through to General Jackson. He was so close!"

"Well," she breathed, "our army is going to whip them anyhow."

"I sure hope so," said Malachi. "I'd like to see Meade and Hooker eat dirt."

"Yeah," said Matthew, "and that guy that hit me with the rifle butt too."

★★★★★

On April 30, Jackson was up before dawn, ready to meet with
General Lee and form battle plans. Lee was at the I Corps camp
nearby. After breakfast, Jackson went back to his tent to await
Lee's appearance for their meeting and fell on his knees to pray.

Corporal Lewis, who was the general's "shadow" and devoted
aide, stationed himself near the opening of the tent to keep anyone from disturbing him.

Lee and Jackson met just after sunrise, and put their heads
together to come up with a way of impeding, if not crushing,
Hooker. They knew they were outnumbered far more than two to
one, and in place of manpower they would have to come up with
ingenuity. They would have to outguess Hooker and anticipate
what he was going to do.

As they discussed the situation, Lee said, "General, I think the
best plan for us is to fortify ourselves and simply let Hooker come
to us."

"I don't think so, sir," said Jackson. "It's my opinion that we
ought to go on the offensive and attack Hooker while we're trying
to outguess him. Let's take the battle to him."

Lee scratched his beard. "Well, my friend, you know I have
the utmost confidence in you. If this is how you feel, then make
your plans and take the battle to ol' Fighting Joe!"

"As you know, sir, our scouts say Hooker has bivouacked
some of his men in tents at Chancellorsville, and they think
Hooker is staying inside the mansion. Unless there's some kind of
major move today, I'd like to do a little reconnoitering after dark
tonight. Should be a new moon. I need to take a look at the situation when no Yankee could possibly see me."

Lee nodded. "Whatever you say. In the meantime, if Hooker
makes an aggressive move, we'll have to counter."

"Yes, sir. I have a feeling he's not quite ready. Let's hope we
can beat him to the punch."

Lee chuckled. "Well, if it's good ol' Stonewall doing the punching, I'm all for it!"

ELEVEN

It was after ten o'clock that night when Lieutenant General Thomas J. Jackson mounted Little Sorrel.

"I appreciate your offer to ride with me, men," he said to the earnest faces looking up at him. "But this is something I must do alone. I can move much quieter by myself."

"But General, there could be Yankee snipers out there and—"

"I'll be very careful, Major Dayton," Jackson said with a smile.

The other men were Dayton's Antietam heroes, Corporals Everett Nichols, Hank Upchurch, Chuck Carney, and Buford Hall.

It was Hall who said, "Sir, what if we ride a half-mile or so behind you? At least then, if you got into trouble, we could help you."

A few other men of the North Carolina Regiments were starting to gather around the small group, curious as to why their commander was leaving camp at this hour.

"Men, I appreciate your concern, but this reconnaissance must be done by one man, and since General Lee has placed the responsibility of planning the battle strategy on me, I'm the one who has to look the situation over. See you at dawn, if not before."

The soldiers watched their leader trot away along the bank of the Rappahannock. Then Private Bo Gentry said, "He's the best, fellas. I'd follow him into the devil's lair if he asked me to."

"Me too," said Private Chad Lynch. "The man's going down in history as a military leader the likes of Napoleon and Alexander the Great."

"Except Stonewall Jackson will be head and shoulders above them," said Corporal Ken Dykstra.

"You hit the nail on the head," agreed Corporal Myron Flynn. "I believe General Lee will be amongst them, too, but there's just something special about General Jackson."

"Hard to put it into words, isn't it?" said Rance Dayton. "I felt that way when he was my favorite professor at V.M.I., and I feel even stronger about him now that I've been on the battlefield with him." Dayton looked in the direction where Jackson had ridden, and said, "Take care of him, Lord."

Stonewall Jackson kept to the bank of the river and under the trees, all the way to the edge of the wilderness. The four-mile ride was uneventful, and the night air was peaceful and quiet as he guided Little Sorrel to a high knoll.

Before him lay the open fields that were part of the Chancellorsville estate, the Orange Turnpike, Ely's Ford Road, and the dark area, which was the Spotsylvania Wilderness.

The area ran north to south from the Rappahannock and Rapidan Rivers to some three miles south of Chancellorsville. East to west, it extended from Tabernacle Church to beyond Wilderness Tavern, a local hotel. Jackson could make out parts of the old plank road that wove its way through the wilderness, along with the turnpike. The only cleared ground was along the sides of the roads.

Jackson studied the wilderness—a dense forest of scrub oak, pine, hickory, and cedar. He had been told that no one left the roads to enter the woods. For there was nothing there but mucky marshes and sloughs in dark, eerie, impenetrable undergrowth.

Stonewall stroked his beard thoughtfully. "You know what, Little Sorrel?" he said aloud. "I just got an idea. That wilderness would be a perfect place to hide my II Corps and pull a surprise on ol' Joe Hooker."

Little Sorrel nickered softly as if he understood and agreed.

Jackson left the knoll, riding slowly, and ventured closer to Chancellorsville, where he could make out the Yankee tents near the mansion. He dismounted and scanned the open fields that edged up to the dark forest. With his experienced eye he judged the artillery range from the edge of the wilderness and measured the ground his men would have to cross before meeting the enemy with bayonets.

Suddenly he gave a decisive nod and mounted up, putting Little Sorrel to a moderate gallop across the moon-sprayed land. If General Lee approved, Jackson would move his II Corps the four miles to the edge of Chancellorsville and position them in the dark shadows of the wilderness. Joe Hooker would never expect that.

Robert E. Lee sat in his tent after midnight, stifling a yawn as he listened to Jackson's plan. He liked it immediately and said, "Go to it, General. Move your men out as soon as you can. I will position I Corps accordingly. We'll give ol' Joe a little surprise."

"Surprise is half the victor's battle," said Stonewall. "But even then, sir, this will likely be a bloody fight. I suggest we move our medical staff close to Chancellorsville, which will no doubt be the field of battle. Wilderness Tavern would be the best spot."

"I agree," said Lee. "And the folks at the hotel will open their arms to them, I'm sure."

The generals concurred. Medical directors Dr. Jason Franks of I Corps and Dr. Hunter McGuire of II Corps, along with their staff and supply wagons, would move immediately to Wilderness Tavern.

The calm, resolute, sensitive, and scholarly Robert E. Lee, and his fiery but calculating Stonewall Jackson were ready to take on an army more than twice the size of their own.

In I Corps, under Lee, the divisions were commanded by Major Generals Lafayette McLaws and R. H. "Dick" Anderson. The cavalry division was led by Major General J. E. B. "Jeb" Stuart.

In Jackson's II Corps, the division commanders were Major Generals A. P. Hill, Jubal Early, R. E. Colson, and D. H. Hill. The artillery was commanded by Colonel Stapleton Crutchfield, who had been trained with the big guns by Stonewall Jackson himself at Virginia Military Institute.

Within half an hour, Jackson and his II Corps were ready to leave the camp on the Rappahannock and march two hours northward to the wilderness.

By 4:30 A.M. Jackson had his men well situated in the marshes and sloughs of the dark forest.

At daylight, General Hooker set in motion the deceptive moves he had revealed to his men inside Matthew Chancellor's bedroom. However, Generals John Sedgwick and John Reynolds, who were to feign a major attack on Stonewall Jackson's II Corps on the Rappahannock, found the camp deserted.

There were a few skirmishes that day between small bands of

troops, but as the sun ran its arc through the Virginia sky, it was evident there would be no major battle that day.

Inside the Chancellorsville mansion, Fannie and her children were gathered in the library with the door closed. The mother had spoken with General Hooker and convinced him that she and her family deserved some privacy. Two soldiers, however, stood guard outside in the hall.

Fannie's daughters were Naomi, nineteen, Ruth, seventeen, Sarah, fifteen, Martha, fourteen, and Rebecca, thirteen. While the family talked about what might have happened if Malachi had reached General Jackson with the information, the youngest of the siblings began to sniffle.

Matthew, who was sitting next to her, gently took her hand and said, "What's wrong, Rebecca?"

Her lips quivered as she spoke. "When General Jackson finds out the Yankees are staying in our house and in our yard, they'll start shooting their cannons. We'll all be killed by our own army."

"Our soldiers won't shoot at the house if they know we're in here," said Malachi.

"I'm sure you're right," said Naomi. "But since we're kept inside, and they can't see us, they might figure the Yankees have run us off. If that's what they think, they'll bombard the house for sure."

"Well, let's hope and pray that it never gets that far," said Fannie. "Maybe General Lee will outsmart Hooker and it will all be over before any guns are fired around here."

"Speaking of guns," said Matthew, "if those dirty Yankees hadn't taken ours, I'd break through my bedroom door and use one to shoot Hooker."

"Yeah, and I'd blast him too," put in Malachi. "I'd kill him deader'n a doornail."

The widow looked at her sons aghast and said, "Boys, you shouldn't want to kill anybody, not even Hooker."

"You told Hooker you'd poison him, Mama," spoke up Martha.

Fannie's face tinted. "Well, I didn't mean it. I couldn't really take anyone's life unless they were trying to kill one of you, or if I had to in self-defense."

"But this is war, Mama," said Matthew. "I'd poison any one of those dirty Yankee soldiers if I had the chance. Or I'd kill them any way I could…especially Hooker. If he didn't want to be in danger of being killed, he should've been a store clerk or a farmer instead of a general. Besides, I don't like the way he looks at you."

"I don't either," said Naomi. "He's got evil, shifty eyes."

"I don't have a gun," said Malachi, "but if he ever comes near you, Mama, I'll climb on his back and ram my fingers in his eyes."

"And I'll kick him in the shin," put in Ruth.

"And I'll kick him in the other shin," said Sarah.

"And I'll kick him in the stomach," Martha growled.

"Yeah, and I'll kick him where he sits down!" said Rebecca, who had long since stopped sniffling.

Fannie covered her mouth to hide her grin.

"And if there's anything left of him," said Matthew, "I'll finish him off!"

Fannie gave up trying to hide her amusement and laughed out loud.

That night, Stonewall Jackson, Rance Dayton, and Chaplain B. Tucker Lacy entered Jackson's tent to pray about the impending battle.

All the tents were set up deep in the wilderness along the edge of the old plank road. No lanterns or fires were allowed.

A dozen men of the Eighteenth North Carolina Regiment stood watch near the edge of the wilderness where II Corps was hiding. A buttermilk sky partially covered the moon, and the men peered into the gloom, watching for any kind of movement on the open field that lay between them and the Chancellor mansion a half-mile away.

All was still, except for a slight breeze that rustled the trees, and the repeated hoot of an owl somewhere deep in the dark regions of the forest.

Sentries Everett Nichols, Hank Upchurch, Buford Hall, and Chuck Carney were huddled together, with their friends Chad Lynch, Bo Gentry, Ken Dykstra, and Myron Flynn close by, watching the road.

Out of earshot from the others, the Fearless Four talked in low tones of the coming battle.

As he ran his gaze to the south, Upchurch said, "The artillery is ready for action. How I hate to see that beautiful Chancellor mansion get blasted. But with Hooker in there, I'm sure Colonel Crutchfield will unleash his guns on the house to flush Hooker into the open."

"I wonder where the family went?" said Carney.

Hall shrugged his shoulders. "Probably staying with a neighbor, I would imagine. Isn't that the way it usually is when the Yankees take over somebody's house as headquarters?"

There was silence for a moment, then Nichols said, "I've got a feeling this move to the wilderness is going to throw Hooker for a loop. Maybe the surprise will be all we need to catch him off guard."

"Yeah," put in Hall, "especially when General Lee hits him from the other side."

"You gotta hand it to General Jackson, fellas," said Carney. "He's one smart cookie, if you'll pardon the expression. I have no doubt his ingenuity will lead us to victory in this battle."

✳✳✳✳✳

It was nine o'clock in the evening on May 1 when Jodie McGuire answered a knock at her apartment door. Mary Anna Jackson was in the spare bedroom, checking on little Julia. A neighbor had loaned Jodie a crib for the baby.

"Good evening, Mrs. McGuire," said a young soldier at the door. "I'm Corporal Justin Porter. I have a message for Mrs. Thomas Jackson from the general. He said she was staying here."

"Yes, Corporal," said Jodie. "Please come in. I'll get Mrs. Jackson."

Porter removed his cap and stepped just inside the door. "I'll wait right here, ma'am."

Seconds later, Mary Anna appeared alongside Jodie and said, "Good evening, corporal. Mrs. McGuire said you have a message?"

"Yes, ma'am. A messenger from II Corps arrived at our camp outside Richmond about an hour ago. General Jackson asked him to send someone to let you know the situation at this time."

The women exchanged glances, and Mary Anna said, "We've been wondering what's happening."

"General Jackson wants you and Mrs. McGuire to know that there will be a big battle tomorrow, and it's certain to take place at the crossroads of the Orange Turnpike and Ely's Ford Road."

"That would be near the Chancellor mansion, then," said Mary Anna.

"Yes, ma'am. General Jackson's corps is set up very close to Chancellorsville. And Mrs. McGuire, your husband and Dr. Franks of I Corps and their staffs are stationed at Wilderness Tavern to care for the wounded."

Mary Anna's brow furrowed. "Do you know how many men the Yankees have there?"

"I'm told about a hundred and forty thousand."

"And we have less than half that number," she said.

"Yes. About sixty-five thousand. But we still have the advantage, ma'am. We have General Stonewall Jackson's military skill to plan the strategy. The Yankees only have Joe Hooker."

"Of course," said Jodie. "So that gives us the edge, no matter how many troops the Yankees have!"

Porter nodded, bade the ladies good evening, and left the premises.

When Jodie closed the door, she turned and put a hand on Mary Anna's shoulder. "I know it's a scary thing to have your husband on the battlefield, no matter what the odds are, but our army has had to fight almost every battle outnumbered by the Yankees. And look how many we've won!"

"And we'll win this one too," said Mary Anna, forcing a note of confidence into her voice. "Of course, that doesn't mean there won't be casualties. Thank the Lord, when you're saved you know that all death can do is usher you into the arms of the Saviour."

"I wouldn't trade that precious truth for anything this world has to offer," said Jodie.

"That makes me think of the Scripture Tom always reads before he goes into battle." Mary Anna turned toward the spare bedroom. "I'll get my Bible and read it."

Moments later the women sat side-by-side at the kitchen table, and Mary Anna opened her Bible to 2 Corinthians 5:1-8.

"That's the passage where Paul deals with the Christian's earthly body compared to his or her heavenly, glorified body, isn't it?" asked Jodie.

Mary Anna nodded.

Jodie followed along, reading silently, while Mary Anna read the passage aloud. When she came to verse 4, she said, "Here is Tom's favorite verse. 'For we that are in this tabernacle do groan, being burdened: not for that we would be unclothed, but clothed upon, that mortality might be swallowed up of life.'"

Jodie nodded solemnly. "It's good that the general can face each battle with this passage firm in his heart. Think of all the men who go to the battlefield and have no such claim on heaven."

Tears misted Mary Anna's eyes. "I'm so glad that both of our husbands are saved, Jodie. If God should allow either or both of them to be taken from us, we know we'll meet them again in heaven."

Sudden tears sprang to Jodie's eyes. "Thank God for Calvary."

"Yes, thank God," said Mary Anna, closing her Bible.

Rising from her chair, Jodie said, "Well, prayer time, then bedtime."

To avoid disturbing little Julia, the two women went to Jodie's bedroom, knelt beside the bed, and asked the Lord to keep their husbands safe.

At the edge of the dark, shadowy Spotsylvania Wilderness, the clouds were drifting away from the moon, allowing its silver rays to shine down clear and bright. The Confederate sentries stood alert and still as they scanned the area for any sign of the enemy. Suddenly Chuck Carney stiffened and squinted.

"What's the matter?" Hank Upchurch asked, following his line of sight.

Carney raised his rifle and snapped the hammer into firing position. "Movement down there on the field at the edge of the woods, to the right."

From a few yards away, Bo Gentry whispered hoarsely, "What's up?"

"Down there!" Carney said, pointing with his rifle muzzle. "Riders!"

Other rifles cocked as three horsemen became visible, their horses hugging the edge of the woods.

Carney led the others out of the shadows to face the oncoming riders. At twenty yards out, the one in the lead saw them and pulled rein. "Hold it, men!" he said. "Don't fire! It's Jeb Stuart!"

"Come on in, sir," said Carney. "Who you got with you?"

"Couple of scouts. We need to see General Jackson."

Stonewall Jackson's prayer time with Rance Dayton and Tucker Lacy was over, and the three men now stood in front of Jackson's tent in the moonlight, speaking in low tones. The conversation stopped abruptly when they heard a tiny jingling sound and a metallic clank. They turned to see four men coming their way.

"What do you suppose this is, sir?" asked Lacy.

"Sounds like a cavalry officer in the bunch," said Jackson. "Only a saber on a man's side makes that kind of noise."

As they drew up, Corporal Chuck Carney said, "General Jackson, I have General Jeb Stuart here, along with a couple of scouts."

Stuart and Jackson greeted each other quietly, then Stuart said, "General, these men are scouts from Brigadier General Fitzhugh Lee's cavalry brigade. General Lee sent them with news you need to hear."

Jackson thanked Carney and sent him back to his post, then took Stuart and the scouts inside his tent.

"General, do you mind if Major Dayton and I listen in?" Lacy said through the tent wall.

"Not in the least. Whatever I'm about to be told, you'll know about it anyway."

The scouts told Jackson about General Hooker's series of planned deceptions, including his move on the spot where Jackson's II Corps had been camped on the bank of the Rappahannock.

When he had the entire picture, Stonewall said, "Thank you, men, and please take my thanks to your commander for sending you tonight. This information is invaluable."

Jeb Stuart chortled. "Looks like the mighty Joe Hooker is

going to get the surprise of his life tomorrow!"

Lacy and Dayton shook hands as Lacy exclaimed, "Praise the Lord! He's already answering prayer!"

When Stuart and the scouts were at the edge of the forest, mounting up, Jackson held a sheet of paper on which he had drawn a crude map and marked the Union army's positions, according to the scouts. "I wish General Lee was still close by," he said to Dayton and Lacy.

Lee had gone to Fredericksburg to stay in the hotel and get a good night's rest. His heart was bothering him again, just as it had before the Antietam battle.

"It's too far to Fredericksburg," said Jackson. "I'll have to make the decision to counter Hooker's moves without General Lee's approval, then send a messenger to tell him what I've decided to do so he can maneuver I Corps accordingly."

Rance Dayton scrubbed a hand over his mustache. "I doubt General Lee would disagree with your strategy, sir, whatever it is."

"I appreciate your confidence, Major."

"You've got that a thousand percent, sir."

Lacy chuckled. "You've got that with all of your men, General."

Jackson smiled and looked at the slip of paper by moonlight. "I've got to figure the routes to send my corps to counteract Hooker's moves. Problem is, I'm not very familiar with the area."

"I can help you with that," said the chaplain. "I've preached in this area many times, and I know it well."

"Good. What we'll need to do is move on the Federal rear, and God willing, not be seen by them till it's too late for them to counter. When I Corps joins us, the element of surprise in this entire operation will carry a heavy weight toward bringing off a victory against such great odds. Let's sit down in the tent and—" Jackson turned his head, covered his mouth, and sneezed. "Excuse me, gentlemen. I think I'm coming down with a cold."

"Maybe we should send for Dr. McGuire, General," said Dayton.

"You're probably right."

"I'll send one of my men for the doctor, sir," said Dayton, and hurried away.

Jackson pulled a handkerchief from his hip pocket, wiped his nose, and said, "As I was about to suggest, Chaplain, let's sit down in the tent and you tell me some things I need to know so I can get them down on this map."

TWELVE

Rance Dayton returned to Jackson's tent within a few minutes and informed him that a messenger was on his way to fetch Dr. McGuire. Jackson thanked the major and invited him to stay while he questioned Tucker Lacy about the lay of the area.

It was near midnight when Jackson finalized his strategy. In the morning I Corps would join II to launch an offensive on the Union forces. He sent a messenger to Fredericksburg to inform General Lee.

After the messenger had gone, Jackson leaned back and began rubbing his tired eyes.

"Sir," said Rance Dayton, "something's been on my mind since Hooker moved into the Chancellor mansion."

"What's that?"

"Where did the Chancellor family go?"

"Well, we've had no report of the family moving about the grounds. Certainly Hooker's aware of the great possibility of a battle right around the mansion. I would think the man has enough character and good sense to have allowed the Chancellor family to go elsewhere for safety's sake."

Lacy cleared his throat gently. "Ah…General, from what I've heard about Hooker, I doubt he has. He likes to bully people, and he doesn't care who it is. You're aware that there's no man of the house—that the widow Fannie Chancellor lives there with seven of her nine children?"

"Yes, I am aware of that," said Jackson. "But do you really think Hooker would hold them captive?"

"Yes, I do. Tell me…would turning your howitzers on the mansion be part of the plan?"

"Yes, if it comes to that."

"Then I want to go over there right now and ask the sentries if the family is still in the house. If they are, I'll demand to see Hooker and put pressure on him to let them go."

"You wouldn't get within thirty yards of the mansion, Chaplain," said Jackson. "They'd cut you down."

"Not if I go in carrying a lighted lantern."

"I don't know…they might shoot first and ask your dead body questions later."

"I'm willing to take the risk," said Lacy. "I must make sure Mrs. Chancellor and those children are safely placed elsewhere before the battle begins."

Jackson shook his head in wonder and glanced at Dayton, then said, "Too bad I don't have you in a uniform with a gun in your hand, Chaplain Lacy. You'd make a great soldier."

"I am a soldier, General. A soldier of the cross."

"You sure are, my friend, and God bless you for the way you preach the cross."

Lanterns burned late in Matthew Chancellor's bedroom as General Hooker stood before his seven corps leaders.

The Chancellor boys had been moved upstairs so they couldn't listen in on any more of Hooker's private conversations.

On the second floor, Fannie Chancellor lay awake, unable to get her mind off the pending battle.

Joe Hooker was lighthearted as he stood before his generals and said, "Gentlemen, we're ready to take on Bobby Lee and Stonehead Jackson in the morning. Some surprise we have in store for those boys!"

None of the generals seemed to share their leader's attitude. While Hooker waited for a show of enthusiasm from his generals, a knock at the door interrupted the silent tension.

A sentry looked around the door and said, "General Hooker, there's someone on the front porch who would like to speak to you."

Hooker scowled. "Who wants to see me at this time of the night?"

"A preacher."

"A preacher?"

"Yes, sir."

"Well, I don't need a sermon at this time of night! What's he want?"

"He asked the sentries on the porch if the Chancellor family was being held as captives. They didn't want to lie, so they told him they are. He wants to see you."

Hooker snorted in disgust and said, "Tell him I'm not seeing visitors tonight."

The disapproving frowns on the faces of his corps leaders made him lift a hand. "On second thought, Private Selby, bring the reverend in."

While Selby was gone, General Meade said, "General Hooker, I've been thinking about the Chancellor widow and her children. We told them no harm would come to them if they cooperated with us. But if the Rebels should shell this house, and any of them are injured or killed, that makes us liars. I'm sure this reverend, whoever he is, is going to ask you to release them. I, for one, think you should do it."

There was a rumble of agreement among the generals.

Hooker frowned. "But I had in mind that if we let it be known the family was here, the Rebels wouldn't turn their guns loose on the mansion."

Major General Darius Couch looked at his commander with disdain. "You mean hide behind a woman and her children?"

Hooker saw the same look in the eyes of the other men. "Well, I—"

The sentry appeared at the door. "Chaplain Tucker Lacy of II Corps, Army of Northern Virginia, sir."

As the chaplain entered, Hooker moved toward him. "I'm Major General Joseph Hooker, Reverend."

"I know," said Lacy. "I've seen your photograph in the papers, sir."

"What is it you wish to see me about, Reverend?"

"I came here to see if Mrs. Chancellor and her children were being held captive in this house, sir, and your sentries outside confirmed that they are. I would like you to let me take them away from here until this conflict is over."

"Well, isn't that a coincidence?" Hooker said, smiling. "I was just talking to my corps commanders here about that very thing. We'd certainly like to get the lady and her children off our hands."

"May I talk to Mrs. Chancellor, please?" asked Lacy.

Fannie was awake when the knock came. She opened the door and clutched at the neck of her robe, glancing at Hooker and the sentries, and then at the man in their midst. Her gaze stayed riveted on the man, and she said, "I know you, sir. You're evangelist Tucker Lacy. I heard you preach when you were at Bonner Grove Presbyterian Church."

Lacy smiled. "That's right, Mrs. Chancellor. I am presently Chaplain General of II Corps, Army of Northern Virginia."

"That's General Jackson's Corps."

"Yes, ma'am. You are aware there could be a battle right here in this area…"

"Yes, I am."

"Well, I came to ask General Hooker to let me take you out of here."

Fannie's eyes flicked to Hooker's face.

"I've given permission," he said quickly.

"Do you and the children know somebody who would take you in, ma'am?" asked Lacy.

"We have some close friends who live just five miles down Ely's Ford Road. An elderly couple—Jack and Elsie Courtman. They have a large house, and I know they would welcome us."

"All right," said Lacy. "How long would it take you to get the children up and ready to go? I'm sure General Hooker will provide a wagon, and I'll go along to make sure the Courtmans are home."

"We can be ready in less than an hour," said Fannie.

"All right. We'll be waiting in the room General Hooker is occupying."

"I'll hurry," said Fannie. "And…and thank you, Reverend Lacy."

"My pleasure, ma'am."

She set her gaze on Hooker. "And thank you for allowing us to leave, General."

Hooker nodded silently.

Fannie had her children packed and ready to go in forty-five minutes. General Meade had appointed four men to ride as escorts, and since Chaplain Lacy wanted to go along, he was assigned to drive the wagon.

Captain Miles Carlton was in charge, accompanied by Lieutenant Errol Waters, a sergeant, and a corporal. Meade and Hooker stood on the porch of the mansion and watched them move away in the moonlight toward Ely's Ford Road.

*****

Jack and Elsie Courtman were unruffled by being awakened after midnight. They welcomed Fannie and her children, glad to offer their home as a place of safety.

Fannie thanked Lacy again for risking himself on her and her children's behalf.

When the widow and her children had entered the Courtman house, the Yankees mounted their horses and Lacy climbed back in the wagon.

"Chaplain," Captain Carlton said, "you go on and take the wagon back to General Hooker. I've heard a lot about the wilderness north of the mansion, and I'd like to take a look at it in the moonlight. If General Hooker is still up, tell him we'll be along in a few minutes."

"Will do," said Lacy, and put the wagon in motion.

"Come on, men," said Carlton, "let's take a little ride.

The captain left the road and guided his men toward the darkness of the wilderness. As they trotted along, Sergeant Mel Finch said, "Captain, what about the forest on the south side of the mansion? Is that part of the wilderness too?"

"No. That's just a normal forest. Lots of trees and brush, but not the sloughs and marshes that make the wilderness a spooky place. I'd just like to take a look at it while there's a chance. May not get another opportunity."

At the edge of camp, the Fearless Four continued their watch of the Chancellor mansion, wondering what was taking Chaplain Lacy so long to return.

Chad Lynch, Bo Gentry, Ken Dykstra, and Myron Flynn were still positioned nearby where they had kept watch since going on sentry duty. There would be a shift change at three o'clock.

Keeping his voice low, Buford Hall said to his three companions, "Maybe those Yankees took Lacy prisoner."

"Why would they do that?" asked Nichols. "He's no threat to them."

"Yeah, but from what I hear about Hooker, he's the kind that just might lock up a preacher."

Hank Upchurch chuckled. "I don't think there's anything that mean, lowdown Hooker wouldn't—"

"Sh-h-h!" came Chuck Carney's hiss. "Look!"

The other men followed the direction Carney pointed and saw four riders trotting along the edge of the wilderness.

"S-s-s-t!" came the sound from their friends nearby. "Riders coming!"

"They're Yankees!" Hank said. "Dark uniforms!"

"Yankees sure enough," said Everett, raising his rifle.

Bo Gentry held up his hand. "Wait a minute! If you fire, they'll hear it over at the mansion and it'll give away our position!"

"But what if they decide to ride the plank road in here?" said Buford. "They'll see the tents! Hooker'll find out anyhow!"

"Let's capture 'em," said Dykstra.

"We can try," said Chuck, "but if they make a break for it, we'll have to cut 'em down. We sure can't let 'em get back to Hooker. Better that Hooker hears a few shots and wonders what's going on than to have even one of 'em tell him we're in here!"

The riders were coming close now, and the sound of hoofbeats was getting louder.

"Okay, men," said Everett. "Guns ready?"

Each man cocked his rifle.

"Follow the leader," he said, and ran out of the shadows to intercept the riders.

Captain Miles Carlton saw the movement in the shadows

first, drew rein, and shouted, "Rebels!" as he whipped out his revolver.

Lieutenant Errol Waters followed suit, and the other two soldiers brought up their rifles.

"Hold it right there!" shouted Nichols, the other seven men on his heels.

Carlton's horse was startled, and when he fired into the advancing group that had stepped into full view in the moonlight, the bullet went astray, plowing sod several feet from them.

The eight Rebels unleashed their rifles on the Yankees.

Moments later, as the Rebels stood over the dead Yankees, Flynn said, "We'd better get their horses. They couldn't have gone far."

When Chaplain Tucker Lacy arrived at the Chancellor mansion, he explained to a sentry why Captain Carlton and his men would be a few minutes behind him. The sentry, unwilling to believe that Carlton would want to investigate the wilderness so late at night, told Lacy he would have to stay until Carlton and his men returned.

General Jackson stood in the moonlight, looking down at the dead Union soldiers, whose bodies had been dragged into the wilderness to a spot near his tent.

"We can be sure they heard the gunfire at the mansion," he said to the eight sentries. Some of the men disturbed from their sleep by the gunshots had gathered around.

"We really had no choice, General," said Chuck Carney. "It was them or us."

"I know you had to defend yourselves," said Jackson, "but I

sure wish these men hadn't come here. It could ruin part of our surprise. I wonder what they were doing, riding here at this time of night?"

"Who knows?" said Rance Dayton.

"Guess when it comes to Yankees riding around our camps at night, we should shoot first and ask questions later," said Buford Hall.

Stonewall Jackson was eating a cold breakfast in his tent about an hour before dawn when he heard the voice of General Robert E. Lee. He pulled back the tent flap as Lee drew near in the waning moonlight.

"Good morning, General Jackson," said Lee. "I received your message and thought it best that I cut my sleep a little shorter and join you."

"I'm glad you're here, sir, but I'm a bit surprised. How's the heart?"

Lee rubbed his chest as he sat down. "Better. Dr. Franks gave me some powders last night. The pain has eased up quite a bit."

"I'm glad. I prayed that it would," said Jackson, sitting down in a facing chair.

"Thank you. The sentries were telling me about the shooting incident."

Jackson shook his head. "I'm also praying about that. Hooker no doubt heard the gunfire, and by now he's wondering where his four men are."

"Well, at least he can't see you in here. He won't have any idea how many—"

"General Jackson..." came the voice of Corporal Jim Lewis.

"Excuse me, General." Stonewall got up and pulled back the flap. "Yes, Jim?"

"Just wanted to let you know that Chaplain Lacy is back.

He'll explain it to you later, but he wanted me to tell you that Mrs. Chancellor and her children are safe with neighbors a few miles from here. The Yankees tried to hold him after the Chancellors were placed with the neighbors, but he managed to escape. Said to tell you that no one followed him."

"Good. Thank you for letting me know, Jim."

When Stonewall sat down again, Lee said, "Chaplain Lacy was able to get that dear widow and her offspring out of the mansion?"

"Sure enough. Don't know how he persuaded Hooker to let them go, but as you just heard, he did."

"I'm glad. Now, General, let's get down to business. I want to say that I concur with your battle strategy 100 percent. So you've already moved troops during the night?"

"Yes, sir. They're in position as I described in my message." As he spoke, Jackson pulled a handkerchief from his hip pocket and turned his head away to sneeze.

"You all right?" asked Lee.

"Yes, sir. Just a head cold."

"You doing something for it?"

Jackson nodded and slipped the handkerchief back in his pocket. "I sent for Dr. McGuire last night. He came over and gave me some medicine. Anyway, General, we're ready to give Hooker a big surprise on his rear flank."

"You sent twenty-eight thousand men to do that…and you've kept fifteen thousand here in the wilderness, right?"

"Right."

"Okay. This leaves me with twenty-two thousand embedded on two sides of the Chancellor estate, and we both have sufficient artillery. Do you still feel sure we've got our numbers placed correctly?"

"I do. As I told you in the message, sir, you are left with an actor's job. You will have to make Fighting Joe believe your troops make up the main army—the bulk of it embedded in the forest on the south side. And you'll have to convince him that your twenty-two thousand are actually sixty thousand."

"And how do you propose I do that?"

"I already explained it to Generals McLaws, Anderson, and Stuart, sir, just in case you weren't able to be with them."

"And what did you tell them?"

"You will have to have sharpshooters running back and forth in the trees, with men there to reload for them as they fire rapidly, making one man appear to be a company. It will take precision timing between firing and loading, but it can be done."

Lee nodded. "And the same thing, in essence, with those men in the low spots behind the hills to the west?"

"That's correct. You'll also have to shift the artillery batteries around on the fly, in the forest and the low spots in the fields, confusing the bluebellies about your positions. You have to hold Hooker's attention from those two sides so we can come at him from behind, and from right here in the wilderness."

Lee chuckled, shaking his head. "General Jackson, my friend, you are indeed a genius. I never thought of Robert E. Lee as an actor."

"You will when we win this battle, sir." Jackson whipped out his handkerchief just in time to sneeze into it again.

"You take care of that cold," said Lee.

"Yes, sir. And you take care of that heart."

Lee grinned. "Yes, sir."

As dawn broke over the Virginia countryside, General Joseph Hooker was astride his prancing horse, riding before his troops who were standing at attention. He tried not to show it but he was concerned about the gunshots he'd heard the night before, and the fact that his four men had not returned. To make it more annoying, the preacher had gotten away before he could get out of bed and question him.

Hooker looked his army over with pride. He was plagued with uncertainty as to where Stonewall Jackson had gone with his II Corps, but with more than twice as many men as Lee and Jackson, he would make short work of them. He figured Jackson had somehow covertly joined Lee near Fredericksburg and had been able to hide his army from Union scouts. Lee and Jackson would come marching toward Chancellorsville with their relatively small numbers and meet up with Joe Hooker's great Union Army of the Potomac for a final showdown. Soon this war would be over.

Hooker was the picture of a confident warrior chief: ramrod straight in the saddle, cheeks rosy, spiffily clad in tailored dark blue. When the inspection was over, he dismounted at the front porch of the Chancellor mansion, where Generals John Gibbon and Oliver Howard waited for him.

"Did you gentlemen get a good look at that marvelous army?" Hooker asked as he dismounted.

"We did, sir," said Howard.

"They seem more confident now, General," said Gibbon. "You've instilled it into them."

"Part of the reason President Lincoln gave me the job. Those are the finest troops in the world out there, and the best prepared. It's taken me some time, but I have no doubt I've gotten the job done."

Both generals nodded.

"Yes, sir," said Hooker, "those men out there are spick-and-span, healthy, alert, and ready to take on those slow-talking, laid-back Southerners. Bobby Lee will have to use every man, woman, child, dog, horse, and mule in Dixie to even make a dent in my army!"

When Hooker had gone inside the mansion, Gibbon and Howard walked toward the troops.

"I'm not exactly fond of the general's frequent gasconade," said Gibbon, "but his confidence is reassuring...far better than Ambrose Burnside's lack of it."

"I appreciate that, General. But his boasting that even God Almighty can't keep him from whipping the socks off Bobby Lee has me a bit disturbed."

"You figure God just might decide to show him?"

"Something like that."

THIRTEEN

G eneral Robert E. Lee, escorted by a group of Jeb Stuart's cavalry, met up with the leaders of I Corps and explained the role they would play in the battle plan, then sent them to assemble their men accordingly.

At the same time, Stonewall Jackson was getting his II Corps ready, placing them strategically to launch the rear attack on Joe Hooker's much larger army.

Jackson could see only a small part of his corps where he sat his horse at the edge of the wilderness. But he knew that out there in the hills and forests were thousands of gray-clad men—some little more than boys—who were eager to attack the unsuspecting Union army. The general let his gaze take in the multiple guns, wagons, and animals close by as his men made last-minute preparations.

He guided Little Sorrel deeper into the trees to meet Brigadier General James H. Lane of the North Carolina Brigade, who was walking toward him from the deep shadows.

When they came together, Jackson dismounted. "Everything ready, General?"

"Yes, sir," replied Lane. "I just wanted to say, sir, that I like your battle plan. Even if it takes two or three days to whittle down Hooker's massive numbers, I believe we will come out the victors. And when we do, it will be your ingenuity that did it."

Jackson shook his head. "Not without brave and dedicated men to execute the plan, General. And that victory will cost many of them their lives."

"I know that, sir," said Lane, "but I just wanted to express my deep appreciation to you for coming up with the plan, and to say how I admire you as a military leader."

Humbled by Lane's sincere words, Stonewall nodded and thanked him. He cast a glance toward the brightening eastern sky and said, "Well, General, the sun will be up shortly. It's time to take the battle to the enemy."

The sun's brilliant rays spread a fan-shaped light in the eastern sky as Stonewall Jackson waited in readiness to launch his surprise assault. As he stood by, a courier from General Lee came riding in with a dispatch, which read:

Lieutenant General Thomas J. Jackson.

Be assured that at the first sign of your engagement with the enemy from the wilderness in front of Chancellorsville, I will vigorously begin my actor's task with infantry and artillery from this position so as to make Hooker think the larger Confederate force is on this side. You then can surprise him by hitting him hard from the rear with your other forces. May God speed us the victory.

Robert E. Lee

Jackson smiled as he stuffed the paper in his pocket and turned to the courier. "Corporal, tell General Lee I'll be expecting a full show, and that maybe someday he and I can do a Shakespeare play on some stage together."

The corporal cocked his head, his brow furrowed. "Pardon, sir?"

Jackson chuckled. "General Lee will understand. Just tell him what I said."

"Yes, sir," said the courier, and galloped away, keeping within the shadow of the trees.

Major General Joseph Hooker stepped out on the wide porch of the Chancellor mansion, attended by Captains Harry Russell, William Candler, and Delbert Binkley. Only two sentries were near the porch, and they vigilantly scanned the fields as the brilliant sun peeked over the eastern horizon.

Hooker leaned an arm against one of the massive white pillars and watched Major General Darius Couch's approach. Couch's II Corps was situated in the hills to the northeast.

Couch dismounted and was about to speak to Hooker when sudden rifle fire came from the northwest. There were more rifle shots, as if the firing were being answered.

Hooker squinted toward the sound then looked around at the others and said, "Skirmish somewhere beyond those hills."

"Appears to be, sir," said Couch, moving toward the porch steps. "Couple of things I need to ask you…"

In the forest about a half-mile to the south, General Lee was in conversation with Major Lafayette McLaws when the sound of rifle fire came rolling across the hills.

"General McLaws!" shouted one of his men, who thought the firing was coming from the wilderness. "Stonewall Jackson has started his assault!"

"Excuse me, General!" McLaws ran toward his brigade. "Open fire, men! Make it sound like there's a million of us! Yell, too! Yell your lungs out! Jackson is in their rear!"

The other brigade leaders gave the same command, and rifles and cannons cut loose amid the bloodcurdling sound of the Rebel yell.

In the deep shadows of the wilderness, General Stonewall Jackson was studying the sounds of the skirmishers when suddenly Lee's guns opened up and the men of I Corps were giving out the Rebel yell.

Jackson realized Lee had mistaken the skirmishers to be his corps opening up on Hooker. He looked through the dense trees where his artillery was hidden, with guns aimed toward the Chancellor house, and gave a hand signal.

Instantly, the cannons began to roar.

Joe Hooker and the men with him now had their attention on I Corps's guns to the south. By some mysterious fluke of acoustics, the roar of Jackson's assault did not meet their ears. Seemingly from out of nowhere, and without warning, a shell landed close by the Chancellor porch and exploded.

A rain of smoking shrapnel ripped into the house and the pillar where Hooker stood. Chunks of brick flew in every direction, one of them striking Hooker and knocking him down.

At the same instant, while the men were diving for cover,

Captain Delbert Binkley took a hunk of shrapnel in the chest and went down with a grunt.

Cannon and rifle fire roared and rattled from the wilderness, shells exploding all across the front yard of the mansion. Bullets spent their force, ripping at foliage and crashing through trees as well as striking the big brick structure.

"Help me get the general inside the house!" Couch shouted at Russell and Candler as he bent over to grasp Hooker's arms.

The two sentries lay crumpled on the ground, and Captain Binkley was sprawled on the porch floor. All three had been killed instantly.

Sounds of Rebel guns seemed to be coming from every direction as Joe Hooker's men laid him on the bed in Matthew Chancellor's room. He was regaining consciousness and moaning as Couch examined the purple knot on his temple.

"One of you bring a wet towel," Couch said. "He's cut."

Candler disappeared into the hall, and Russell bent close to examine the wound.

The sounds of Confederate guns and exploding cannonballs were deafening.

When Hooker's eyelids began to flutter, Couch said, "General, sir! Can you hear me?"

Fighting Joe moaned and opened his eyes to give Couch a glassy look.

"Do you know where you are, sir?" asked Couch.

Hooker closed his eyes, then opened them again. "Mmm?"

"Do you know me, General?"

Hooker worked his mouth, trying to focus his eyes on Couch. "Y-you are Darius Couch."

"Yes, sir! You were just struck by a brick, sir. A Rebel cannonball hit the house. Lee's army is firing at us. We must counterattack immediately. Do I have your permission to signal our army to counterattack?"

Still glassy-eyed, Hooker mumbled, "No. Have…to…ask President Linc— President Lincoln."

Captain William Candler rushed in with a wet towel, and Couch stepped back, allowing him to press the towel to the wound. Hooker jerked, swearing with a thick tongue.

To Russell, Couch said, "He's not coherent. I've got to order a counterattack. When his mind clears, tell him what I'm doing. I'll be back once I've got all units involved in the fight."

By eight o'clock that morning, the battle of Chancellorsville was in full swing. The battle area, covering sixteen square miles, shook with the heavy fire of artillery punctuated with musketry. The shrill whistling of cannonballs and bullets gave an adrenaline rush through soldiers' veins on both sides of the conflict.

The hostile artillery batteries of the Confederates blasted away from the wilderness, and the Federals' big guns were masked in ravines and small patches of dense thicket as they answered with deep-throated roars.

White sulfurous clouds rose slowly in the air from every spot where artillery fired.

So far, Stonewall Jackson's surprise attack on the Union rear had not been activated. Jackson would wait till the enemy grew complacent, thinking that the heaviest fire was coming from Lee's I Corps. Then he would unleash his deadly artillery on them.

The din of battle reached the people of Fredericksburg and the small villages and settlements that surrounded the Chancellorsville area. People stood on their porches and in their yards, and many farmers had even climbed on their barn roofs to get a glimpse of the battle.

The rising smoke from cannons and rifles filled the sky and could be seen for miles around.

At the Jack Courtman place, a worried Fannie Pound Chancellor stood with her children and the Courtmans on their front porch. She and the girls wept, while Matthew and Malachi gazed in the direction of the mansion, their faces stiff and pale.

Elsie Courtman draped her arm around Fannie's shoulders, trying to give her strength.

"Oh, Elsie," Fannie sobbed, "I just know our house is going to be destroyed, if it isn't already."

"Maybe not, honey," said the elderly woman. "Maybe our men won't fire on it."

Fannie sucked in a sharp breath and swallowed hard. "They'll have to, Elsie. Getting Hooker will be at the top of the list."

Silver-haired Jack comforted Rebecca and Martha, while Naomi, Ruth, and Sarah huddled together in a tight knot, weeping as if their hearts would break. Their brothers stood next to them, wordlessly patting their shoulders.

"We've lost it all!" sobbed Sarah. "Everything is probably blown to bits by now!"

"The horses will be killed or stolen by those horrible Yankees!" wailed Naomi. "Oh, why does there have to be war? Why? Why? Why?"

The weather was warm that spring morning as twenty-eight thousand Confederate men lay low in the woods at the rear flank of Hooker's army. Stonewall Jackson was there with his unit leaders, who were prepared on a moment's notice to move the infantry out, as well as the cavalry and artillery.

Jackson stood near the edge of the woods, listening to the battle as it grew more fierce by the moment. With him stood cavalry division commander Major General Jeb Stuart and one of Stuart's aides, Corporal Richard Austin. Both men knew Jackson was bidding his time, waiting for the proper moment to pull off his surprise. He had just sent four scouts to appraise the situation and bring him word as to all enemy positions.

Jeb Stuart knew Stonewall well and could feel the fire building in him as water builds behind a dam. Thomas Jackson was eager to hit the Yankees with his surprise, but it had to come at just the right time.

"I'd say Hooker's got most of his troops in the battle now, sir," said the cavalry leader.

"Most, but not all," replied Jackson, his eyes fixed on the smoke of battle to the south. "He'll keep some reserves. And, of course, we'll have them to contend with once this bunch gets into the fight."

Stuart grinned. "I like your plan, General. Gonna be a real shocker."

"General Jackson," Corporal Austin said, "there's some kind of fancy word for what you're doing. I can't remember it right now. Know what I mean?"

The general smiled and said, "It's called *en échelon*."

"That's it! My father fought in the Mexican War, and I remember him using that description."

"It means 'in steps' or something planned or arranged in continuous order."

"Yes, sir. I remember now. Do we have time for you to explain the strategy in more detail?"

Jackson nodded. "You begin on one side…like I had planned to do from the wilderness, until General Lee was confused by the skirmish that broke out unexpectedly. Turns out it still worked pretty well. Anyway, when you set up en échelon, the enemy sees you coming at him from one side. He naturally begins to move his troops there to meet you. At the right moment, your attack opens in another place.

"The enemy leaders don't know where to move their troops

next, or if they should move any at all. They'll usually delay because of the uncertainty of it. What you hope they will do is go on the move. That's the best way to catch them—on the move. They aren't situated for battle then.

"But while the enemy is delaying and trying to decide what to do, your own situation strengthens. He doesn't know the attack is en échelon. He just might figure you're throwing a diversion at him, and you'll hit him at another flank. If he decides that indeed it could be a diversion, he waits till he can find out for sure. In the meantime, you've surrounded him where he stands. You look for where his line is the weakest and hit him hard and fast. If you've executed your plan correctly, you've got him."

Austin looked admiringly at Lieutenant General Jackson, who had the air of a man who knew what he was doing. It was no wonder General Lee had so much confidence in him.

At the Chancellor mansion, no more bombardment had rained down since the initial one that killed three men and rendered General Hooker unconscious. The Confederate troops were now occupied with a swarm of Yankees advancing across the open field, guns blazing.

By nine o' clock Hooker was clear-minded, and he stood at a window on the third floor, observing what portion of the battle he could see. Captains Russell and Candler had wrapped a makeshift bandage around his head to stay the flow of blood.

Hooker rubbed his head and swore vehemently. "I wish General Couch would show up!"

"He said he would be back as soon as he could, sir," said Russell.

"Well, it's not soon enough. We've got to change our tactics out there."

"Should I see if I can find some powders downstairs for

your headache, sir?" asked Candler.

"Forget the powders. There's a bottle of whiskey in my saddle-bags down in the kid's bedroom. Bring it to me."

"But, sir," said Candler, "President Lincoln—"

"I know, I know! I'm not gonna get drunk! I just need something to ease the pain of this headache. Get the whiskey for me. That's an order!"

Moments later, Captain Candler returned with the bottle. Hooker downed several big gulps, then smacked his lips and belched. As he replaced the cork, he saw a small group of Union men on horseback gallop by and quickly vanish from sight.

"Sir," said Candler, who was standing at Hooker's shoulder, "wasn't that General Sickles?"

Hooker nodded. "Yes, and I don't understand what he's doing this close to the mansion." He swore again and growled, "Where is that Couch?"

The sounds of battle continued to roll across the Virginia countryside as Russell moved up to Hooker's other side. "Sir, could you clear something up about General Sickles?"

"What's that?"

"I've heard he killed Francis Scott Key's son."

Hooker pulled the cork on the bottle, took a short swig, and said, "That was back a few years…when Dan Sickles was a U.S. congressman from New York. He was well known for his explosive temper, just as he is now. He found out Mrs. Sickles and Key's son were having an affair, and he shot and killed the man. Sickles pleaded temporary insanity and was acquitted."

"So that's it," said Russell. "I'd heard bits and pieces, but never had the whole—"

"General Hooker!" a sentry called from the bottom floor. "General Couch is here, sir!"

Hooker rubbed his head as he went to the door and called back, "I'll see him in my office! Be right down!"

Hooker's line, at present, formed an arc that ran southwestward from the Rappahannock River, curved around Chancellorsville, then jutted northwestward to its terminus along the Orange Turnpike, just beyond Wilderness Chapel—a small settlement centered by an old stone church building. Meade's V Corps, anchored on the Rappahannock about a mile downstream from a crossing called United States Ford, held the left. Howard's XI Corps manned the right, with the corps of Sickles, Couch, and Major General Henry Slocum deployed in the immediate area of the Chancellorsville crossroads.

Major General Daniel Sickles had his First Division brigade commander, Brigadier General David Birney, at his side as they galloped past the Chancellor mansion and veered off to the left into a part of the wilderness where there were no Confederates. Three other officers were with them, Major Eli Worth, Captain Eldridge Buckman, and Lieutenant Milo Dartt.

Birney had spotted Stonewall Jackson's twenty-eight thousand troops as they swarmed out of the forest like a horde of insects coming for the kill and had told Sickles, but the general had to see for himself.

Pointing to the southwest, Birney said, "Look right there, sir!"

Sickles's eyes bulged and his jaw slacked. "Lieutenant Dartt, get to the mansion as fast as you can and tell General Hooker we're being flanked on the rear! Hurry! We'll get back to the men. I need to know the general's orders…fast!"

Dartt gouged his horse's sides and headed for the mansion. Sickles led the others back toward their position at a gallop.

✳✳✳✳✳

As General Couch sat down in Matthew Chancellor's bedroom, Hooker took another swig of whiskey. When he saw Couch frown, he grinned and said, "Medicinal purposes, General. I've got a whopper of a headache."

Couch eyed the bottle, noting it was half full. He wondered how much of it Hooker had consumed since the bandage had been put on his head.

"All right," said Hooker, "what can you tell me?"

"Thus far, we have suffered comparatively little damage anywhere, sir. Our officers responded quickly when the attacks came, and we've gained some strong positions on high ground. We're ready to—"

Couch was interrupted by a loud knock at the door.

"Come in!" called Hooker.

A young private appeared at the door, opening it just wide enough to stick his head in. "General Hooker, I have Lieutenant Milo Dartt of II Corps out here. General Sickles sent him, and the lieutenant said his message is urgent."

"Tell him to hold on a few minutes," said Hooker, clipping his words. "I've got General Couch in here, and I can only talk to one man at a time."

Suddenly the door flew open all the way, and Lieutenant Dartt plunged into the room. "General, we're being flanked from the rear by a massive force of troops! General Sickles wants to know how to react, immediately!"

General Couch banged his fist into the palm of his hand, swearing angrily. "I should have known it! That's Jackson's troops! Hid those men and their equipment somewhere after pulling them away from the Rappahannock, and now, after decoying us with the other troops, he's coming in on our rear flank!"

Joe Hooker's face was pallid as he opened a map of the area

and spread it out on the desk. "Show me, Lieutenant! Where are those troops, exactly?"

When Hooker saw the position of Jackson's twenty-eight thousand, he quickly sent a courier to General Oliver Howard, whose XI Corps was deployed to the south. He sent Dartt with orders for Sickles, then said to Couch, "Take your corps and join Howard. Do it fast!"

Couriers from unit leaders all over the area came to the Chancellor mansion, reporting on Jackson's massive force and their move on the rear flank. And the battle raged on as the hours passed.

Lieutenant Dartt returned to the mansion with a message from his commanding general. General Sickles was asking Hooker for permission to swing around on Jackson's rear flank and attack him. Hooker's reply was for Sickles to stay close to General Howard's corps and fight alongside them.

Sickles knew from Lieutenant Dartt that Hooker had been drinking and figured his mind was muddled. Leaving one of his three divisions to fight alongside Howard, he took the other two and assaulted the rear of Jackson's Confederate force. The Union attackers overwhelmed the Twenty-Third Georgia Regiment, inflicting some three hundred casualties in a matter of minutes.

Like snarling dogs who had been bitten on their tails, regiments from Major General Robert Anderson's division and from Major General A. P. Hill's division turned on Sickles's troops and drove them off, killing dozens before they could get away.

As noon came and went, reports came to General Hooker in rapid succession that the assault by Jackson's troops out of the south was taking a horrible toll. Hooker's army was being whittled down by the smaller number of Rebels.

Joe Hooker was taking a swallow of whiskey when Captains Harry Russell and William Candler entered the office. He looked up at them and said, "This stuff isn't helping my headache at all."

"Be best if you threw the rest of it away, sir," said Candler.

Hooker gave him a look of disdain, then said, "Because of the reports I've been getting, I've decided to make a rash change in this battle. I want you two to send my couriers to every corps leader and tell them to abandon whatever ground they hold and to return to the positions they occupied last night around Chancellorsville."

"Are you sure, sir?" asked Russell. "That wouldn't be a wise thing to do. It—"

"Don't tell me what's wise!" said Hooker, the whiskey making his eyes watery. "Just do what I tell you!"

It was almost three o'clock when Major General George Meade received his orders. He was among a stand of trees on the ridge he had gained in the battle that morning. Glancing up at the courier who had handed him the written order, he swore and spit on the ground. "Has Hooker lost his mind? If we can't hold the top of the hill, what makes him think we can hold the bottom of it?"

The courier shrugged. "Sorry, General. I'm only delivering the message. I have nothing to do with its contents."

Major General Darius Couch was so angry when he received his orders to retreat to Chancellorsville that he left his corps in charge of Major General Winfield Hancock and rode his horse across the battlefield, dodging bullets and shrapnel amid thick clouds of gun smoke.

Joe Hooker was alone in his office when the door burst open and Couch barged in.

"General Hooker, what on earth has happened to your mind?" he fumed. "Why are you ordering us to retreat to Chancellorsville? Sure, we've been taken by surprise, and we're having ourselves a tough fight, but what can we gain by falling back here? You're taking us completely off the offensive and putting us totally on the defensive! You don't win battles by fighting defensively!"

Hooker wiped a hand across his face and said, "You don't understand, General. I'll have Lee and Jackson just where I want them. By pulling my army back here, I'll make them fight me on my own ground."

"Is that you talking, or is it the whiskey? If you do this, General Hooker, we're going to lose the battle…and it'll be all your fault!"

Hooker rose to his feet. His voice was ragged as he snapped, "You just do what I tell you, Couch!"

The commander of II Corps clamped his mouth shut, pivoted, and stormed across the room, slamming the door behind him.

FOURTEEN

As the afternoon wore on, Stonewall Jackson rode Little Sorrel up and down the ranks, shouting encouragement to his men. One of his main objectives was to take the high ground at a farm owned by a family named Taylor and situated a thousand yards down the Orange Turnpike from the Chancellor estate.

About the time Darius Couch was slamming the door of General Hooker's office, Brigadier General James Lane and his North Carolina brigade positioned themselves in the forest just east of the Taylor farm.

A brigade of General John Sedgwick's VI Corps under Union Colonel Hiram Burnham was occupying the farm's high ground.

The North Carolina men stayed far enough in the forest to remain unseen and watched General Lane as he met with his regiment leaders.

They could see that the Yankees who had taken possession of the farm were facing an angry farmer and his family. The farmer was waving his arms and apparently telling Burnham and his troops to get off his property.

Keeping his eyes on the scene, Lane said, "Seems a shame

those Yankees can just take the place over and give those nice people a hard time. Since General Jackson told us to take it and secure it for the Confederate cause, I think we'd best do it."

"I agree," said Major Rance Dayton, who stood next to him. "We need that high ground right now…and those nice Southern people need to be shed of those bluebellies."

Seconds later the North Carolina Brigade rushed through the trees with the bloodcurdling Rebel yell reverberating through the dense woods. The attackers ran forward, ignoring the underbrush that tugged and ripped at their clothes and flesh, as the surprised Federals turned to meet the onslaught.

The farmer and his wife made a mad dash for the house.

Occupying the farm was the First Division of Major General Oliver O. Howard's XI Corps. Spread around the area was the rest of XI Corps in fields, ditches, gullies, and small wooded patches. Jackson's charging Rebels drove brigade after brigade of Yankees into hasty retreat.

When the fleeing men descended on the astonished men of the One Hundred Fifty-third Pennsylvania and Fifty-fourth New York—the two regiments on Howard's flank that were facing west—they formed ranks and were able to fire three volleys, momentarily checking the Confederate advance before giving ground. They were hit by a murderous volley, then broke for the rear without firing another shot.

Another unit in the Union XI Corps, the Seventy-fifth Ohio Regiment, commanded by Colonel Robert Reilly, opened fire when the oncoming Confederates were only thirty yards away and kept at it until they were overwhelmed by the Rebels, who were bearing down on them like an avalanche. In a matter of minutes, Colonel Reilly was killed, and 150 other officers and men were killed or wounded. The rest of the regiment was swept away in retreat.

✠✠✠✠✠

General Howard waited nearby in his headquarters at Dowdall's Tavern on the plank road. When he heard the firing, he leaped on his horse with two aides following and rode to the top of a nearby hill. At first he saw only rabbits, foxes, and deer tearing through the woods toward him. But then came the panic-stricken men of his entire First Division.

Howard and his aides sat their horses, observing the rush of men in blue and the swarm of gray coming at them like quick lightning. The roar was doubled in volume by the echoes through the forest.

The general felt sick to his stomach observing the panic of his men as bullets and shrapnel ripped into them, the dead and dying crumpled and sprawled on the ground, and the wounded straggled along—the frantic efforts of a surprised corps attempting to flee an angry Rebel storm.

"General!" gasped Lieutenant Michael Davenport, one of the aides. "They mustn't retreat from Jackson's troops! They're whipped unless they stand and fight!"

His features resolute, Howard said, "You have a flag in your saddlebags, don't you, Lieutenant?"

"No, sir," said Davenport. "I gave mine to one of the regiments who lost theirs."

"I have one, sir," said the other aide, a sergeant named Bill Kopatich. He pulled the flag from his saddlebag and handed it to Howard. The general clutched it under the stump of his right arm, which he had lost in the Battle of Fair Oaks ten months before, and galloped down the slope until he was within thirty yards of his retreating troops. Dropping the reins, he raised the flag high with his left hand, waved it, and shouted, "Halt! Don't run! Turn and fight them! Turn and fight them!"

Most of the frenzied men didn't see their leader, but Colonel Adolphus Buschbeck, commander of a Second Division brigade, saw the fluttering flag in the hand of General Howard and called for his men to turn and make a stand.

Buschbeck's brigade had been deployed in reserve in a line of rifle pits at right angles to the plank road near Dowdall's Tavern. They halted at the colonel's command and managed to produce enough fire power to delay the Confederate onslaught for a brief moment, cutting many of the Rebels down with musket fire and canister fired by their artillery.

But Stonewall Jackson's men would not be denied their victory. With a yell, they kept coming, and closed in, blasting away with a deadly series of volleys. The blue line gave way, and the Rebels continued their attack.

As the Confederate tide swept past the spot where General Oliver Howard sat his horse, waving the flag and calling for the fleeing soldiers to turn and fight, General Daniel Sickles and his III Corps, on the opposite side of Chancellorsville, were unaware of the disaster befalling Howard's XI Corps.

Distracted by a demonstration mounted by General Lee's I Corps at a small settlement called Catherine Furnace, Sickles doubted the word of an aide sent by General Howard to get help. It took the aide a few moments to convince Sickles that such havoc and loss could come from the enemy's smaller army. When the truth of it took hold in his mind, Sickles ordered a cavalry regiment—the Eighth Pennsylvania under Major Pennock Huey—to ride to Howard's assistance.

Huey and his regiment galloped down a country lane toward the area where Howard's XI Corps was under siege. They topped a gentle rise and skidded to a sudden halt as they ran head-on into Brigadier General R. E. Rodes's brigade, who were in battle position in a half circle, waiting for them.

Although his cavalry unit was vastly outnumbered, Huey gallantly shouted for his men to charge and led them into the teeth of Rodes's guns.

A deadly Confederate volley halted the cavalry unit in its tracks. Major Peter Keenan, commander of Huey's First Battalion, went down in a hail of enemy fire, along with the regimental adjutant, thirty men, and eighty horses.

Caught in the same volley, Union Sergeant John Collins had his horse shot out from under him. He leaped to his feet amid gunfire and smoke and dashed away through the woods as fast as he could run. Gaining the plank road, he found himself in a scene of terror and confusion like he had never experienced in any battle before. Panting for breath, Collins crossed the road and made for the woods on the opposite side.

Men and animals were dashing against one another in wild dismay before the line of assault that came crackling and crashing after them. The smoke was so thick in the forest that Collins wondered if it was on fire. The thunderous roar of exploding cannon-balls seemed to come from every direction, and he was confused as to which way was safety.

When a shell struck a few feet to his left, Collins felt something claw at his left leg as the concussion of the explosion knocked him down. Stunned, he lay there until his head cleared. He could hear wild screaming above the crackle of flames devouring trees. The forest was aflame, and through the smoke Collins could make out his Union comrades dashing about in frenzied terror, stumbling, falling, and screaming—their clothing on fire.

Collins struggled to his feet. It was then that he looked down and saw a dark chunk of metal embedded in his left thigh, and blood soaking his pant leg. He took a halting step forward; he had to get out of the woods before the fire consumed him!

His eyes smarted from the smoke, and the heat of the flames scorched his uniform. He looked around in confusion. Which way had he come into the woods? Which way was closest to the edge of the woods and safety—at least safety from the blazing forest?

With the screams piercing his eardrums, Collins chose a direction and limped as fast as his wounded leg would let him. He gripped his thigh just above the place where the shrapnel was embedded and stumbled in the direction where there seemed to be the fewest flames.

Some twenty yards outside the forest to the west, Brigadier General James Lane had his North Carolina Brigade in position to unleash artillery and musketry on the Yankees who came along the old plank road. Lane's artillery had been shelling the woods for an hour, mercilessly killing the Yankees still in there and capturing those who came running out to escape the shelling. Twenty-nine Federals were already held as prisoners in a nearby gully.

A few yards down the infantry line from Lane were Major Rance Dayton and his Eighteenth North Carolina Regiment. Flanked on each side by his hometown friends, Corporals Everett Nichols, Hank Upchurch, Buford Hall, and Chuck Carney, Dayton was concentrating on the road, waiting for more Yankee troops.

The nearby forest was ablaze, and the men could feel the heat from it where they hunkered down. Massive billows of black smoke boiled toward the sky, darkening the sun.

Suddenly, a dark clot of blue uniforms appeared on the plank road, and General Lane shouted for his brigade to open fire. The Yankees were part of General Howard's routed XI Corps and were seeking another place to take cover since the woods were aflame.

Lane's order brought a thundering roll of musketry, and an increase of noise that was almost deafening. Shouts and loud commands were drowned out in the awful noise as the Yankees dashed to the opposite side of the road to take what cover they could find and return fire. Many of them didn't make it across the road.

While muskets barked and bullets whizzed through the air,

sounding like angry hornets, the screams from the blazing forest were heard above it all.

As he knelt to reload his musket, Corporal Upchurch let his gaze swing toward the nearby forest where wounded Yankees were burning to death. Amid the smoke and flames, he caught sight of a stumbling human form at the edge of the woods.

Sergeant John Collins was in severe pain from the hunk of shrapnel in his thigh, but he limped as fast as he could toward the edge of the forest. Just a few more steps and he would be out of the blazing woods!

Collins staggered forward, gripping his leg and trying to keep his senses. His brain felt as if it were on fire. Suddenly the wounded leg gave way, and Collins fell to the ground amid burning leaves. He rolled to escape the flames, but his pants began to smoke.

Struggling to rise, Collins beat at the hot spots on his trousers. He made it to his feet and stumbled toward the edge of the forest, where he could see Rebel troops dug in and firing toward Yankees on the road. Two more steps and he fell again. A wild cry forced itself from his lips as he slapped at the flames taking hold of his uniform.

Hank Upchurch watched the man in the blue uniform stumble and fall. Dropping his musket, he said to Dayton, "Major, there's a wounded Yankee over there in the woods about to burn to death! I'm going after him!"

Before Dayton could respond, Hank was dashing across the open field toward Collins.

"Hank! Come back here!" Dayton shouted. "You'll get yourself killed!"

But if Upchurch heard the major, he didn't show it.

Chuck Carney, who had just emptied his rifle at Yankees on the road, bent down to reload. When he heard Hank's words, he let his musket fall and sprang to his feet.

"Chuck!" said Dayton, grabbing his arm. "Don't try it!"

"Have to, Major!" said Carney. "Hank might need help, and I can't let that Yankee burn to death either!"

Hank was aware of someone on his heels as he reached the edge of the burning forest. He paused briefly, trying to pick the best route to the fallen man.

Chuck drew up beside him. "This way!" he cried, and took off, zigzagging around burning trees and grass.

When Chuck reached Collins, he saw the bloody pant leg and realized the man was seriously wounded. Collins was trying as best he could to put out the flames. Chuck pounced on him, smothering the flames with his own body, and when Hank knelt beside him, he used his hands to beat out the flames.

Sergeant Collins thought he must be dreaming. He blinked against the smoke and squinted to make sure he was seeing correctly. Two Rebel soldiers had come to his aid!

"Let's get him out of here!" yelled Chuck above the din of battle and the roar of the fire.

Together, they lifted the wounded Yankee into their arms.

"What are you doing?" gasped Collins.

"We're taking you to a safe place, Sergeant," said Chuck. "This whole forest is going to be a hot box in a few minutes!"

"Are…are you taking me prisoner?" asked Collins.

"You might say that," said Hank. "But if we don't take you out of here, you're going to be burned meat! Would you rather stay?"

"No! Let's go!"

The battle raged on as the two men from Fayetteville, North Carolina, carried their wounded enemy across the field. They saw their regiment commander watching them, along with Everett Nichols and Buford Hall.

Bullets hissed and zipped about them as Upchurch and Carney hurried to relative safety with their prisoner. When they eased him down next to a huge bush behind the firing line, Major Dayton appeared beside them. He looked at the shrapnel in the Yankee sergeant's thigh and thought of the similar wound he had suffered at Antietam.

Running his gaze between the two men, Dayton said, "You boys did a very humane thing. Even though you disobeyed me when I told you not to do it, I won't report you."

Hank hunched his shoulders. "I didn't hear any command not to do it, Major."

Dayton grinned. "I'll never know whether you're telling me the truth or not, will I?"

Hank grinned back at him.

The major knelt beside the wounded Yankee and said, "I guess you know these two brave soldiers saved your life, Sergeant."

Gritting his teeth, Collins said, "Yes, sir. I know that. I don't understand why, but…" He looked up at Carney and Upchurch. "But I sure do thank you."

"It's something our major has taught us, Sergeant," said Hank. "When an enemy soldier is wounded and out of the battle, he's no longer our enemy. He's a human being in need of help."

"What's your name, Sergeant?" asked Dayton.

"Collins, sir. John L. Collins."

"Well, Sergeant John L. Collins, I hereby declare you a prisoner of the Confederate States of America. And since you are our prisoner, you will now be taken to our corps medical staff so they can get that shrapnel out of your leg and patch you up. Did you suffer any burns?"

"Must not have, sir. I don't have any pain except in my thigh. These men must've put the flames out before they burned through my clothing."

"Good. Well, we'll get you to our medical people right away."

"I appreciate that, Major," said Collins. Then he looked at

Upchurch and Carney. "I am forever in your debt, gentlemen. You risked your lives to save mine. I wish there was some way I could express my gratitude."

"Well," said Chuck, "maybe someday, when this crazy war is over, we can meet together somewhere at the Mason-Dixon line and talk about what happened here today."

Collins managed a grin. "Hey, that would be great. I…I don't know your names."

"Hank Upchurch."

"Chuck Carney."

"Well, Corporal Upchurch…Corporal Carney, I owe my life to you."

Moments later, Sergeant Collins was carried away on a stretcher by a pair of Rebel soldiers who made it plain they were taking him to Dr. Hunter McGuire and his staff only because Major Rance Dayton was ordering them to do so.

Soon the Yankees either lay dead on the plank road or had retreated far enough to get out of the line of fire. General Lane's North Carolina Brigade was able to pull back from the road for a brief respite in the fighting.

The sounds of fierce battle on the other side of Chancellorsville still rode the air.

After a few minutes, General Lane approached Lance Dayton and said, "Well, Major, our rest period is about up. We've got to head down the plank road and find more Yankees to fight. We'll pull out in five minutes. I'll go pass the word along to the other regiments."

Dayton hurriedly moved among his men, telling them General Lane wanted to pull out in five minutes.

The Fearless Four were gulping water from their canteens when a half-dozen infantrymen of the Twentieth North Carolina drew up. One of them had a sneer on his face as he looked at Upchurch and Carney and said, "Big heroes, aren't you? Went to the trouble to save that stinkin' bluebelly so he can fight us again…maybe even kill some of us."

"Yeah," said another, "you glory boys sure did us a bad turn today."

Buford Hall's face went a deep crimson. "What's the matter with you guys? I suppose you'd have let that Yankee burn to death!"

"You bet! And why not? If he could've done it, he would've killed us. Why should we lift a finger for him? We're here to kill 'em, ain't we?"

"Killing them in battle is one thing," said Chuck Carney, "but letting a man die a horrible, agonizing death when you can prevent it is another."

"Bah! You fools should've let him die! War is war!"

When the six soldiers were gone, Everett said, "Don't let 'em bother you. You did the right thing."

Chuck Carney spit on the ground and said bitterly, "Too bad when your fellow soldiers have to upbraid you for saving a human life."

"Don't let a few soreheads get to you," came the voice of Corporal Ken Dykstra.

They looked around to see Dykstra standing close with Corporal Myron Flynn and Privates Chad Lynch and Bo Gentry. As the four stepped closer, Gentry said, "That sergeant isn't going to be killing any of us. He'll be a prisoner till the end of the war."

The North Carolina Brigade was back in the thick of the battle when Dr. Hunter McGuire stood over Sergeant John Collins at Wilderness Tavern after examining the man's wound.

"I'll have to put you under with ether, Sergeant," McGuire said. "There'll be quite a bit of cutting to do to get that metal out of your leg."

Collins nodded. "Whatever you say, Doctor."

McGuire nodded to the middle-aged nurse who stood on the other side of the table. As she turned away to get the ether, he looked down at his patient and said, "According to the men who carried you in here, it was a couple of soldiers of the North Carolina Brigade who pulled you out of the burning woods."

"Yes, Doctor. Couple of corporals. Names are Hank Upchurch and Chuck Carney."

"Doesn't surprise me," McGuire said with a chuckle.

"What do you mean?"

"They are two of a group of five who won themselves presidential commendations for saving their major's life on the battlefield at Antietam."

"That I can understand, but I'm still having a hard time believing they hazarded themselves to save me."

"They're great men," said the doctor as the nurse moved up to the table with the bottle of ether in one hand and a folded white cloth in the other.

Forty minutes had passed when Dr. McGuire and an assistant, Dr. Floyd Vickers, carefully lifted the Yankee sergeant from the table and laid him on a cot across the hotel conference room where the medical staff was set up to do their work.

McGuire turned to the nurse, who was coming through the door, and said, "Who's next, Hilda?"

"We were to work on a lieutenant who had a finger blown off, Doctor, but they just brought in a young sergeant who has a bullet lodged next to his heart."

"Bring him in!"

When the sergeant was laid on the table, he was conscious, though his face was sheet-white. Sweat beads covered his brow. Doctor McGuire pulled the shirt open to expose the wound, examined it carefully, and said to Hilda, "Laudanum."

While Hilda was preparing the pain medication, McGuire looked down at the wounded soldier, who said weakly, "It's bad...isn't it, Dr. McGuire?"

Hunter nodded. "Yes, I won't try to kid you, Sergeant. The bullet's dangerously close to your heart."

"Sir...?"

"Yes?"

"If I don't make it...would you tell General Jackson something for me?"

"Sure, but don't give up. I—"

"Doctor. Please. My name is Ryan Colston."

"Yes."

"Please...tell General Jackson that if he had not cared for my soul...and led me to Jesus—" He choked, swallowed with difficulty, and his eyes began glazing over. "Tell General Jackson...I will meet him...in heaven."

Ryan Colston's eyes closed. His head rolled to one side and his breathing stopped.

Hilda stepped up with the laudanum, took one look at the doctor's face, and halted. "Is he...?"

"Yes." Hunter looked down at Colston and said, "I'll tell General Jackson for you, Sergeant. And...I'll meet you there too."

As darkness fell over Chancellorsville, General Hooker paced the floor in his office. Major General John Sedgwick and Captains Harry Russell and William Chandler were in the room with him. Sedgwick had come to tell Hooker that the First and Second Divisions of his VI Corps had been cut to shreds.

Hooker had been given similar information from a good number of his corps leaders.

Hooker still wore the head bandage, and there was despair in his voice as he said, "We've lost the battle. We're beaten. Lee and Jackson beat us. They beat us."

General Sedgwick sat in silence, his head bowed and resting in his hands.

"We can't give up yet, General Hooker," said Russell. "We still have almost twice as many men as Lee and Jackson do."

"It doesn't seem to matter," said Hooker. "Oh, we won't surrender. We'll keep on fighting…but there's no way around it. We're whipped, I tell you. This battle is lost."

A haggard-looking John Sedgwick rose from his chair and quietly headed for the door. Hooker stopped pacing, looked toward him, and said, "Where are you going, General Sedgwick?"

The commander of VI Corps stopped, turned, and said, "Back to my men. But before I go, let me remind you of what you said in my hearing—that even God Almighty couldn't keep you from winning the victory in this battle. Maybe you'd better apologize to Him."

With that, Sedgwick passed through the door and closed it behind him.

Hooker stood mute, staring at the door.

FIFTEEN

The Union Army of the Potomac was being routed on all fronts around Chancellorsville when twilight finally gave way to darkness. The fighting dwindled, and soon all was still across the valley.

Stonewall Jackson, who could taste victory, met with his division leaders: Major Generals A. P. Hill and Jubal Early, Brigadier General R. E. Rodes, Colonel Stapleton Crutchfield, Brigadier General William Pendleton, and Major General Jeb Stuart.

"Gentlemen," he said, "I know that night fighting is almost unheard of in this war, but I believe if we keep up our attack tonight, we'll finish Hooker off by morning. The moon will be up shortly and give us some light. We've got those bluebellies just about whipped. We need to stay after them."

"General Jackson," said Hill, "I noticed some clouds in the west just before the last glimmer of sunlight, and the breeze is coming from the west. In two to three hours the winds could drive those clouds this way and cover the moon. We'll lose most of our light if they do."

"Well," said Jackson, "we just might have this battle won in two or three hours. The quicker we get after it, the quicker we can finish it. Now, here's the plan...."

Twenty minutes after Jackson's meeting with his division leaders, the Yankees were settled down in their camps for the night, expecting to get some rest.

Major General Hooker stood on the wide porch of the Chancellor mansion in conversation with his corps leaders, Major Generals John Reynolds, Darius Couch, Daniel Sickles, George Meade, John Sedgwick, Oliver Howard, Henry Slocum, and Brigadier General George Stoneman.

Though the generals could barely see their leader in the darkness, they knew by the sound of his voice that he was a whipped man.

"Gentlemen," Hooker said, "I know there's plenty of fight left in you in spite of the heavy losses we've incurred, and I'm not going to tell you to pull out and retreat back to Washington. But after we give Bobby Lee and Stonehead Jackson everything we've got in the morning, if we don't put a dent in their army we won't have any choice but to turn and run for home.

"It hurts me to even have to say this, but Jackson's surprise attack on our rear flank was a staggering blow. Are you willing— after a good night's rest—to meet Johnny Reb with everything you've got?"

There was an affirmative rumble of voices.

Darius Couch, who was still upset at Hooker for calling the troops back to Chancellorsville and giving up ground they had gained, said, "General Hooker, are we going to just sit and wait for the Rebels to come at us, or are we going to launch an attack?"

"We'll get us a good night's rest, General Couch, and take the battle to the enemy. Let's put our heads together now and work out a plan."

Suddenly the sharp blast of a bugle cut through the soft evening air. Every head whipped around toward the sound. A series of bugle calls came from brigade after brigade, left and right. Then an etched moment of pure silence.

"They're going to attack us!" Couch gasped.

Joe Hooker glanced at the rising moon in the east. "I can't believe this! Are Lee and Jackson so foolish as to attempt a night battle?"

"If I read those bugle signals correctly," Meade said, "that's exactly what they're doing!"

"We'd better get to our men!" said Oliver Howard.

"Do it!" Hooker said, almost in a daze. "Give those Rebels a reason to be sorry they've been so foolish!"

The moon was spreading its silver beams across the Virginia country-side as the Confederates attacked. All around Chancellorsville, Union soldiers were in a state of confusion as Rebel skirmishers came at them, guns blazing. Then came the solid battle lines on the run, determined men in gray, surging forward like ocean waves in a storm. They held their red battle flags out front and unleashed their high and eerie Rebel yell.

Frightened deer and rabbits scattered before the Rebels as they kept coming, their bayonets flashing in the moonlight and rifles spitting fire.

In several places, the startled Yankees became as wild as the deer and rabbits. Many stumbled and fell in their rush to get away. Some took time to drop their knapsacks and gear so they could run faster.

Stonewall Jackson was with General Early's division a few hundred yards east of the Chancellor mansion. In the moonlight, hundreds of Yankees could be seen running ahead of the Rebel lines, many dropping to earth as bullets tore into them.

As the troops swept by him, Stonewall cried, "Press on, men! Press on! Don't let them get away!"

Wild cries of victory resounded across the fields and through the wooded areas. Little Sorrell snorted and danced in the excitement. "Whoa, boy," said Jackson, tightening the reins. "You can't chase those bluebellies. You have to stay here."

Abruptly, a young lieutenant drew up beside Jackson on his horse and said, "They're running too fast for us, General! We can't keep up with them!"

Stonewall turned a stern gaze on the young man and said, "They never run too fast for me! Press them! Press them!"

High, thin clouds were floating eastward, carried by the wind, as General Hooker stood on the porch of the mansion with his two aides. He paced, swearing and muttering, with the near-empty whiskey bottle in his hand. He had heard nothing from his corps leaders since they'd gone to join their troops.

The heavy brush and trees in the surrounding forests muffled the firing and the cries of the combatants. Hooker paced for over an hour before Harry Russell pointed to the south side of the mansion and shouted, "General! Here they come!"

Hooker cursed when he saw a swarm of Rebels charging across the open fields from the south, chasing a wild mob of crazy-eyed Yankees. As the Rebel guns spit fire, Yankees fell, and many were trampled by their comrades. The closer they came, the louder the din of booming guns and the bloodcurdling Rebel yells.

It was Brigadier General R. E. Rodes and his brigade chasing the fleeing Federals.

Joe Hooker swore again, popped the cork of the bottle, and drained its contents. He threw the bottle away, pulled his saber from its sheath, and headed for the porch steps.

Captain Candler watched his leader, aghast. "General! Where are you going? What are you doing?"

Hooker didn't reply. Down the steps he went toward the running troops. As he drew near his fleeing soldiers, he swung the saber to get their attention and shouted as loud as he could, "Halt! Halt! Turn around and give them the bayonet! Do you hear me? Halt! Turn around! Give them the bayonet!"

It was as if Major General Joseph Hooker did not exist. Not one man even showed that he saw or heard him. This infuriated Hooker, and he continued to shout commands.

Captains Russell and Candler looked on, wide-eyed, as the rushing Confederates closed in on the spot where Hooker stood and swallowed him up in the melee.

Amazingly, the rout passed right by Fighting Joe. Not one Yankee had stopped for him, and he became so engulfed in the mob of Rebels chasing the Yankees that no one noticed him. Indeed, it was as if he didn't exist.

When the swarm of Confederates had passed, Hooker stared after them and raised his saber, swearing at the top of his lungs.

The Rebels chased the scurrying Federals until they reached the woods, where the dense trees engulfed them. The moon was still clear in the sky, but Rodes's men had sprinted for miles and were exhausted. Unwilling to let the Yankees go without further pursuit, Rodes called for General A. P. Hill's fresh troops, who had taken a breather. Hill sent his men into the woods, shouting commands to press the battle to the Yankees.

At his position to the east, Stonewall Jackson decided now was his opportunity to claim full victory. He was not going to let it slip by. As he watched A. P. Hill's division thunder into the woods after the Yankees, he made a decision.

Next to Jackson sat his brother-in-law, Lieutenant Joseph G. Morrison, who was in Jubal Early's division and had come to make a report. Jackson had hardly laid eyes on Mary Anna's brother since they'd arrived at Chancellorsville.

With Jackson and Morrison was Captain Keith Boswell, whom Jackson knew had grown up in the area. Corporal Jim Lewis was nearby, talking to a small group of men.

"Captain, you know the countryside around here pretty well, don't you?" Stonewall said to Boswell.

"Yes, sir."

"I want to find the enemy's stronghold and demolish them. The last concentrated firing from the Yankees came from over in that direction." He pointed southwest.

"Yes, sir."

"I want you to pick the best route and guide me over there. I want to get a look at their position."

"I can do that, General," Boswell said.

Jackson hipped around in the saddle. Speaking to the small group, he said, "Captain Boswell's going to lead me to where the Yankees are concentrated the heaviest. I'd like you men to ride with us."

General Hill rode up, having sent his men into the forest in pursuit of wild-eyed Yankees. Jackson explained to Hill what he was doing, and Hill said he wanted to ride along too.

Brigadier General James Lane and his North Carolina Brigade chased Union troops until they spread out and disappeared in the deep shadows of the woods on the west side of the Chancellor estate. When it became obvious they were wasting their time to pursue any farther, Lane took his brigade back to the main

Confederate camp at the edge of the wilderness, which was settled deep in the trees along the plank road.

Upon arriving at the camp, Lane found others coming in from different units, and there were little pockets of excited conversation as the men talked of the rout they were giving the Yankees.

General Lane and Major Rance Dayton dismounted near a spot where several of the Eighteenth were collected, including the Fearless Four and some of their closest comrades.

Lane looked back toward the open fields and said, "Major, did you notice there are no sentries guarding this position out there?"

"Yes, I did," said Dayton. "I guess nobody's thought to set them up since we're routing the Yankees."

"Probably so, but those bluebellies might have a few brave ones who'd like to come charging in here and see how many of us they can kill."

"I agree, General," spoke up Everett Nichols, moving toward the officers with his friends following. "Who knows what those four who rode in here last night had in mind? Never know what those Yankees might do."

"Yeah," said Ken Dykstra. "Maybe those guys last night were on a suicide mission. I wouldn't put it past them."

"Be even more likely for them to do it tonight," said Chuck Carney. "Since they're being routed, they're probably pretty desperate by now."

Dayton nodded and said, "We'd best keep a sharp eye."

"How about us volunteering to do the sentry duty tonight, men?" said Myron Flynn, looking around at the others.

"I'm in," said Buford Hall.

The rest volunteered quickly.

"All right," Dayton said. "Let's see...there are eight of you. Should be enough. Take your usual places along the side of the road."

"And thanks," said General Lane.

Lane and Dayton headed for the tents on the back side of the camp, and the sentries checked their weapons in preparation to take their posts.

They were about to head toward the edge of the wilderness when some unidentified Rebel deeper in the woods called out, "Hey, Barney! Is General Jackson in camp?"

"I think so!" Barney called back. "But I don't know where he is at the moment!"

"Okay! I'll find him!"

The sentries eyed each other.

"I wasn't aware the general had returned," said Everett Nichols.

"Me neither," said Chad Lynch. "Guess he got in ahead of us."

Captain Keith Boswell led the small group along the old plank road in the moonlight. General Jackson noted that all gunfire had ceased; there weren't even any sounds from I Corps some five miles to the southeast. He hoped General Lee's heart wasn't acting up.

Riding next to Jim Lewis in the group was Sergeant Bill Cunliffe, who was in the signal corps. "General Jackson," he said, "if you find the stronghold out here as you suspect, are you going to wait till dawn to hit them?"

"No, Sergeant. We're going to hit them tonight. I want this battle settled and won as soon as possible."

"I like your style, General," said Cunliffe, chuckling.

"We all do," said Hill.

"What's this up here, Captain?" Stonewall pointed with his chin to a small building a few yards off the road.

"Schoolhouse, sir," replied Boswell. "Colonel Crutchfield has an artillery battery set up here. He wanted to make sure any

Federals who might come along this road got a taste of Southern hospitality."

Major Sandie Pendleton of Early's division rode next to General Hill. Pendleton, a brilliant young man who had not yet reached his twenty-second birthday, let his eyes roam the moonlit fields on both sides of the road. There were grassy patches and dark spots where ditches threaded their way across the fields. Such places would be excellent spots for snipers, he thought.

They could see sentries standing at the corner of the old schoolhouse, watching their approach.

General Hill pulled his horse up a step or two ahead of Little Sorrel and called out, "I'm General Ambrose P. Hill! General Jackson is with us!"

"Come in slowly!" came the reply, as the sentries stood, guns ready.

Jackson and his companions knew that somewhere in the deep shadows around the schoolhouse were howitzers. No doubt some were trained on them.

Seconds later, the group hauled up and one of the sentries said, "Welcome, General Jackson! And all of you."

"Thank you," said Stonewall. "I'm looking for a Yankee stronghold in this direction."

"Yes, sir," said the sentry. "They came in late this afternoon and set up their guns about a mile and a half down the road. We watched them battling with some of our troops until it got dark. They didn't come by here, or we'd have blasted 'em."

Jackson smiled. "I'm sure of that. Thank you. We'll be moving on."

The general led the group another mile or so down the road, then halted and looked at the Union camp laid out on both sides of the road.

Sandie Pendleton scanned the moonlit fields and noted all the dark spots. "General Jackson," he said softly, "don't you think this is the wrong place for you?"

Jackson glanced at him and smiled. "The danger's over, Major. The enemy is routed." Then to A. P. Hill: "General Hill, let's go back to camp, gather our forces, and attack Hooker's last stronghold while they're licking their wounds. Let's finish it for good ol' Dixie tonight."

"We'll all be happy when it's done," said Hill.

Jackson turned to his aide and said, "Jim, by now news has reached Richmond that there's been a lot of fighting going on around Chancellorsville today. I'd like for you to ride to Fredericksburg and have them send a wire to Mary Anna. Let her know I'm all right."

"Certainly, sir. I'll be back as soon as possible."

With that, Jim Lewis galloped away, angling in the direction of the Rappahannock River, whose west bank he would ride to Fredericksburg.

The group wheeled about and headed back up the plank road. They were within three hundred yards of the wilderness camp when a single rifle shot shattered the stillness of the night. Jackson raised a hand, signaling for the group to stop.

Lieutenant Joe Morrison turned to his brother-in-law and said, "Sir, that might be a Yankee sniper out there somewhere."

"We need to get the general to camp as fast as possible!" Pendleton said.

At that instant, there was a second shot, a third, then a smattering of shots. Bullets were buzzing through the air, but they couldn't tell from which direction they were coming.

"Let's go, General!" Morrison said.

Stonewall Jackson gouged Little Sorrel's sides, and the others surrounded him as they galloped toward the camp. A few clouds were drifting overhead, covering the moon and cutting down its light.

✯✯✯✯✯

At the Confederate camp, Rance Dayton's sentries were firing at what they believed were Union skirmishers along the plank road, though they couldn't see them. Others joined them quickly, firing blindly.

The firing kept up for several minutes, then Major Dayton appeared and said, "Hold it! Nobody's firing back! Don't waste your ammunition."

There was a period of silence. When it remained so, Dayton said, "Keep your eyes open, but don't shoot unless you can see what you're shooting at."

The major moved back into the trees, followed by the men who had jumped in to help.

Chuck Carney looked around at the other seven men, and said, "Okay. Load your guns and stay sharp."

The muskets were reloaded and the sentries hunkered down in silence.

Not long after, they heard a rumble of hooves coming from the same direction where the gunfire had been moments before. They raised their rifles and waited, squinting past the dark shadows cast by the trees to the open field.

"Riders!" said Buford Hall.

They could all see the vague figures in the flat white light of the moon. The horses were trotting straight toward them on the plank road. When the horses reached the dark shadows beneath the trees, Hank Upchurch—skittish from the experience with the four Yankee riders the night before—raised up, put his musket to his shoulder, and shouted, "Yankees!"

"Don't shoot!" said Ken Dykstra. "You don't know it's Yankees!"

"I can tell it's Yankees!" Upchurch said. "We can't let 'em get any closer!"

"Wait!" said Bo Gentry. "It may be some of our men!"

"It's Yankees!" Everett Nichols shouted. And fired.

"No! Wait!" a voice cried.

Hall's nerves were strung tight. At the sound of Nichols's rifle, he squeezed the trigger and his gun belched fire.

One of the incoming riders peeled out of his saddle and hit the ground as the others pulled rein. The horses were whinnying fearfully and dancing about.

A voice from the group of riders shouted, "Cease firing! You're firing into your own men!"

Hall shouted back, "Who gave that order? Some stinkin' Yankee? Pour it into 'em, boys!"

Nerves jangled, Carney and Upchurch opened fire. One man jerked in the saddle and bent over as a bullet hit him, and another fell to the ground.

A rider came thundering at them, screaming, "I'm General A. P. Hill! Stop firing! Stop firing!"

When Hill drew up, the Fearless Four recognized him. Their blood froze in their veins as he bawled, "You fools! You've shot General Jackson!"

SIXTEEN

Captain Keith Boswell and Sergeant William Cunliffe lay on the ground—one dead and one seriously wounded. Major Sandie Pendleton's horse, fighting its bit, stepped on Cunliffe, who was unconscious, and Lieutenant Joe Morrison's horse reared in fright. Morrison struggled to contain his terrified animal as he tried to see how bad General Jackson was wounded.

Little Sorrel, alarmed by the gunshots, shouting men, and frightened horses, bolted, carrying the slumped general into the forest.

A low branch struck the general, nearly knocking him out of the saddle. But in spite of a wounded right hand, he grasped the reins and regained control, then wheeled Little Sorrel about.

As he trotted the horse toward the plank road, nearby Federals—assuming all the firing within the shadowed wilderness was aimed at them—cut loose with a fierce barrage of artillery.

Cannonballs struck trees and sod all around, and shrapnel hissed through the air.

When General Jackson had reached the road, his men were there to meet him, in spite of the bombardment. Two of them took Little Sorrell's reins, and A. P. Hill and Joe Morrison lowered

Jackson from the saddle. His right hand was bleeding, and the left sleeve of his coat was soaked with blood. Bullets had hit him in the upper arm near the shoulder and in the forearm, as well as the right hand.

The Union guns suddenly went quiet as Jackson was being carried to the shelter of a huge oak tree. When they started to lay him down flat, he protested.

"No, no," he said through clenched teeth. "Let me sit up with my back to the tree."

While General Hill dispatched two men to ride to Wilderness Tavern for Dr. Hunter McGuire, Captain Jack Wilbourn of the signal corps moved in and said to Morrison, "I have some medical experience. May I look at him?"

"That all right, General?" asked Morrison.

Stonewall nodded.

Wilbourn looked around. "Could we get a lantern over here?"

As a soldier hurried away to bring the needed lantern, Hill returned and knelt beside Jackson. "We'll have Dr. McGuire here as soon as possible, General. Are you in much pain?"

Jackson grimaced and spoke with effort. "I fear my left arm is broken. There's some pain, yes. My right hand was hit too."

Hill nodded. "We'll get you fixed up as soon as possible."

Stonewall licked dry lips. "Others were hit, too, weren't they?"

"Yes, sir. Captain Boswell and Sergeant Cunliffe."

"How bad?"

"Sergeant Cunliffe is still alive. But Captain Boswell was killed instantly."

"I've got the sergeant resting comfortably, sir," said Wilbourn. "Dr. McGuire will have to treat him too."

"First," said Jackson.

"Pardon me, sir?"

"I want Dr. McGuire to take care of Sergeant Cunliffe first."

Wilbourn looked at Morrison and Hill, who both shook their heads in admiration for the general.

The sergeant arrived with the lantern, and Wilbourn cut away Jackson's left sleeve for a quick examination. To stop the flow of blood he wrapped strips of the general's sleeve around the wounds, using double cloth on the wound in the upper arm.

"So what do you think, Captain?" asked Jackson.

"Nothing life-threatening, sir," said Wilbourn. "But it doesn't look good. The bullet that hit your forearm has shattered bone, but the upper wound is worse. From what I can tell, the bullet shattered the bone just below the shoulder and all the way to the elbow joint. It severed an artery, and you've lost a lot of blood. But I think I've got it wrapped good enough to hold you till Dr. McGuire gets here."

Jackson let the news settle in his mind. "Then Dr. McGuire will have to take off the arm, won't he?"

Wilbourn wiped a hand over his face. "I really can't say, General."

Jackson closed his eyes. "How did this thing happen? It was our own men who shot us, wasn't it?"

"It was, sir," said Hill. "It's best that you don't talk now. Just sit there and rest. Dr. McGuire should be here in a few minutes."

General Hill moved about the camp, telling the men they must keep General Jackson's wounds a secret. It would only harm the morale of the Army of Northern Virginia if the troops learned that he was out of commission.

Hill then approached Captain Wilbourn and Lieutenant Ted Ransom, who were kneeling over Sergeant Cunliffe. The wind had blown the clouds away, and once again the moon was shining in its fullness. "How's he doing, Captain?" Hill asked.

Both men rose to their feet, their faces drawn.

"He just died, sir," said Wilbourn. "I thought he would make it, but he must have been bleeding internally."

Hill drew in a deep breath and let it out slowly. He looked to the spot nearby where Keith Boswell's body lay covered by a blanket. "I'll have him placed over there by Captain Boswell."

"We'll do it, sir," said Ransom.

"I have another job for you two, and I need you to move on it immediately. I need you to take the news of General Jackson's wounds to General Lee. As commander-in-chief, he must be told."

"Certainly," said Wilbourn. "We'll go right now."

"I told you earlier that we've got to keep the news from spreading…so talk with the general privately."

"Yes, sir."

"And make a wide circle so you don't get caught by the Yankees."

"We'll do that, sir," Wilbourn assured him.

"Come back as fast as you can so I'll know the message was delivered."

As Wilbourn and Ransom headed for their horses, Corporal Jim Lewis approached the sentries at the plank road.

"Hi, Jim," said Bo Gentry. "Where you been?"

"Fredericksburg. General Jackson sent me. He knew Mrs. Jackson would learn about the battle here today. I wired her to let her know he was all right."

Gentry looked away, a pained expression on his face.

"What's the matter?" Lewis asked, frowning.

The other sentries stood near, looking on.

Lewis scanned their faces. "What's happened?" he demanded, sliding from his horse's back.

"We're not at liberty to say, Jim," said Myron Flynn.

"Has something happened to the general?"

"We're not at liberty to say," said Chad Lynch. "You'd best find General Hill and ask him."

"I'll just do that!" said Lewis, leading his horse toward the camp at a fast pace.

Captain Wilbourn and Lieutenant Ransom trotted past Lewis, nodding a greeting, and soon were galloping away.

Lewis saw General Hill standing with two privates over a lifeless form on the ground. His heart lurched, and he dropped the reins and dashed toward the body. When he saw that the dead man wasn't Stonewall Jackson, he breathed a sigh of relief, and said to Hill, "General, what happened—"

Lewis broke off as he saw the second form a few feet away, covered by a blanket. He hurried to it, pulled the blanket from the face, and recognized Captain Keith Boswell. Turning back to Hill, he said, "Where's General Jackson? What's happened here?"

Hill moved up close to Jackson's aide and said, "We've had a horrible stroke of misfortune, Jim. Some of our sentries mistook a group of our men for Yankees when they came riding in. General Jackson was leading them."

"Wh-where is he, sir? Is he…all right?"

"He's been wounded. Come. I'll take you to him."

As Hill guided Lewis toward the spot where II Corps' commander leaned against the large oak, there was a sudden boom of cannons from the Union positions, and the shrill whine of cannonballs came to their ears. Thunderous explosions followed as men began scurrying about. Shrapnel cut the air, chewed into tree bark, and rattled bushes.

"Come on!" said Hill, breaking into a run.

More cannonade followed as Hill and Lewis approached Jackson, who was surrounded by several men. Joe Morrison was kneeling beside him.

"Litter!" shouted Hill. "Somebody bring a litter! We must take General Jackson deeper into the woods!"

Lewis elbowed his way through the press and knelt on Jackson's other side. Morrison smiled at him and said to the general, whose eyes were closed, "Jim Lewis is back, General."

Jackson opened dull eyes and tried to focus on Lewis.

"How bad is it, sir?" Jim asked.

"I'm glad you're back safe," said the general, gritting his teeth in pain. "You got the wire off to Mary Anna?"

"Yes, sir."

"Good. She won't have to know about this till Dr. McGuire gets me all patched up."

Running his eyes over Jackson, Jim said, "Your right hand and left arm. Is that it, sir?"

"Please step aside, Corporal!" came Hill's voice above the sound of more exploding cannonballs.

Lewis looked up to see a man carrying a stretcher and three other men with him.

"Hurry!" said Hill to the stretcher bearers. "We've got to move the general!"

Jackson winced as the four men picked him up and placed him on the stretcher. He tried to find Jim Lewis, but his eyes were glazed over. He was going into shock.

The forest rocked from multiple explosions, and suddenly a cannonball hit close by, sending hissing shrapnel through the air. One of the bearers was hit in the side and collapsed, dropping his corner and Jackson with it. Stonewall landed hard on his wounded arm and groaned.

Lewis and Morrison were beside him instantly. "Let's get him on the litter again," said Lewis. "I'll carry this corner."

Just as they were ready to keep moving, Brigadier General William Pender, of A. P. Hill's division, rushed up to Hill. "General! We're getting heavy bombardment in several places! The Yankees are giving it to us! I need permission to pull back!"

Even in Stonewall Jackson's state of shock, he heard Pender's words and roused himself. "You must hold your ground, General Pender!" he said hoarsely. "Do not fall back! You must hold your ground!"

General Hill set level eyes on Pender. "You have your orders, General."

"Yes, sir," said Pender, then wheeled about and was gone.

Federal cannonballs continued to strike in the wilderness as Hill led the stretcher bearers through a swampy area to a spot that had dry ground amid dense trees. The Union shells had not come that far into the forest.

As they gently put Jackson down, a voice from behind called, "General Hill. Dr. McGuire is here, sir. He has an ambulance, and Chaplain Lacy is with him."

Union artillery pounded the area as Hunter McGuire and Tucker Lacy rushed in. However, Confederate artillery was now answering, and the bombardment in the wilderness was easing up.

The chaplain went to Jackson's side while McGuire opened his medical bag.

Jackson met Lacy's gaze and moved dry lips to say, "Little setback, Preacher."

Lacy smiled. "For a tough guy like you, I'm sure that's all it is. You'll be up calling the shots in no time."

A soldier set a lantern next to the stretcher, and McGuire moved up beside the general and knelt down.

"Hello, Doc," Jackson said weakly.

"Hello, yourself, my friend. Looks like we've got some work to do on you."

"Maybe a little."

The sounds of artillery battle were gradually lessening.

Hunter reached for the lantern and placed it to get a better look at the wounds, then removed the makeshift bandages. After a quick examination he took a bandage roll out of his black bag and began rewrapping the wounds. His voice was heavy as he said, "Tom—ah…General, I may have to amputate the arm."

Jackson nodded.

"We brought an ambulance. We'll take you to Wilderness Tavern and I'll do whatever is necessary to make you better."

✶✶✶✶✶

The artillery battle soon ended as the ambulance bearing General Jackson, Dr. McGuire, and Chaplain Lacy left the wilderness and headed across open land for Wilderness Tavern.

Major Rance Dayton was with the four heroes of Antietam as they watched the ambulance rattle by and disappear from sight. The four men sat on the ground at the base of a tree and wept.

"Look, men," said Dayton, "nobody's going to punish you for what happened. You didn't know you were firing into our men."

"But Major," Buford Hall said in a tear-thickened voice, "we killed two good men! And...and if General Jackson dies, how are we going to live with ourselves?"

Hank Upchurch looked at the major with an expression of despair. "The South could lose the War...because we robbed them of General Jackson!"

"How are we gonna face anybody?" said Everett Nichols. "I mean, our fellow soldiers, and the people back home?"

Dayton prayed in his heart for wisdom. "You only did what you thought was right. After all, four Yankees came riding in here last night, and we don't know what they had in mind. You were naturally on edge."

"But two men are dead because we reacted too quickly, sir," said Carney. "And General Jackson will probably die!"

"Now, listen to me. All of you proved what you were made of when you saved my life at Antietam without batting an eye. You were willing to risk life and limb for me. Your fellow soldiers and thousands of civilians heard President Davis lift you up as examples of what true Confederate soldiers ought to be. Sure, you hate what happened. But that doesn't change what you are.

"And what about the Yankee sergeant in the burning woods? It would've been easy to say, 'Let him burn; he's the enemy'...but you didn't. Hank...Chuck...you hazarded your lives to save another human being from a horrible death, even though he's your enemy. You other two would have done it too. Now, don't give up on yourselves."

The Fearless Four continued to hang their heads low. The major's words had little effect.

After a few moments, Dayton said, "Listen to me, men. From what I was told, the worst that could happen to General Jackson would be to lose his left arm. He's in no danger of dying from his wounds."

Hank sniffed and ran a sleeve over his nose and mouth, then said shakily, "But we love and admire the man so much, Major! We'd never knowingly do anything to cause him harm!"

"Everybody in our brigade knows that," said Dayton.

Footsteps sounded nearby, and the group looked up to see Brigadier General James Lane. All five jumped to their feet and saluted. Lane sent a glance to Dayton, then looked at the four distraught men.

"I couldn't help but hear what was being said as I came over here," Lane said. "I'm sorry you men will have to live with what you did for the rest of your lives, but let me remind you of something. You were told before you started firing that those riders could be some of our own men. Were you not?"

The four men stood in silence, remembering all the warnings from their comrades.

"And didn't one of the riders cry out, telling you that you were shooting at your own men?"

Silence.

"And didn't one of you—in spite of that voice—shout something about some stinking Yankee giving the order, and then say, 'Pour it into them, boys'? You men should have been more cautious, as were the other sentries—the ones who tried to get you to hold your fire till the riders could be identified."

When there was still no response, Lane snapped, "Well, shouldn't you have?"

Chuck Carney finally broke the men's silence. "Yes, General

Lane. We should have. But what's done is done. We can't turn the clock back and start over. It was an honest mistake. We thought we were being invaded by enemy riders tonight, and we did what we thought was right. We were wrong, and we're very sorry. We'll be even more sorry if General Jackson dies. We've got enough on our consciences to last for a dozen lifetimes without that."

Dayton took a step closer to Lane. "Sir, we must not forget what these men did at Antietam, and even today in the forest fire. Don't they deserve some consideration here?"

Lane rubbed his jaw and peered at Dayton in the moonlight. "Even if you and I give them consideration based on past performance, Major, I'm afraid the rest of this army will not." With that, General Lane walked away.

"Men," said Dayton, "this war isn't over. You'll have another opportunity to show what you're really made of. Keep your chins up, and be yourselves."

At Wilderness Tavern, Dr. Hunter McGuire cleaned and bandaged Stonewall Jackson's two minor wounds, telling the general that his hand would heal completely in time, as would the forearm.

They were alone at the moment, and Jackson looked up at his friend and said, "But Hunter, if you have to take the arm, it won't matter about the forearm healing."

Hunter's lips pulled into a thin line and he nodded. "You're right about that."

Once more, Hunter did a close examination of the wound in the upper arm. With a shake of his head, he said, "I can't let gangrene set in and kill you, Tom. And there's no sense in my leaving your arm to hang like a dead piece of rope from your shoulder."

Jackson met his gaze without flinching. "So you're going to take it?"

Hunter sighed. "Not without conferring with the other doctors on my staff."

Moments later, Dr. McGuire stood with his three staff doctors as they examined the wound together. When they had each taken a good look, he said, "Tell me if I'm wrong, gentlemen. The humerus, in my opinion, is shattered beyond repair. Even if by a miracle we could get him past the danger of gangrene, he would have nothing here but a useless, dead limb."

All three doctors were in full agreement.

Hunter excused them and once again was alone with his best friend. "You heard them, Tom. I have no choice but to amputate. I'll have to take it off two inches below the shoulder."

Jackson pondered McGuire's words for a moment, and said quietly, "God's will be done."

Tears misted Hunter McGuire's eyes. He swallowed hard and gently cleared his throat. "I've got to get started, Tom. It will take a little preparation, then we'll get this over with."

He called Hilda from a room where she was resting, and asked her to prepare the chloroform, then probed with experienced fingers around the area where he would cut.

Wincing, the general said, "Hunter, I haven't asked who it was that shot me, and nobody's volunteered their names."

"I'd say it would be better if you never knew. Those men made a horrid mistake, yes, but it was an honest one."

"That's how I look at it," said Jackson. "I don't want to know who they are. And I don't want them punished or charged in any way."

Footsteps sounded at the door, and Hilda looked past Dr. McGuire to say, "Hello, Chaplain Lacy."

B. Tucker Lacy remained at the door, and Jackson's pain-filled eyes struggled to bring him into focus.

"Dr. McGuire," said Lacy, "the other surgeons told me you're going to take the arm."

"Yes," said Hunter, without looking up. "His life could be endangered if I don't."

"That's what they told me. How about we have a little prayer meeting before you begin the surgery?"

The doctor raised his head, set kind eyes on the preacher, and said, "Of course. Come over here and lead us."

General Jackson managed a weak smile as Lacy drew up to the operating table. "Thank you, Chaplain," he said. "My Jesus is close, and if something should happen that is beyond my doctor's control…I know He will take me to be with Him."

After Lacy led them in prayer, asking for God's hands to guide the doctor's, he left the room.

Hilda administered the chloroform, and when the man known as Stonewall was under, Dr. Hunter McGuire began cutting.

General Robert E. Lee was sleeping soundly in his tent, having taken powders to relieve the pains in his chest. At first the voice calling his name seemed part of his dream, but finally it broke through and awakened him.

Lee raised up on his cot and looked toward the flap. He saw the vague shadows of three men against the tent wall. One was standing closer than the other two. "Yes?" he called.

"General Lee, sir, it's Corporal Clifford Wyatt."

"What is it, Corporal?"

"I have two men from II Corps out here, sir. Captain Jack Wilbourn and Lieutenant Ted Ransom. They have something very important to see you about, or I wouldn't have disturbed you."

"All right," said Lee, "I'll be right there."

Lee had slept in his trousers and shirt. He quickly put on his boots, slipped into his coat, then pulled back the flap. "Thank you, Corporal Wyatt. Step in, gentlemen."

Lee turned to his portable desk where the lantern sat and struck a match. As the two officers stepped in behind him, they pulled the flap down.

When the wick was aglow with yellow flame, Lee dropped the glass chimney in place and said, "Now, gentlemen, what can I do for you?"

"We have a message from General Ambrose Hill, sir," said Wilbourn in a subdued voice. "I speak in a low tone because General Hill said you were the only man in this camp to hear the message."

"All right," said Lee. "I assume that what you're about to tell me has been sanctioned by General Jackson."

"Well, no, it hasn't, General. It's about General Jackson."

Lee frowned. "What do you mean?"

"General Jackson has been shot, sir."

Lee's eyes widened. "Is he alive?"

"Yes, sir. He has three wounds, sir. One in his right hand, and two in the left arm. General Hill had already sent for Dr. McGuire when we left."

"Thank God it's not worse. The Lord be praised that he wasn't killed."

"We both thank God that General Jackson is still alive, sir," said Ransom.

Shaking his head, the silver-haired general said, "So how did it happen? Snipers or what?"

Wilbourn and Ransom looked at each other.

"Captain Wilbourn," said Ransom, "since you outrank me, I'll let you answer his question."

Jack Wilbourn scrubbed a hand over his mouth and said, "Some of our sentries shot him, General."

"Our sentries!"

"Yes, sir."

Wilbourn then explained how it happened, and told Lee of the deaths of Captain Keith Boswell and Sergeant William Cunliffe.

Lee looked down at his hands, which he had unconsciously balled into fists. "Does General Lane know who did this?"

"Yes, sir," said Wilbourn.

The general rubbed his chest and said, "How goes the battle over on your side?"

"You no doubt would have had a report by now if General Jackson hadn't been shot, sir. Right now, all of General Hill's attention is on him."

"I understand. Tell me how it's going."

"We've about got the Yankees licked over there, sir," said Wilbourn. "It looks like we're going to win this one."

Lee rubbed his chest again. "Gentlemen, any victory is dearly bought that deprives us of the services of our beloved Stonewall Jackson...even temporarily."

"I agree, sir," said Wilbourn. "Well, sir, we must be getting back. General Hill asked us to return as soon as possible."

Lee nodded. "Of course. I..."

"Yes, sir?"

"From what you've told me, I believe those sentries made an honest mistake. I don't want them charged."

"We'll pass your words on to the generals, sir."

SEVENTEEN

J odie McGuire and Mary Anna Jackson were finishing
kitchen cleanup after supper when they heard a knock at the
apartment door.

"I'll get it," said Jodie. She opened the door to a uniformed
man with corporal's stripes. "Yes, Corporal?"

"I have a wire for Mrs. Jackson, ma'am. It came to the camp
about an hour ago. I believe it's from the general."

"Mrs. Jackson's in the kitchen. I'll get her."

"No need, ma'am," said the corporal, extending an envelope.
"You can give it to her."

"Oh…all right. Thank you."

"My pleasure, ma'am."

Jodie closed the door and headed for the kitchen, calling out,
"It's a message from your husband! It came to the camp about an
hour ago."

Mary Anna rushed through the kitchen doorway and inter-
cepted Jodie, plucking the envelope from her hand and tearing it
open. When she had finished reading, Mary Anna said, "It's actually from Jim Lewis. Tom asked him to wire me from
Fredericksburg and let me know he was alive and unscathed after

the battle today near Chancellorsville."

"Praise the Lord!"

"And Jim adds that Hunter has set up a hospital in the Wilderness Tavern, close to Chancellorsville, and he's just fine."

"Praise the Lord again!" Jodie said.

"And we're giving the Yankees a good whipping, Jim says."

"Good! Maybe they'll go back to Washington and stay there."

"Wouldn't that be wonderful?"

"It sure would."

Mary Anna folded the paper and slipped it back into the envelope. "It was sweet of Tom to make sure I knew he was all right." Her features took on a pinched look. "Jodie, I don't know what I'd do if something happened to him…I just love him so much."

"I understand, honey. Even though Hunter isn't in the same kind of danger the general is, I still have thoughts about some cannonball dropping where he stands, or a bullet finding him. I'll be so glad when this horrid war is over."

"Won't it be wonderful when we can all live in peace?"

"It sure will," Jodie sighed. "It sure will."

Hunter McGuire finished surgery on Stonewall Jackson at 2:30 A.M., and he left Hilda to keep an eye on the patient while he met with Jim Lewis and Chaplain Lacy. The surgery had gone well, with little loss of blood, and he urged the two men to get some sleep. When he returned to the surgery room, Major Sandie Pendleton and Hilda were talking just outside the door.

"Dr. McGuire," said Hilda, "Major Pendleton insists on seeing General Jackson. I told him that even though the general is conscious, he's in no condition to talk."

"Doctor," said the youthful major, "the fate of the army and the Confederate cause itself depends on my being allowed to talk to General Jackson. Please."

"I'll let you come in and try, since you put it that way, Major," said McGuire, "but his mind can't be very clear yet."

"I must try, Doctor."

As the three moved up to the operating table, Pendleton's gaze fell on the bandaged stump of Jackson's left arm and he felt a wave of nausea.

Hunter bent over his patient. "General Jackson…"

Stonewall's eyelids fluttered, and he opened them, trying to focus on the face that went with the voice.

"General, it's Dr. McGuire. Can you understand what I'm saying?"

Jackson nodded.

"Who am I?"

Stonewall's eyes lost some of their glassy look, and he said thickly, "You're…my best friend. The best doctor…in the world."

Hunter smiled. "Listen, General. Major Pendleton is here. He needs to talk to you. Can you talk to him?"

Pendleton moved up beside McGuire to stand within the general's line of vision. "Hello, sir."

Jackson slowly moved his eyes to the major's face. "Sandie…glad to see you. What is it you need?"

"Sir, General Hill took over II Corps after you were shot."

"Yes. Good man."

"Yes, sir. But General Hill has been wounded. We suffered an artillery attack after they drove you away in the ambulance. General Hill was struck across the back of the legs by shrapnel. They're bringing him here right now."

Jackson licked dry lips. "I'm…sorry to hear that. Who's in charge now?"

"Jeb Stuart, sir. General Hill assigned command to him, even though he's never commanded anything larger than his cavalry unit. General Hill wanted Jubal Early to take his place, but he's off on a reconnaissance somewhere."

"I see," said the general.

Hilda stepped up on the other side of the table with a tin cup in her hand. "Here, General. Drink this water."

After Jackson had drained the cup, he put his attention back on the major.

"Sir," said Pendleton, "General Stuart asked me to come and talk to you if at all possible. He doesn't know the overall plan to finish off the Yankee stronghold. What instructions can I take back to him?"

The general's brow furrowed, and his eyes seemed to fog up. The effect of the chloroform was still on him, and he struggled with his thoughts. His lips quivered slightly as he said, "Major, I...can't tell you. Tell...tell General Stuart he must do...what he thinks best."

With that, Jackson's eyes closed, and he sank into a deep sleep.

"Major," Dr. McGuire said, "I suspect he'll be like this for several hours."

Pendleton nodded. "Well, I guess I'd better get back and tell General Stuart it's up to him to carry on."

At dawn, on Sunday morning, May 3, Major General Jubal Early showed up from his reconnaissance of the area only moments before Jeb Stuart was ready to launch his attack on the last Union stronghold. When Early learned of General Hill's wounds, and that Hill had assigned Stuart to head up II Corps, he told Stuart to proceed as commander of the corps. He would gladly follow his orders.

Stuart informed Early that he had ridden to General Lee and spent a few minutes showing him his battle plan, and Lee had approved it. Stuart had also learned only moments ago that somehow word of General Jackson's wounds had leaked out. Everyone in both corps knew their beloved Stonewall lay wounded at Wilderness Tavern. The news, however, did not affect them as A. P. Hill had thought it would. Instead of lowering their morale, it served to instill a greater determination to take the fight to the enemy and win.

The sun had not yet risen when both Lee and Stuart unleashed their fierce onslaught on Joe Hooker's army, which was sandwiched between the two Confederate corps. As the battle grew hot and heavy, Stuart displayed amazing proficiency, and the Federals were soon fighting like cornered, wounded animals.

Stonewall Jackson awoke just after 9:00 A.M. to a beautiful morning. He was clearheaded and sitting up in the bed in one of the hotel rooms where Hunter had had him carried in the middle of the night. Hunter and Chaplain Lacy stood beside the bed while Hilda fed him a light breakfast.

A heavy dew lay on the grassy fields. Just outside the general's window, multicolored fruit blossoms moved in the gentle breeze, and whippoorwills and robins sang. But in the distance was the rumble of cannons.

Jackson could barely remember Sandie Pendleton's visit. Hunter reminded him of it and filled him in on General Hill's wounds and the fact that Hill had turned II Corps over to Jeb Stuart. Hill was in a room down the hall and doing well now that he had been patched up.

Jackson swallowed the last of his breakfast, and Hilda left the room, carrying the tray.

"So all I told Sandie was to tell General Stuart to do what he thought best?" Jackson said.

"That's it."

Jackson turned his attention toward the window and the

rumble of the big guns. He sighed. "Well, I hope Jeb makes the right decisions."

"We all do," said Lacy.

In spite of his discomfort, Stonewall said, "What a beautiful Sunday morning! I've always hoped that when it comes my time to leave this world, the Lord would let me go home on a Sunday."

Lacy chuckled. "Well, General, you're not going to heaven today. Is he, Doctor?"

"No, he isn't. In fact, in a few months he'll be back leading II Corps."

Stonewall set affectionate eyes on Hunter. "You think so, eh?"

"Tough as you are, my friend...yes."

"Dr. McGuire," came Hilda's voice from the doorway, "there's a courier here from General Lee. He would like to speak to you."

"All right. I'll talk to him out there." Then to Lacy he said, "Chaplain, you keep an eye on my patient. I'll be back shortly."

As Hunter moved toward the door, Jackson said, "Doctor...I'll want to know what this is about."

"Of course."

"And tell the courier to get a message to General Stuart. I don't want those sentries who mistook us for Yankees to be charged with any wrongdoing."

"I'll tell him, sir."

Chaplain Lacy sat down beside the general's bed and read to him from the Psalms. He had just closed his Bible again when Hunter returned and stood over Jackson.

"General Lee sends his regards to you, Tom—ah...sir."

Lacy smiled. "You two don't have to keep up formalities in my presence."

Hunter smiled. "Anyway, General Lee sends his regards and says he's praying you will recover quickly and be back at the head of II Corps soon. In the meantime, he and the Army of Northern Virginia are going to give the Yankees a whipping they will not soon forget."

Jackson tuned his ears to the thunderous sounds of cannonade some five miles away. "Sounds like he's busy at it right now."

"Another thing, Tom," said Hunter. "General Lee has ordered me to move you farther from the battlefield. He wants you totally out of danger from the fighting, and I am to stay with you at all times. The choice of where you go is up to you, as long as getting you there won't impede your recovery."

Jackson pondered Lee's order, then said, "Well…I have some dear Christian friends who live near Guiney's Station. Thomas and Clara Chandler. Is that far enough away?"

"I'm sure it is," said Hunter. "You think there will be any problem if we show up there and ask them to take us in?"

"None at all. They'll be happy to let me recuperate in their home. They have a large house and several spare bedrooms."

"All right, then. I'll have an ambulance ready shortly."

Jackson nodded. "Hunter, you did give my message to the courier for General Stuart?"

"Sure did."

He looked out the window again toward the sounds of battle. "Have you sent word to Mary Anna?"

"No. I figured to leave it up to you when you wanted her to know."

"Mmm-hmm. Well, since we're going to the Chandlers' house, Mary Anna and the baby can come see me. When we get to Guiney's Station, you could wire her."

Hunter nodded. "I'll do it. Now let me go order that ambulance."

"General," said Lacy, "I'd like to stay with you too. Do you suppose the Chandlers would let me do that?"

"Of course. They'll feel honored to have a preacher in their home." He let a sly grin curve his lips. "The Chandlers will welcome a Presbyterian preacher…but they'll only tolerate a Baptist doctor!"

Hunter gave the general a mock scowl and left the room.

On Tuesday morning, May 5, Presidential Secretary John Hay was at his desk when the door opened and an army courier entered.

"Good morning, Mr. Hay," said the courier. "I have a message for Mr. Lincoln from Major General Joseph Hooker."

Hay frowned. "I hope it isn't bad news."

"I'm afraid it is, Mr. Hay."

"I really hate to give the president more bad news...but I guess there's no choice."

"It wouldn't appear so, sir."

Hay waited until the young man was gone, then carried the sealed envelope to the door and tapped on it before easing it open. Lincoln was at his desk.

"Sir," said Hay, "I have a message from General Hooker."

Lincoln nodded solemnly.

Hay waited as the president opened the envelope and read the message. His countenance sagged, then he looked up and said, "The Union Army of the Potomac has retreated from Chancellorsville. They've pulled back to Falmouth. We've been defeated by Lee and Jackson."

"I'm sorry, sir."

Lincoln scanned the page again and said in a low tone, "Hooker is trying to shift responsibility for the defeat to the corps leaders under his command. Says they didn't do their jobs."

"But you don't think it was that way?"

"Those major generals are soldiers tried and true. I could accept that maybe one or two of them might have failed...but all of them? I think Hooker's leadership may have been hindered by a whiskey bottle."

Lincoln placed the tips of his fingers to his temples. "What a tragedy! An army less than half the size of ours has whipped us at Chancellorsville. Oh, John...what will the country say?"

*****

On Tuesday afternoon, General Robert E. Lee sat his horse before the weary Army of Northern Virginia, near the Chancellor mansion. The wounded who could not stand sat on the ground.

Lee raised a small Confederate flag over his head, waved it, and said so that all could hear, "You men are to be commended for a battle well fought! Outnumbered more than two to one, you showed Billy Yank how a real army can fight when they put their minds to it!"

There were cheers.

"I am aware," said Lee, "that we owe a great deal to our beloved General Stonewall Jackson for engineering this victory. It was his genius that bewildered General Hooker and his leaders and made this triumph possible. And I commend Generals Hill and Stuart for their vital efforts in carrying on when General Jackson was wounded."

The cheering was loud and prolonged.

When they quieted down again, Lee said, "I have word from Dr. Hunter McGuire that General Jackson's condition is good, for all he has been through. We plan to have him back within two or three months."

The cheers were louder yet, punctuated with wild Rebel yells, then the men went into a loud chant, crying, "Stonewall Jackson! Stonewall Jackson! Stonewall Jackson!"

Amidst the jubilation, General Lee dismissed the men to get some much-needed rest. In a few days, they would return to Richmond.

The Fearless Four stood huddled together, off to the side. They had already suffered caustic comments from many of their comrades and had been snubbed by most.

"I think I can survive this ordeal," said Chuck Carney, "now that I know General Jackson is recuperating."

"Yeah, me too," said Hank Upchurch. "It helps a whole lot

to know he's going to be all right."

Buford Hall rubbed his chin. "I'd sure like to talk to General Jackson and tell him how sorry I am for all this. I think I'd feel better if I could just say it to him."

The others murmured agreement.

"And I wish there was some way we could tell the families of Captain Boswell and Sergeant Cunliffe how sorry we are."

Hank shook his head. "But how could we look them in the eye?"

"Wouldn't be easy," Buford said, "but it sure would relieve the pressure I feel down inside."

Hank's peripheral vision caught movement to his left. "Brace yourselves, boys," he said. "Here comes more trouble."

A group of some eight or nine soldiers were walking toward them. Leading the bunch was a burly corporal from Chattanooga, Tennessee, named Mike Robinson.

"Well, lookee here, boys!" Robinson sneered. "We have the great heroes of Antietam before us!"

"Heroes?" said Private Gifford Henderson. "Hah! They oughtta be hung for what they did to General Jackson, Captain Boswell, and Sergeant Cunliffe!"

"Look," said Carney, "we made a mistake. We know that. But—"

"You made a mistake, all right!" came the voice of Bo Gentry as he and Chad Lynch, Ken Dykstra, and Myron Flynn drew up. "We tried to tell you not to fire till you could see who it was, but you wouldn't listen! As far as I'm concerned, you're heroes, all right...but for the wrong side! Wouldn't surprise me if Abe Lincoln pinned a medal on you boys for what you did!"

"You know ol' Abe will be happy when he learns General Jackson has lost an arm!" said Flynn. "He won't have to worry about fighting Stonewall for a long time!"

"If we end up losing the War," said Dykstra, "it'll be because you guys put our greatest military commander out of commission!"

"Maybe we oughtta just take these trigger-happy guys out in the swamp and forget to bring 'em back!" Robinson said.

"Hold it right there!" came the commanding voice of Major Rance Dayton.

Every eye was on the major as he crowded in between the Fearless Four and the others. His face was stern as he said, "Let me explain something to you. Both General Lee and General Jackson have said these men are not to be punished in any way for what happened, nor are they to be charged for any wrongdoing. They've declared it an honest mistake. This isn't the first time someone has been shot by his own men. And it won't be the last. It happens in every army in the world. These four men have suffered enough mental agony over this to do them for a lifetime. As their fellow soldiers, you should understand. And remember, we're all on the same side in this war. Our fight with the Union isn't over. So pull yourselves together."

The accusers gave the major an angry look, then turned abruptly and walked away.

"They're not through with us, Major," said Carney.

"Well, they'd better be!"

"It's in their eyes, sir," said Upchurch. "They'll be on us again."

"If they do, above all, don't fight them. It'll only make you look bad. Hold your tempers, and let me know it's happening."

"We'll try, sir," said Carney, "but a man can only take so much of that kind of stuff."

EIGHTEEN

The courier stood at the open door of the apartment, looking downcast, as Mary Anna read the message from Dr. Hunter McGuire.

"Oh, no!" she gasped, and her whole body seemed to sag.

Jodie rushed to her side with Julia in her arms. "Mary Anna, what is it?"

Mary Anna's voice quavered as she said, "The wire's from Hunter, Jodie. Tom's been shot.... He's been shot!"

Jodie tried to see what was written on the piece of paper. "But he's alive, isn't he?"

"Yes, thank God." Mary Anna held the wire so Jodie could read it. "Read the rest of it for me, will you, Jodie? I couldn't get past the part where Hunter said he had to amputate Tom's left arm...but at least Tom's on the road to recovery. Praise the Lord!"

Jodie quickly took in the message and noted that Stonewall was staying at the Thomas Chandler home near Guiney's Station, and Hunter and Chaplain Tucker Lacy were with him. "Do you know the Thomas Chandlers, where the general is staying, Mary Anna?"

"Yes. They used to live in Lexington and belonged to our

church. We're very close friends. I know Tom feels comfortable there."

Jodie read the last few lines. "The general wants you and Julia to come to him. And Hunter wants me to come."

"We'll go immediately! Can you get off work, Jodie?"

"I'll have to ask, but I'm sure the hospital director will let me."

Both women had forgotten the courier's presence at the door. Now, as he shuffled his feet, Mary Anna gave him a startled look.

"Mrs. Jackson," he said, "would you like me to send a wire back to Dr. McGuire?"

"I'll have to go to the railroad station and get our tickets first," she replied. "I'm not sure which train they can put us on."

"Well, ma'am, since I'm a great admirer of General Jackson, let me go to the station and make reservations for you. I'll be back shortly. Then I'll know what to tell Dr. McGuire about your arrival when I wire him."

Mary Anna thanked him, and he hurried away.

Jodie encircled her friend's shoulders and said, "Now, don't you worry, honey. The general is a strong and healthy man. He'll pull through this and be back leading his men in no time."

Mary Anna raised her apron to teary eyes. "I know this is self-ish of me, but I wish the loss of his arm would be enough to send him back to V.M.I. to teach."

"I know," Jodie said, giving her friend's shoulders a squeeze. "But the Lord has His mighty hand in all of this. He'll do what is best for the Jacksons."

On Wednesday morning, May 6, Dr. Hunter McGuire was at Stonewall Jackson's bedside. Jackson had slept little the night before. He was having difficulty breathing and felt intense pain in his left side.

McGuire did a thorough examination of Jackson's chest, abdomen, back, and rib cage. When he had finished, he said, "Tom, I can't find any sign of a broken rib…not even a bruise."

"So what do you think is causing the pain?"

"Well, it could be that you have some fluid in your left lung. I really don't want to put you through it yet, but it looks like I've got to go ahead and give you a menthol steam treatment. I'll have to sit you up, drape a towel over your head, and put a steaming pan of water below your face. It would be a lot easier at a table, but you can't get up and move around yet. I'll just have to rig it here on the bed."

"Well, if it'll help, I guess you'd better do it. The pain in my side is pretty bad."

There was a knock at the door, and Hunter quickly pulled the covers up on his friend before calling out, "Come in!"

Thomas Chandler and Tucker Lacy entered. Chandler had a piece of paper in his hand.

"How's our patient, Doctor?" asked Lacy.

"No broken ribs, I can tell you that. I think he's got some fluid in the left lung."

Chandler held up the paper and gave it a little shake. "Look here, Tom! A wire from Mary Anna!"

Jackson's dull eyes brightened, and he said, "Don't hold me in suspense, my friend!"

Chandler grinned. "She and Julia will arrive at Guiney's Station at 9:45 tomorrow morning!"

"Wonderful!" said Jackson, and then winced from the sudden pain in his side.

Chandler turned his gaze toward Hunter. "And guess what, Doc? Somebody you're married to is coming!"

A big smile lighted Hunter's face as he said, "Well, I wonder who that could be?"

Hunter reached into his medical bag and took out oil of peppermint, then excused himself and went to enlist Clara Chandler's help to keep hot, steaming water on the stove.

Soon, Hunter had Tucker Lacy running up and down the stairs, replenishing the cooled water with hot, as he gave Stonewall the menthol treatment.

Late in the afternoon, the general awakened to see his brother-in-law, Joe Morrison, sitting at his bedside along with the doctor and others.

"Joe!" he said. "What brings you here?"

Morrison rose from his chair and stood close to the general. "It's not what brought me here, Tom, it's who brought me here. I came to see how you're doing."

Jackson tested his lung by taking a deep breath. "Well, it still hurts a little, but it's better than before this quack gave me the menthol treatment."

Hunter grinned. "He must be feeling better, Joe. He's jabbing at me again."

"So," Morrison said, "I'm told that if I hang around till morning, I'll get to see my sister and my new little niece."

"Yes," Stonewall said, "and I can hardly wait!"

"And I guess I get to meet Mrs. Hunter McGuire, too."

Jackson smiled. "That means you'll see one of the prettiest little Southern belles you ever saw in your life!"

Joe looked at Hunter. "I'm sure she is. Opposites attract, you know."

Stonewall started to chuckle, then winced with pain. "Oh! Joe, don't crack funny stuff around me just yet. It hurts to laugh."

"So you think that was funny, do you?" said Hunter. "Maybe I'll just let you find a better-looking doctor!"

"That wouldn't be hard to do," said the general. "But I think I'll keep you just the same."

Joe's face took a more serious look as he said, "Tom, I was

with General Lee just before coming over here. He gave me a message for you. He said, 'Tell him to make haste and get well, and to come back to me as soon as he can. He has lost his left arm, but I have lost my right arm!'"

The general blinked against sudden tears and was about to reply when Clara stepped into the room and announced, "Your number-one aide is here, General Jackson."

Jim Lewis moved past her and drew up beside the bed. "Hello, General."

"Hello, Jim! How did Mrs. Chandler know you were my number-one aide?"

"He told me so, General," said Clara, chuckling.

Jackson grinned. "So, Jim, what brings you here?"

"The main reason, of course, is to see how you're doing. Mrs. Chandler filled me in on that. But also, if I know Dr. McGuire like I think I do, he's been running short on sleep."

"Yes, he has," spoke up Lacy. "I've tried to get him to let me sit up with the general through the night, but he only let me do it for an hour and a half last night."

"Well, he's going to get himself a full night's sleep tonight," said Jim. "And that's that."

McGuire rubbed his tired eyes. "I won't argue as long as you'll promise to wake me if I'm needed."

Lewis shrugged and flashed his palms. "Hey, I'm no doctor. If you're needed, I'll call you."

Late that night, Jim Lewis was sleeping in an overstuffed chair beside Jackson's bed. A single lantern burned in the room.

His head came up with a jerk when he heard the old grand-father clock in the hall give off its double chime, signaling 2:00 A.M. He heard a moan and looked toward the general, who was drawing up his knees and rolling his head back and forth in his sleep.

Jim bolted out of the chair and laid a hand on Jackson's brow. It felt hot to the touch, and Jackson's face was flushed.

Suddenly the general's eyes opened and he squinted to bring Jim into focus. "Jim…?" he said weakly.

"General, you're running a fever, and you look pale too."

"Just a little nausea. It'll pass."

"I'm going to get Doc," Jim said, starting away.

"No! Let him sleep. He's a very tired man."

"I promised him I would call him if you needed him, sir. You're nauseated and you're running a fever. That's plenty of reason for me to wake him."

"No! I-I'll be fine. Let him sleep."

"But you're shaking, sir, and your teeth are chattering. You're fever is going higher."

"Just find a b-blanket and put it on me."

Jim went to the closet and pulled out a blanket. As he started to place it over Jackson, the general clutched his midsection and clenched his teeth in pain. Suddenly his hand went to his chest, and he moaned.

Jim quickly spread the blanket over his commander and said, "I'm going to get Doc, sir."

This time the general didn't argue.

Moments later, a weary Hunter McGuire was working furiously on Stonewall Jackson, trying to bring his temperature down. He and Jim Lewis took turns dipping cloths in cold water to bathe his wrist and the sides of his neck.

Tucker Lacy, who had been awakened by the sounds in McGuire's room when Lewis had come for him, also entered Jackson's room. "What's wrong, Doctor?"

Hunter answered without looking up. "His temperature went up, he's having pains in his stomach and chest, and he's nauseated." He wrung out water and placed the cold, wet cloth against Jackson's neck.

"What do you make of it, Doctor?" asked Lacy.

"He's had trouble breathing and increased pain in his rib cage on the left side. Those symptoms, combined with the fever, makes me think he's got pneumonia."

"Gentlemen," said Lacy, "I want to have prayer for him right now. You keep working, and I'll pray."

McGuire and Lewis continued their ministrations but followed every word in their hearts as Tucker Lacy prayed, asking God in the name of His Son to reach down and clear the pneumonia from Jackson's lung.

By sunrise, the general's temperature was almost down to normal, the nausea was gone, and the pain in his chest was less severe.

Clara Chandler brought in breakfast, and McGuire was pleased to see Jackson eat.

When Jackson had finished eating, Clara fed the other men in her large kitchen—pancakes, sausage, and hot oatmeal. Hunter, who was unwilling to leave the general alone, stayed by his side and ate his breakfast from a tray.

At 9:15, Thomas Chandler and Joe Morrison left the house in a carriage to pick up the ladies and baby Julia at Guiney's Station.

Thirty minutes later, Clara Chandler was at the door, welcoming Mary Anna, little Julia, and Jodie. She told them Dr. McGuire wanted to see them before they went upstairs to the general's room.

Joe Morrison, who was holding his little niece, placed her in Mary Anna's arms, and said, "I'll run up and stay with Tom while Doc and Jim Lewis come down."

Moments later, Hunter and Jodie were in each other's arms and stole a kiss even though they were in public. Hunter then turned to embrace Mary Anna and tweak Julia's fat little cheek. Jodie greeted Jim Lewis, whom she had met during the battle at Antietam.

When Mary Anna glanced upstairs, Hunter said, "He's had a cold for several days, Mary Anna. I've treated him for it, but it just hasn't gotten any better. That, along with his wounds, has brought on the pneumonia. We were able to get the fever down, and he's feeling much better now."

"But what about the pneumonia, Hunter?" she asked, fear touching her eyes. "Is it going to get worse?"

"Not if I can help it. I'm watching him closely. Now…even though you know his arm has been amputated, it's going to be a hard moment for you when you first see it. Stay as calm and act as normally as possible. Understand?"

"Yes," said Mary Anna, nodding her head.

Jodie laid a hand on her forearm, and said, "You'll do fine. Would you like for me to carry Julia, so you can go to him and have your moment together?"

"Yes, please," Mary Anna said with a flutter in her voice.

Jodie took the baby, kissed her forehead, and said, "Julia, we're going to take you upstairs to see your papa now."

When the group topped the stairs and moved to the door of the general's room, they stood back and let Mary Anna go in ahead of them.

Her brother was standing by the bed, and when she came in, he said to Jackson, "Look, Tom. Here she is."

The general's face lit up and a smile graced his lips as Mary Anna moved toward him.

Joe stepped aside as his sister wiped tears and leaned over to kiss her husband, and Stonewall wrapped his arm around her neck and held her close.

They remained that way for a long moment, then Mary Anna said, "Darling, I'm so thankful to the Lord that He spared your life." She kissed him again, then said, "Your little daughter came to see her papa."

Jackson looked past her and saw Jodie holding the baby. He smiled again. "Hello, Jodie."

"Hello, General," she said, handing the baby to her mother.

Mary Anna lowered little Julia so Stonewall could kiss her.

While he spoke soft, sweet words to his daughter, tears flowed down his cheeks.

Mary Anna studied his drawn features while his attention was on Julia. Her heart ached as she noted the dark circles around his eyes, and it was all she could do to keep from weeping as she saw the bandaged stump where his left arm used to be.

After a few minutes, Mary Anna lifted Julia and stepped back from the bed, allowing Jodie to move closer.

As she bent down to kiss his cheek, the general squeezed her hand and said, "Thank you so much for keeping my family in your home."

"It's been my pleasure, General," Jodie said softly. As she stepped back, Hunter curved an arm around her waist.

Mary Anna placed a cool hand on her husband's brow and looked up at Hunter. "I think he's still got some fever."

"Yes, he does. But it was much higher last night. You've got a strong man there, Mary Anna."

Jackson began speaking tender, loving words to his wife and daughter as if they were the only ones in the room.

Jodie and Hunter and the others looked on, touched by the heartwarming scene.

That night, as Jodie was brushing her hair at the dresser in Hunter's room, she heard the door open and saw her husband come in. She continued to brush her hair as he crossed the room and moved up behind her. She met his eyes in the mirror and said, "All set for the night?"

"Mmm-hmm. Jim will take the first shift, Joe the second, and Tucker the third. I feel a little guilty, not taking a shift with Tom myself."

"Well, you shouldn't. From what Jim told me, you've been staying with him almost around the clock. You've got to get some rest, darling. Even rugged, handsome doctors need rest."

Hunter bent down and lifted her hair, kissing the back of her neck. She laid down the hairbrush and stood up, turning around to wrap her arms around his neck. She kissed him soundly and said, "I love you, Dr. McGuire."

He chuckled with pleasure, kissed her again, and said, "And I love you, Mrs. Dr. McGuire."

Jodie moved back in the circle of his arms so she could look him square in the eye, and said, "Hunter, I get the feeling that you're not telling the Jacksons how you really feel about his condition."

His face took on a bleak look. "You know me too well, don't you?"

"A wife is supposed to be able to read her husband. The Lord set it up that way."

"Oh, He did, eh?"

"Mmm-hmm. Now, tell your wife what you really think about the general."

Hunter sighed. "Well…I'm afraid Tom may not be strong enough to pull through."

"So the pneumonia is getting worse?"

"Yes. I've been thinking about the one and only thing I could do to possibly break the congestion."

"Cupping?"

"Yes."

"And you've held back because you would have to give him opiates?"

"Yes. If I'm going to make a positive move to save his life, I've got to do the cupping. But I don't like putting the drugs in his body. It could be dangerous."

"If you don't do it, what are his chances of pulling through?"

Hunter swallowed hard. "Nil. At best the opiates will make him delirious. He'll have some lucid moments, but he'll talk crazy until they wear off completely." He shook his head. "Jodie, I keep telling myself if I could have cured his cold before he was wounded, this pneumonia might not have happened. But then I've seen so many wounded soldiers die of pneumonia when they had no cold to begin with."

Jodie gripped his upper arms and gave him a gentle shake. "Darling, don't go blaming yourself for the general's condition. You've done everything a doctor could do."

Hunter bit his lower lip and nodded. "Cupping is the only chance he has, Jodie. I'll have to ask Tom and Mary Anna for permission to do it."

"Do you have everything you need with you?"

"Yes…in my medical bag."

"Then shouldn't we talk to them now, and do it right away, if they give permission?"

"It won't hurt to wait till morning. The cupping will wear Tom down. It's best for him to get his rest tonight."

"Oh…you're right. But maybe we should talk to Clara right now, so she'll be prepared with the hot water in the morning."

"Good idea."

"And we ought to go ahead and talk to Mary Anna tonight. If she agrees, then all we have to do is explain it to the general in the morning and go to work if he agrees."

Jodie, who was in her nightgown and robe, changed into a dress, and they went downstairs together to talk with the Chandlers.

Afterwards, when Hunter and Jodie were on their way to talk with Mary Anna, they heard voices in the general's room. They paused at the door and realized it was Mary Anna's voice they were hearing. Hunter knocked softly on the door, and they were met by Jim Lewis, who explained that the general wanted to see Mary Anna once more before he went to sleep.

Jodie took Hunter's hand and looked into his eyes. He answered her unspoken question with a nod and entered the room, pulling her gently in his wake.

While Jim Lewis stood by, Hunter told the Jacksons about the cupping treatment—the most drastic yet effective treatment to help alleviate the pneumonia. He explained that the general would be given a mixture of mercury, antimony, and opium. With the opiates in him, Hunter and Jodie would bathe the general's chest with hot water and use glass cups to draw blood to the affected area for the purpose of breaking up the congestion.

Hunter carefully explained the dangers involved with the opiates. But in spite of the risk, both Jacksons gave their permission.

By Saturday morning, some forty-eight hours after the cupping treatment, Stonewall Jackson appeared to be rallying.

Jodie was taking care of Julia elsewhere in the Chandler house, leaving Mary Anna free to stay with the general. She now stood beside his bed, holding his hand. He had been drifting in and out of a mental fog since the opiates had been administered on Thursday.

Often he would give some command as if he were on the battlefield, then he would mumble something she couldn't understand. At other times, he was lucid.

In one of his better moments, he looked up at her with lackluster eyes and said, "Mary Anna, my condition is very serious, isn't it?"

"Yes, sweetheart, but you're doing better."

"I am?"

"Yes. Hunter seems encouraged, at least, and he's the doctor."

Stonewall closed his eyes for a long moment, then looked up at her again. "Mary Anna, if somehow I don't make it…if it's God's will to take me, I'm ready to go."

"Of course," she said. "But the Lord knows little Julia and I need you. He's going to let you get well."

Jackson's eyes suddenly widened, and he cried, "General

Early! Form that line! Bring the artillery up! Don't let those Yankees get away!"

Mary Anna gripped his hand tightly and felt his body trembling. His eyes closed, and he coughed hard. She could hear the rattle in his chest, and perspiration formed on his brow.

At that moment, Dr. McGuire and Mary Anna's brother came in.

"How's he doing?" asked Hunter.

"I think the fever's coming back," she said.

Hours passed, and the general only grew weaker.

Late in the afternoon, Jackson was asleep while every occupant of the house but the Chandlers sat silently in his room. Baby Julia was asleep in her mother's arms.

Suddenly they heard footsteps, and the Chandlers entered the room.

"How's he doing?" whispered Thomas.

"No need to whisper," said Hunter. "He won't wake up until the opiates allow it. He isn't doing very well. I've done everything in my power to break the pneumonia, but at this point, it's worse."

"Tell them what we learned, dear," said Clara.

All eyes were on Thomas Chandler as he said, "We found out in town that word has spread all over the South about the general. Prayer services are being held everywhere—in cities, towns, and hamlets. The Southern people love this man."

Mary Anna managed a weak smile and murmured, "God bless them."

Suddenly the general jerked awake, opened glassy eyes, and shouted, "Press on, men! Press on! We've got Hooker on the run! Tell Major Hawks to send forward provisions for the men! They can't fight if they don't eat!"

Just as abruptly he went quiet, and the glaze left his eyes. He looked up to see Mary Anna standing over him with the baby in her arms. Julia had been startled from her sleep, but only cried for a few seconds.

"Papa," said Mary Anna, "here's your daughter. Want me to hold her so you can cuddle her close?"

Jackson smiled. "Yes. Please."

He kissed the baby's cheek and then suddenly looked toward the ceiling and cried, "Order General Hill to prepare for action! Pass the infantry to the front!"

That evening, the general was lucid once more, and he asked Mary Anna to read to him from the Psalms. Everyone in the house gathered in the room. When Mary Anna finished reading, Chaplain Lacy called for a circle around the bed, asking that all join hands. Little Julia was across the room, asleep in her crib.

Many tears were shed as Lacy prayed. When he said the "Amen," Stonewall Jackson ran his eyes around the circle and smiled at each one.

While Mary Anna held his hand, he talked of that moment in his life when as a youth the gospel light shined into his darkness and he opened his heart to Jesus. With tears on his cheeks, he said, "Mary Anna, I wouldn't trade the life I've had with the Lord for anything this old world could offer in its place."

"None of us would, General," said Lacy, stepping closer to the bed. "Knowing Jesus in this life is only a prelude to the wonders of heaven."

As the hour grew later, the general's fever increased. Hunter and Jodie gave him a cool sponging, which seemed to help, but he slipped into deliriums again, and once more shouted commands to his men.

Mary Anna broke down and cried, and Jodie took her in her arms.

When the rays of the rising sun lighted the windows on Sunday morning, General Jackson was sitting up in the bed and sipping tea that Clara was spooning into his mouth. Mary Anna sat next to the bed, holding the baby.

Dr. Hunter McGuire had treated too many dying patients to be fooled by the temporary rally. He gave Jodie a meaningful look and then said, "Mary Anna, do you suppose you could get Uncle Joe to hold Julia so Jodie and I could talk to you in private for a few minutes?"

Moments later, the McGuires and Mary Anna stepped into Mary Anna's room, and Hunter closed the door. He asked her to be seated on the small sofa, and Jodie sat down beside her.

"Mary Anna," he said solemnly, "I can't keep up the facade any longer, and I know you don't want me to."

The gallant woman looked him square in the eye and said, "I know you've been trying to keep me cushioned from the facts, Hunter, and I love you for it. But I know Tom isn't going to make it. How long does he have?"

Hunter took a ragged breath and his lips were pale as he said, "The end will come today. He won't live to see the sunset."

Jodie kept an arm around Mary Anna as the she broke down and sobbed. When she had regained some control, she said, "Tom must be told the end is near. He has a right to know."

Hunter nodded. "Yes, he does. Would you like me to tell him?"

"No. I must do it. But thank you for offering."

As Hunter and Jodie walked Mary Anna back toward the general's room, Hunter said, "I'll get the others out of the room so you can be alone with him."

"No need," she replied. "We're all like family. I would rather all of you were there."

When the McGuires and Mary Anna entered the room, Clara and Thomas Chandler were sitting with Lacy and Lewis while Joe Morrison was holding Julia so her papa could see her.

The tearstains were still evident on Mary Anna's face, and while the others looked on, she silently prayed for help. Suddenly she drew back her shoulders and moved up beside the bed, taking her husband's hand. "Darling," she said, "I have something very important to tell you."

He looked at her with attentive, loving eyes.

Mary Anna gently cleared her throat. "Hunter...Hunter tells me that very soon you will be in heaven."

Without hesitation, the hero of the South said, "I will miss you and the baby, but I prefer it."

The tears began to slip down Mary Anna's cheeks again, and every eye was fixed on the general's calm features.

Mary Anna smiled through her tears. "Well, before this day closes, you will be with the blessed Saviour in His glory."

The general gazed into her eyes and said, "What day is it, Mary Anna?"

"Sunday," she replied softly.

"Then it's all right," he said. "Praise the Lord."

Mary Anna motioned to Joe, who still held Julia. He placed the baby into her hands, and Mary Anna lowered Julia so her papa could see her once more.

"Little darling," he murmured. "Sweet one!" Then to Mary Anna he said, "Would you read my favorite passage? I will soon leave this groaning tabernacle, and mortality will be swallowed up of life."

Jodie quickly took the baby, and Mary Anna picked up her Bible with trembling hands.

Chaplain Lacy stood close by as Mary Anna read aloud 2 Corinthians 5:1–8. When she finished the passage, she repeated verse 4, her voice cracking slightly, and tears coursing freely down her cheeks:

> For we that are in this tabernacle do groan, being burdened: not for that we would be unclothed, but clothed upon, that mortality might be swallowed up of life.

There was a faint smile on the general's lips. His voice was weak as he turned his eyes on the others in the room and said, "God bless you, my dear ones. I love every one of you." He looked at Mary Anna last and smiled sweetly, saying, "I love you, my sweetheart."

There was a hush in the room.

Suddenly, the general's eyes widened and turned glassy. "General Stuart!" he cried hoarsely. "Bring up the cavalry! Hurry! Where's General Longstreet? He's on Marye's Heights with General Lee? Tell him to cut loose with the artillery! We must cross the river! By all means, we must cross the river!"

The man they called Stonewall looked toward the ceiling and said, "The river. Yes, the river…" And then, as if inviting those in the room along, he said, "Let us cross over the river and rest in the shade of the trees."

The great soldier's eyes closed, and his facial muscles sagged. There was a momentary rise and fall of his chest, then it fell and remained still.

Stonewall Jackson was gone.

NINETEEN

That Sunday, as night fell over Virginia, the stars twinkled in the velvety black sky.

The Army of Northern Virginia was camped on the Rappahannock River, just south of Fredericksburg, and the men sat around campfires, talking of their victory at Chancellorsville. Those who happened to be at the mansion when Fannie Pound Chancellor and her children returned told how glad she was that their home had sustained little damage.

Suddenly a rider thundered into the camp and dismounted. The men around the nearest campfire recognized Corporal Jim Lewis, Stonewall Jackson's aide. Lewis stepped toward them and said, "I need to talk to General Lee. Where's his tent?"

One of them pointed downriver about forty yards.

The Fearless Four, who sat alone by a nearby fire, watched Lewis thread his way toward Lee's tent.

"He sure seems in a hurry," said Hank Upchurch. "Just about has to be news about General Jackson. Why else would he ride from over there at this time of night?"

"Doesn't mean it's bad news," said Chuck Carney. "General

Lee has probably given orders to keep him up to date on the general's condition."

Some fifteen minutes passed, and then Lee's aides were summoned to his tent. It wasn't long before they were moving about the camp, announcing that General Lee wanted to meet with all the men.

When the entire army was collected near Robert E. Lee's tent, the general moved to a spot on the riverbank where a large boulder stood, some four feet in height. Campfires cast their flickering light on the silver-haired general as he climbed atop the rock. When he tried to speak, he choked up, pausing for a few moments to compose himself.

"Men…I must be the bearer of very bad news. Our beloved General Stonewall Jackson has died. The general died of pneumonia—a direct result of his wounds. We…must go on in this war without him. Indeed, my right arm is gone."

A pall fell over the thousands of men like a cold, wet blanket.

General Lee forced his words past the lump in his throat and said, "We must be in prayer for Mary Anna Jackson and her baby." Tears began to stream down his cheeks. "A giant has fallen. We shall never forget him!" With that, the general moved off the rock and hurried to his tent.

There was a dead silence as the men began walking slowly back to their campfires.

Numb and sick at heart, Upchurch, Nichols, Carney, and Hall stood like statues, unable to believe that their hero was dead by their hands. Soldiers who passed by them stared with bitter eyes and angry faces.

Major Rance Dayton, who stood close by, saw it all, and his heart was heavy for the four young men. He started to go talk with them. But before he could, a group led by Mike Robinson walked up to them.

"Well, you did it!" Robinson said. "You killed Stonewall Jackson, the greatest soldier who ever put on a uniform! I hope you skunks are proud of yourselves!"

"Yeah," Gifford Henderson said, "when you're old and gray, I hope you still have nightmares about what you did!"

As other men joined the group, Bo Gentry said, "You trigger-happy dogs oughtta hang your heads in shame! We told you not to shoot! Well, I hope your insides rot till they eat you alive!"

"Stonewall killers!" cried someone in the bunch.

At that, Dayton stomped up to the group and pushed his way to the middle. "All right, that's enough! Now move on! These men feel bad enough without you taunting them!"

When the soldiers had gone, Dayton said, "I'm sorry for this, boys. Don't let them get to you."

"How do we do that, Major?" asked Buford. "We're only made of mortal flesh."

Chuck Carney's voice had a brittle edge to it as he said, "They keep it up, somebody's gonna get hurt."

The firelight revealed four bitter faces. Where once Rance Dayton had seen only hurt, he now detected anger and hatred. "Boys, listen to me," he said. "If you get physical, somebody will get hurt, and it could be you. I don't want that to happen."

"Major," Carney said, "we've taken it so far, but every man has his limit how much abuse he can take."

"Look," said Dayton, "I'm going to talk to General Lee. Something has to be done to help the men of this army see that they could have done the same thing in the same circumstances. Please…give me some time to get this situation resolved."

In its Monday, May 11, 1863, issue, the front page of the *Chicago Tribune* declared in bold print:

Under the leadership of "Fighting Joe" Hooker, the glorious Army of the Potomac is becoming more slow in its movements, more unwieldy, less confident of itself, more of a football to the enemy and less an honor to the country than any army we have yet raised.

Other Northern newspapers were saying much the same thing.

President Abraham Lincoln was signally embarrassed. The United States Congressmen could barely hold their heads up in public, and General Halleck would not even appear in public. The morale of the Union army camped at Falmouth was at an all-time low, and the people of the Northern states were losing faith in their cause.

On the other hand, though devastated at the death of their hero, the morale of the Army of Northern Virginia was at an all-time high. The return of Lieutenant General James Longstreet and his two divisions to the camp at Fredericksburg brought General Lee to the peak of strength in manpower. Lee and Longstreet—feeling deeply the loss of Jackson—began forming plans on their next move.

During this time, Major Rance Dayton went to Lee and told him what the four young men who saved his life at Antietam were facing from the soldiers because they had shot Stonewall Jackson.

Lee drew up a document exonerating the four of any mis-deed. The document explained the circumstances under which the "friendly fire" took place, and Lee asked the men of the Confederate army to understand that it could have happened to any of them.

Hundreds of copies of Lee's document were printed and placed in the hands of unit leaders. The leaders were to meet with their men, read them the document, and tell them to heed it.

Major Dayton kept a sharp eye on his four friends to see how it would go after the document had been distributed. Most of the men did ease off. But Mike Robinson and his group, and the four men who had been sentries with the Fearless Four on that fateful night, kept the pressure on.

Dayton was pleased that, in spite of Robinson and his group, his friends had not retaliated.

Some ten days after the victory at Chancellorsville, Dayton was in his tent on the riverbank when he heard loud shouts and curses from upstream. The noise lasted only a few seconds, and Dayton went back to his paperwork.

Several minutes later, a young private appeared at the tent flap and said, "Major Dayton, we've got trouble out here!"

Dayton went outside to find that the Fearless Four had gotten into a fistfight with Chad Lynch, Bo Gentry, and Myron Flynn. The latter three had ended up in the river, and Bo Gentry was lying on the bank with his lungs half full of water. One of the corps doctors was trying to save his life.

Hall, Upchurch, Nichols, and Carney were standing by, and more than a hundred soldiers had gathered to see what had happened. Gentry suddenly started coughing, and the doctor announced, "He'll make it, Major, but he came plenty close to drowning."

Dayton stepped up to his friends. "What happened?" he asked.

"Same old thing, sir," replied Chuck. "They were needling us, and we just couldn't take it anymore."

"Well, you can be mighty glad Gentry didn't drown."

Hank Everett shrugged his shoulders. "If he had, it would've been his own fault." He looked past the major and said, "Uh-oh. It's General Lane."

Lane stopped where the doctor was working on Gentry and listened as Lynch and Flynn, dripping wet, told him the Fearless Four had started an argument then began throwing punches. It took them off guard, and they ended up in the river.

"They're lying through their teeth," growled Buford. "Major, we didn't start it. They did!"

"Yeah," said Everett, "we haven't retaliated before, so they figured we wouldn't this time either. Guess we showed 'em."

General Lane stomped up and said, "Major Dayton, I want you and these four men at my tent in fifteen minutes. Those other three will get dried off and be there too."

Lane gave the four an angry glance and walked away.

"Guess we're in for it now," said Chuck.

Dayton sighed. "Look, fellows, a truly big man will not let little men make him a little man like themselves. You proved at Antietam that you're big men. You mustn't let those few little men who badger you get under your skin."

"We tried that, sir," said Chuck. "We really did."

"Well, you'll have to try harder next time. I just hope General Lane isn't going to be too severe."

When the seven men were assembled before Lane in his large tent, he scolded them for fighting, saying that mature soldiers would not get into fisticuffs. He then warned of disciplinary action if any of them were ever involved in another such affair. When he dismissed them, he said, "You stay a moment, Major Dayton."

Lane waited until the seven were outside the tent, then said, "Major, you must keep a tight rein on your four friends. I mean it. If they get into another fight, I'll make them wish they'd never put on a gray uniform!"

Dayton left the tent and took the four aside. "Men," he said, "you can't ever let anybody prod you into a fight again. General Lane told me it would go very bad for you if it happens. You've got to keep a tight rein on your tempers, no matter what. You do understand what I'm saying, don't you?"

"No offense intended toward you, Major," said Chuck, "but maybe I'll come to the place where I flat just don't care what the general does."

"Chuck, please don't let that kind of attitude get a hold on you. It can only bring heartache and trouble that you don't need or want. You boys know what you mean to me. I owe you my life.

I don't want you to have any more misery than you've already suffered. Just be careful."

"We appreciate your concern for us, Major. And for your sake, we'll try not to get into another fight."

Two days later, the soldiers ate their supper as usual on the riverbank, then went into Fredericksburg to walk the streets, which had become a form of entertainment since the Chancellorsville battle.

General Lee had put the drinking establishments off limits and had promised severe punishment to any man who returned to camp with liquor on his breath.

On this evening, Nichols, Upchurch, Hall, and Carney were walking the lantern-lit streets, talking of the day the War would end and they could go home to Fayetteville and put their lives back together.

Much of Fredericksburg had been destroyed by Yankee artillery back in December, and in many places reconstruction was taking place.

The four friends had reached the business district and were approaching a dark alley where new construction was being done on both sides of the street.

Abruptly, several shadowy figures emerged from the alley and blocked their path. They tensed up as they recognized Mike Robinson's bunch, along with Chad Lynch, Bo Gentry, Ken Dykstra, and Myron Flynn.

Robinson took a step ahead of the others and said, "Well, lookee who we've got here, boys! Stonewall killers!"

"Apparently General Lee's document meant nothing to you," Chuck Carney said. "We were exonerated. Or didn't you listen?"

"Maybe Lee exonerated you, but we didn't!"

"So what does that mean?" asked Upchurch, his anger mounting.

Dykstra moved up beside Robinson. "That means we're gonna punish you on our own."

Carney noticed a small pile of two-by-fours among other pieces of lumber a step or two to his right. "You'd better think twice before you try to do that," he said. "You just go on down the street and forget what you had planned."

Robinson guffawed. "I think we've got 'em scared, boys!"

Carney sprang forward, throwing his full weight into Robinson. The impact sent the big man backpedaling, and he slammed into the others, knocking most of them down.

"Over here, guys!" said Carney as he dashed to the lumber and picked up one of the two-by-fours.

While the other three men went for their own two-by-fours, Robinson charged Carney. But he was too slow. Carney swung the two-by-four, catching Robinson square in the mouth. The big man's head snapped back, and he dropped like a rock, blood pouring from his mouth.

Gifford Henderson took one look at Robinson and lunged toward Carney. But Hank Upchurch decked him with his two-by-four. The others in Robinson's group broke into a run, heading down the dark alley. Buford swore at them and threw his two-by-four as hard as he could after them.

Suddenly they heard loud voices behind them. When they turned, they saw a dozen or more soldiers, who quickly surrounded them, pointing their rifles.

The Fearless Four dropped their two-by-fours and faced the black musket bores on all sides.

Two lieutenants bent over the two men on the ground. One of them straightened up and stepped accusingly toward Carney, Hall, Nichols, and Upchurch. "You can be thankful they're still alive...though just barely."

"It was them or us," Carney said. "They laid in wait for us, here in the alley. They had plans to punish us. They said so."

"You're under arrest," said the lieutenant. "We're jailing you right here in town."

The next morning, the four heroes of Antietam were sitting glumly in their cell when they saw Deputy Sheriff Roy Bates enter the cell block with Major Rance Dayton. The four men had been placed in the same cell, which had only a pair of bunk beds. They rose to their feet at the sound of voices.

Bates gestured toward a wooden chair in a corner of the cell block and said, "You can pull that up to the bars and sit down if you want, Major."

Dayton nodded, but stepped right up to the bars. Bates returned to the office, and Dayton said, "I don't know what to say, men. I really hoped you'd be able to take the harassment without violence. Now you've really done it."

"They were going to attack us, Major," Chuck said. "It was hit first or get hit."

Dayton sighed and rubbed the back of his neck. "General Lane is going to bring assault charges against you. Several of the men in the group have already agreed to testify against you."

"Well, if they'll tell the truth," said Hank, "they'll have to say that they were lying in wait in that alley to jump us."

The major shook his head. "They're not going to admit that, I guarantee you."

"So what will an assault charge bring us?" asked Everett.

"Probably several months, maybe even years, in prison."

At the news, sick looks passed over their faces.

"Fellows," said Dayton, "I can't let you face those charges without trying to get you off."

Hank Upchurch lifted his head slightly. "What do you mean, sir?"

"Since General Lee knows the circumstances surrounding the shooting of General Jackson, Captain Boswell, and Sergeant Cunliffe, and he was partially responsible for your receiving the Presidential Commendation for your valor at Antietam, I'm going to talk to him. I'll explain to him why you went on the offensive last night. I'll see if he'll simply let you be released and allowed to leave the army. It's best that we get you away from the source of the trouble."

The four men were thanking Dayton when Sheriff George Duncan entered the cell block. A stout man of fifty-five, with a generous paunch, Duncan said, "Major, I just found out these are the men who were honored for bravery a few months ago in Richmond by President Davis...for saving your life up at Sharpsburg."

"That's right," said Dayton.

Duncan looked at the foursome, then back at Dayton. "How could they do a thing like that, then shoot Stonewall Jackson and two other Confederate soldiers, and bludgeon two more soldiers last night?"

"It's a long story, Sheriff," said Dayton. "No time to tell it now. But they're not bad men. They got caught up in some extenuating circumstances." Turning to his friends, the major said, "I'll see you tomorrow."

The next morning, Deputy Bates ushered General James Lane into the cell block, then returned to the office. The prisoners rose to their feet and approached the bars.

"I'm here in place of Major Dayton," said Lane. His countenance reflected distaste as he scanned their faces. "I have him on assignment today, and he won't be able to come. I thought it best to inform you that Major Dayton talked to General Lee. The general would not agree to release you from the army and let you go home based on past performance and present circumstances. You're going to stand trial."

With that, Lane started toward the door. He stopped after a few steps and said, "Oh. Major Dayton said to tell you he'll come and see you tomorrow."

When Lane was gone, Chuck swore and said, "I hate this stinkin' army! They're not gonna lock me up!"

"Me neither," said Hank. "We need to bust outta here."

"That's exactly what we're gonna do," said Chuck. "We'll escape when that deputy brings our supper tonight."

"So what'll we do, Chuck?" asked Everett.

"One of us will have to play sick...."

It was after dark when General James Lane and Major Rance Dayton dismounted their horses in front of the county jail, along with the teenage boy who had ridden to fetch them.

George Duncan was waiting for them when they walked into his office. He handed the boy a Confederate dollar bill for his services and dismissed him.

"The kid said the men escaped, Sheriff," said Lane.

"That's right...and I want you to come see what they did."

Duncan took the army officers into the cell block where the body of Deputy Sheriff Roy Bates lay on the floor in a pool of blood.

Both men were stunned.

"Somehow they tricked my deputy into opening the cell door when he brought their supper," the sheriff said. "The trays are usually slid beneath the cell door. You can see the food hasn't been touched. And if you'll look closely, you'll see that they beat him to death with the butt of his revolver. One or two hard blows would certainly have knocked him out. But they must have hit him at least a dozen times. It was murder, gentlemen. Coldblooded murder. I have warrants for their arrest. When we find them, they'll hang for sure."

Rance Dayton felt sick all over, and his face was deathly white. "It's like a nightmare, Sheriff. Those four young men who so gallantly saved my life and basked in glory as heroes have become bitter, coldhearted killers. I guess you could call it a turn of glory."

Sheriff Duncan sent a wire to the sheriff of Cumberland County, North Carolina, advising him of what had happened, and to be on the lookout for the fugitives if they should return to Fayetteville. Other law agencies were alerted, with descriptions of the Fearless Four.

Duncan himself launched a manhunt, wanting desperately to catch the men who had murdered his deputy and see them hang.

Major Rance Dayton often thought of the Antietam heroes as the war continued. As far as he knew, the Fearless Four hadn't been caught. It was as if they had vanished from the earth.

Finally, the Civil War came to an end with the Union the victor on April 9, 1865.

Rance Dayton, still wanting to become a lawman in the West and to build a new life on the frontier, first made a trip to Fayetteville, North Carolina. There he met with the families of the four men who had saved his life. None of them had heard from the men since their escape from Fredericksburg in May 1863.

Dayton's purpose in returning to Fayetteville was to obtain official papers from the sheriff's department that would tell of his accomplishments as a lawman in Cumberland County. With the desired papers in hand, he took a train west.

TWENTY

In early June of 1865, a train carried Rance Dayton across Tennessee, the western tip of Kentucky, and into Illinois. He would change trains at St. Louis, Missouri, and head west to Kansas City.

As the train rolled across the flat land of Illinois, Dayton reached into his valise and took out the most recent letter he had received from Jackson County Sheriff Bart Clifford in Independence, Missouri. He smiled as he read it again, and then carefully placed it back in the valise. *Lord,* he prayed silently, *help me find the place where You want me to live, and the job You want me to have.*

When the train chugged into the depot at St. Louis, Dayton picked up his two pieces of hand luggage and stepped out of the coach. He threaded his way among the people who crowded the station platform and approached a large blackboard on the wall next to the ticket office. The chalk writing told him his train to Kansas City would be on time.

Since it was almost noon, and he had about two hours, Dayton went to the café attached to the station and ate lunch.

The train from Kansas City indeed came in on time, turned

around in the railroad yard, and hissed its way to a stop at its assigned spot in the depot.

Soon the conductor was calling for all passengers to board. Dayton climbed aboard the last car before the caboose and chose a seat about midway in the coach. He placed his luggage in the overhead rack and sat down next to the window. It looked as if the train was going to be quite full. He could see people hurrying to the other cars, and passengers entered the coach he occupied in a steady stream from both ends.

A young woman stopped at the seat directly across the aisle from Dayton, carrying her hand luggage. She sat one piece down so she could lift the other into the overhead rack.

"Excuse me, ma'am," Rance said, "would you allow me to put your luggage in the rack for you?"

The lady smiled. "Why, yes. Thank you, sir."

"You're welcome, ma'am. I'll be glad to take them down for you when we get to Kansas City."

Rance was about to ask if he could sit beside her when she looked past him and said, "Thank you, sir, but that won't be necessary. My husband's here now. Hello, darling. I was afraid you weren't going to make it."

Puffing from an apparent long run, the woman's husband put his luggage in the overhead rack and said, "Last-minute business. Got it taken care of, though."

"Darling," she said, looking at Dayton, "this nice gentleman put my luggage in the rack for me."

The man smiled at Rance and said, "Thank you for your kindness to my wife, Mr...."

"Dayton. Rance Dayton."

"Well, thank you, Mr. Dayton. I'm Lowell Carstairs. This is Lucille."

"Glad to meet both of you," said Rance, then turned and sat down in his seat.

The coach was filling up, and now the bell on the engine began clanging—the signal that the train would soon depart.

Rance noticed a tall, square-jawed man with salt-and-pepper hair and mustache enter the front door of the coach and move down the aisle. As he came closer, the badge on his vest caught Rance's attention. The lawman stopped beside Rance and said, "The second half of this seat taken?"

"No, sir," said Rance with a smile. "Please, sit down." He read the inscription on the badge. *Deputy United States marshal.*

The deputy, whom Rance figured to be in his early fifties, placed his luggage overhead and eased onto the seat.

Outside, the conductor shouted, "All abo-o-oard!"

Rance extended his hand. "I'm Rance Dayton, sir."

The deputy gripped his hand firmly and smiled. "Deputy U.S. Marshal Dan Moore."

"Always glad to meet a lawman," said Dayton. "Before the War I was sheriff of Cumberland County, North Carolina…and had been deputy sheriff before that."

"So you're a veteran of the War. I don't have to ask which side."

"Hardly," Dayton said, chuckling.

"And something tells me you were an officer."

"Yes. Major."

"Major! And you aren't a West Pointer?"

"No."

"Well, that's great. So you fought with a North Carolina out-fit, I assume."

"Yes, sir. I was commander of the Eighteenth North Carolina Regiment in Brigadier General James Lane's brigade."

The lawman frowned slightly and said, "Eighteenth North Carolina…now why does that ring a bell?"

"It probably rings a bell, Marshal, because it was some men of my regiment who mistook General Stonewall Jackson and a group of riders for Yankees, and fired at them."

Moore snapped his fingers. "Yes, that's it. So it was some of your men?"

"Yes. A real tragedy."

"Must've been hard for all of you."

"We all loved and admired General Jackson tremendously."

"Jackson sure was one of my heroes, too, I'll tell you that. So, ah...what are you doing for a living now?"

"At the moment I'm unemployed, but I'm heading west to get back into law enforcement."

"Do you have something lined up, or are you traveling west cold turkey?"

"I've been corresponding with Jackson County Sheriff Bart Clifford in Independence."

"Oh, sure! Bart Clifford. Know him well. Fine man."

"He's going to help me find a town needing a marshal, or even a deputy marshal somewhere in the West."

"Well, Bart has a lot of friends all over the West. He'll have some good contacts, that's for sure."

The train was now moving along the Mississippi River northward. Rance let his gaze settle on the wide river. "The mighty Mississippi," he said in a low voice. "Played a big part in the War."

Soon the tracks veered away from the river and turned due west, and Rance turned back to Moore. "You been a deputy U.S. marshal very long?" he asked.

"Only two months."

"Oh, really? So where did you wear a badge before then?"

"I was Douglas County sheriff in Lawrence, Kansas, up until the end of the War. Had been for ten years. And I was deputy sheriff before that."

"Lawrence..." Rance said. "Then you were there when William Quantrill and his raiders sacked and burned the city in '63."

"Yep. Those wild fools killed a hundred and fifty civilians in that raid. But in spite of the fact that Quantrill was a Confederate guerrilla, I still leaned toward the South in the War."

Dayton smiled. "Well, I'm glad you didn't let Quantrill sway your sentiments toward Dixie."

Moore laughed, then said, "You married, Dayton?"

"No, sir. I was engaged once but...it didn't work out. I'm hoping to find the right one out there where the buffalo roam. You married?"

Moore nodded. "Very happily. Nina and I have been married almost thirty years. Have a daughter and two sons...four grandchildren. A son-in-law and two daughters-in-law, of course."

Rance grinned.

"I'm glad to see you heading out West, Dayton," said Moore. "I admire you for it. The West is going to need a whole lot more like you as more people head for the frontier. It's becoming a haven for ne'er-do-wells, thieves, robbers, and troublemakers. Unfortunately, a good number of those are Civil War veterans. Just got used to violence and can't seem to live without it. So they create their own."

The two men were quiet a moment, listening to the steady clicking of the steel wheels beneath them. Then Dayton said, "Why did you decide to become a federal man? Certainly Lawrence has its share of troublemakers."

"Pressure," Moore said evenly.

"What kind of pressure?"

"The kind from Chief United States Marshal Ben Starke in Kansas City. He and I are longtime friends. Ben showed up at my office in Lawrence a week after the War was over and talked about the big influx of Civil War soldiers heading west...their lives empty and looking for excitement.

"Ben needed to beef up his staff of deputies, so being a personal friend, and knowing my arrest record, he pressured me to resign as sheriff and become one of his deputies. The reason I was in St. Louis was to take a couple of those Civil War troublemakers—

Rebels, by the way—to be tried for murder in St. Louis, where they killed two men who'd beaten them in a series of poker games."

The conversation lulled for a few minutes, and Rance watched the sunlit countryside go by.

Suddenly, Moore said, "You know what, Dayton?"

"Sir?"

"If you have a better than average arrest record in Cumberland County, you ought to consider applying for a deputy U.S. marshal's position."

"Well, maybe I should. Let me get my valise out of the overhead rack, and I'll let you take a look at my record."

"I'll get it for you," said Moore, leaving the seat to stand in the aisle. "Which one is it?"

"Dark brown leather. Has my initials on it."

"Okay. Got it."

Rance took out the envelope that contained the arrest records for his years in law enforcement and handed them to Dan Moore. "Here, sir. Take a look."

Moore carefully read the records. When he looked up from the report, he glanced at Dayton and said, "Whew! My record can't come near yours! You must be plenty good at tracking down and catching fugitives."

Rance shrugged. "Maybe God gave me the nose of a bloodhound."

"I'll tell you right now, Ben Starke would jump at the chance to get a man like you. I mean it. If you decide you'd like to apply, Dayton, I'll be glad to put in a good word for you with Ben. Not that you'd need it with these credentials!"

Rance grinned and nodded slowly.

Moore slid down on the seat, tipped his hat over his face, and said, "Well, ol' Dan here is going to take a little snooze."

Rance did the same, only instead of sleeping, he began to pray silently about becoming a deputy U.S. marshal. After a while, an unmistakable peace encompassed his heart. "All right, Lord," he said in a whisper. "I'll pursue it. Thank You for Your guidance. You know I want to be in the very center of Your will."

People moved up and down the aisles, the conductor came through twice, and children played nearby, but still Dan Moore slept on.

Finally, the train slowed down for a stop at Columbia, Missouri, and the change of speed and the sound of the wheels awakened Moore. He sat up, blinking, and placed his hat on his head. "We must be coming into Columbia," he mumbled.

"That's it," Rance said. "You sleep pretty sound, don't you?"

"Been known to," Moore said, covering a yawn. "'Specially when I've been running a little short on it. And that's the way it's been the past day or two. Want to stretch your legs?"

The two men stepped off the train and walked alongside it.

"Tell you what, Deputy," said Rance, "I'm going to take you up on putting in a good word for me with Chief Starke."

A smile spread over Moore's face. "Well, great! As you know, we won't get into Kansas City until late this evening, but how about I take you and introduce you to Ben first thing in the morning?"

"I'm ready."

"What about Sheriff Clifford? When are you supposed to meet with him?"

"No set time. He knows I'm coming, but we didn't set a particular day or time. He's just expecting me to walk into his office sometime soon."

"Good. Then this won't mess up anything with him."

"Nope. If I get hired by Chief Starke, I'll simply contact Sheriff Clifford and tell him I've got a job."

*****

Chief United States Marshal Benjamin Starke sat at his desk reading Rance Dayton's records from Cumberland County. True to his word, Dan Moore had taken Dayton to the chief's office and now waited with him as the chief considered Rance's prospects.

When he finished reading, Starke shook his head in wonder and looked over his half-moon glasses. "Mr. Dayton," he said, "this is an impressive record. I need your kind. Where have you been all my life?"

Dayton and Moore laughed.

Starke, who was a stout, bald man of sixty, shook his head again and said, "And to top it off, you made major under Robert E. Lee in a very short amount of time. If you want a job, I can place you real fast."

Dayton glanced at Moore and smiled, then said, "I'll take it, sir."

"All right. Now, we have U.S. marshal offices in several places in the West, and every one of them is shorthanded. Each office is headed up by a United States marshal and they're all accountable to this office. And this office is accountable to the U.S. marshal's headquarters in Washington D.C. We have plans for the office in Denver, Colorado, to take over the western territory now under my jurisdiction, but that's a ways off. Anyway, I can list the locations of the offices and let you pick the place you like best. Or, I can tell you where you're needed the most right now and see what you think about it."

"I'm here to serve, sir. Where do you need me the most?"

"Western Montana."

Dayton pursed his lips and cocked his head to one side. "What can you tell me about it?"

"We opened an office in Helena just about a year ago. We've had one in Billings for about five years. Gold strikes and other mining have drawn people for several years, and with population comes lawbreakers. The Billings office handles problems in eastern Montana Territory, and the Helena office handles those on the western side. Helena is situated just east of the towering and majestic Rockies."

"Towering and majestic," echoed Moore. "You really know how to do a sales job, don't you, my friend?"

"Hush up, Dan. I need this man in Helena desperately."

"Chief Starke," said Dayton, "I'll take the job. What's next?"

"You haven't asked me what the job pays."

"No lawman gets paid what he's worth, but I figure it'll be enough to keep me in food, shelter, and clothes."

Starke smiled. "It will."

"Okay. What's next?"

"You need to fill out an application, which from what I've already learned about you will only be a formality. Then you take the oath before me in the presence of two deputies. I'll commission you a deputy United States marshal, and I'll wire your new boss immediately and tell him about you. We'll have you headed west by tomorrow morning. You go by rail as far as Billings, then travel by stagecoach to Helena."

"Let's get on with it," said Rance.

Less than an hour later, all the formalities had been taken care of, and Deputy U.S. Marshal Rance Dayton received his badge and a new rifle, revolver, and gun belt. He would be provided with horse, bridle, and saddle when he arrived at his destination.

Starke sent a wire to U.S. Marshal Douglas Wright in Helena, advising him of the new man assigned to his office, along with a brief description of his qualifications.

Dan Moore looked extremely pleased with himself that he had recruited Rance Dayton for Starke. But duty called, and he excused himself, shook hands with Dayton, and left the office.

Within half an hour after the wire had been sent, Wright wired back, telling Starke to put Dayton on a train as soon as possible.

Chief Starke made reservations for Dayton with both railroad and stage lines, then wired Wright of his new man's arrival time in Helena.

When that was done, the chief sat down with Dayton at his desk, and said, "Rance, I want to explain why we need you at Helena right now. Your experience and success in tracking and capturing lawbreakers fills a real need. There's a bloody gang of outlaws terrorizing western Montana Territory. They're robbing banks, stagecoaches, stores, ranchers, and travelers. And they're heartless and ruthless. They kill anyone who dares to resist them."

"I've dealt with that kind before, sir."

Chief Starke nodded. "They also pride themselves in killing lawmen. They've been pursued by other federal men out of the Helena office. Five, in fact. And they've killed three of them. The other two saw what they were up against and resigned.

"Wright can't go after them personally and oversee the office. He has three deputies, but none of them have your experience behind a badge, or your success record. Doug Wright needs you real bad." Starke paused, then said, "Has what I've said changed your mind about going to Helena?"

Rance looked at the badge on his chest and said, "No, sir. It'll be a welcome challenge to go after that gang. Do you know who they are?"

The chief opened a desk drawer and pulled out the latest issue of *Police Gazette*, an eastern magazine about crime and punishment. Placing it on the desk in front of his new deputy, he said, "Right there on the front page. The Phantom Riders. That's them. The article tells all about what they're doing in western Montana. The article takes up three pages.

"They've also been written up in newspapers all over the West. No one knows who they are. They always wear masks when pulling their robberies and doing their killing. A few of the gang have been killed in gun battles with lawmen, but the dead ones have never been identified."

"I see," said Dayton, running his eyes over the front page. "How many men ride in the gang?"

"Anywhere from seven to ten, depending on how fast they replace a man when one of them goes down. A few times some of the gang members have been wounded when battling lawmen, but they've always escaped and taken their wounded with them."

"Sounds like they're well organized," said Dayton. "It's not going to be easy to bring them in."

"How well I know. Doug'll go over everything with you, but let me say it right here. Though you'll be tracking them alone, when you find them, you're not to try to take them by yourself. You pinpoint their hideout and go to the closest local law for help. Understand?"

"Yes, sir."

"All right," said Starke, rising to his feet. "I'll let you go to your hotel room and get some rest. I'll see you here at eight o'clock in the morning, and one of my deputies will drive you to the depot."

The day was still early, and Dayton borrowed a horse from Starke to ride to Independence. He wanted to thank Sheriff Bart Clifford in person for his willingness to help him find a lawman's job, and to let him know that he was now a deputy U.S. marshal.

The next morning, Rance left for Montana and spent the night in Cheyenne City, Wyoming, then boarded a different train for Billings and traveled all day. The following morning he boarded the Wells Fargo stage that would take him to Bozeman, where he would change stagecoaches and travel north between the Big Belt Mountains and the Rocky Mountains to Helena.

On the final leg of his journey, Rance sat in amazement as the massive Rockies came into view on his left, and the Big Belts raised their jagged peaks toward the azure sky on his right. He thrilled at the Rocky Mountain peaks that lifted their snow-capped heads, even in June, eleven and twelve thousand feet above sea level.

When the stage reached the small town of Gallatin, the passengers were allowed to get off and stretch their legs while the horses were fed and watered. Dayton decided to take a short stroll and look the town over. When he came upon a cluster of men who stood outside the town's only saloon, he heard them talking about the Phantom Riders.

One of the men noticed his badge and said, "Howdy, there, Marshal. You come in on the stage?"

"Just pausing while the horses are being serviced," said Dayton. "I'm on my way to Helena. I heard you talking about the Phantom Riders a moment ago."

"Yes, sir," spoke up a middle-aged man. "You must know about 'em."

"I do. They're part of the reason I'm going to Helena. I'm joining the U.S. marshal's office there."

"Well, good for you. I hope you put a rope around every one of their dirty necks!"

"What were you saying about them?" asked Dayton.

"Those filthy skunks robbed a bank yesterday in Missoula. Killed two bank employees who weren't even givin' 'em any trouble. Just did it outta meanness. They also wounded a bank customer. Got away before the town marshal or his deputy could appear on the scene."

As the stage bound for Helena rolled northward and the other passengers slept, Rance took his Bible out of his valise and started flipping pages. He'd read something in the Psalms recently that came back to him. He'd marked the verses and was now able to find the passage quickly. He read the two verses in Psalm 55 and let their truth grip him.

> Let death seize upon them, and let them go down quick into hell: for wickedness is in their dwellings, and among them.
>
> But thou, O God, shalt bring them down into the pit of destruction: bloody and deceitful men shall not live out half their days....

The new deputy United States marshal rested the Bible in his lap and stared out the window at the majestic Rockies. "Lord," he said in a whisper, "help me to bring these bloody and deceitful men to justice."

TWENTY-ONE

Rance Dayton's stagecoach rolled into Helena at sundown. As the stage squealed to a halt in a cloud of dust, he noticed a small group of men standing in front of the Wells Fargo office. Then he noticed the coffin at their feet.

He stepped out of the coach, helped two ladies to alight, then reached inside for his hand luggage. As he turned around, he found himself facing a lanky man with a droopy silver mustache. The man glanced at Rance's badge and said, "Deputy Rance Dayton, I presume?"

"Yes, sir. Marshal Wright?"

"That's me," said Wright, shaking Rance's hand. "I'll have to ask you to excuse me for a moment. I've got to get a coffin loaded on the stage."

Dayton watched as the U.S. Marshal, the stage agent, and the driver and shotgunner hoisted the heavy oblong box onto the rack atop the coach.

A fresh six-up team of horses was brought from the rear of the stage station while the present team was unhitched. Marshal Wright talked to the driver for a few minutes, then came back to his new deputy and said, "Sorry about that, Dayton, but I had to make sure the driver and shotgunner understood about the coffin."

"No problem, sir."

"Let's go to the office and do what paperwork has to be done. Then we'll get you settled into a hotel room. By then, it'll be time for supper."

"Whatever you say, sir."

After filling out the necessary paperwork to establish Deputy U.S. Marshal Rance Dayton as officially working out of the Helena office, Wright said, "Now, let me tell you about the body in the coffin. That was one of my deputies—Alan Thaxter. He was from Texas, so I'm sending the body home to his family for burial."

Rance nodded. "That seems only right, sir."

"Alan was killed by the Phantom Riders...yesterday."

The marshal shook his head regretfully. "Hindsight always makes a man wise. And I sure wish I hadn't let him go after that gang alone. He really wasn't experienced enough. But when they murdered two bank employees over in Missoula a few days ago, Alan insisted I let him track them down."

"I heard about the Missoula robbery," said Rance. "They wounded a bank customer, too, if I heard right."

"You heard right. So anyway, I gave Alan permission to trail those dirty rats, with the stipulation that he not try to take them on by himself if he caught up to them. He was to get help from the closest sheriff or town marshal."

Rance nodded. "Chief Starke laid down the same orders to me, sir."

"Good. Then I won't have to school you on it, will I?"

"No, sir."

"Well, anyway...Alan caught up with them in the woods outside a town called Duncan, at the south tip of the Flathead Indian Reservation. That's about forty miles north of Missoula."

"Marshal, if he was alone, how do you know what happened?"

"Because of an eyewitness—fella named John Hammett. As instructed, my deputy went to Bob Dardin, marshal at Duncan, and asked for help to capture the gang. Dardin and his only deputy—Hammett—went with him. The three were sneaking up on the camp when they spooked a big bull moose and he charged through the campsite. The gang opened fire, my deputy and Marshal Dardin were killed, and Hammett was wounded. He lived only because the gang took off in a hurry. They probably thought there was more help on the way."

"Do you have any idea which way they're headed now?" asked Dayton.

"No, but their trail won't be hard to find. They leave dead bodies wherever they go."

"Do you want me to head out in the morning, sir?"

"Yes. We'll give you a stalwart horse and turn you loose. And Dayton…please…don't try to capture them alone. Make sure you have help."

"I will, sir."

The next morning, Rance placed his personal items in the saddlebags, strapped on a bedroll, and rode north toward Duncan to pick up the trail of the Phantom Riders. After several miles of riding, he knew he had a strong horse in the bay gelding with the white face and stockings.

The next day, he found that the gang had swung west and begun robbing banks in towns along the east side of the Bitterroot Mountains. Marshal Wright was correct. The Phantom Riders robbed six banks in four days, and left dead people in every town.

On his fifth day out, he came close to the gang at a town

called Stevensville, where they had killed a bank customer and the local marshal. Rance trailed the gang to some nearby woods and even found blood on some bushes, which corroborated an eyewitness account that the marshal had shot one of the robbers before he was killed.

The trail turned east from Stevensville, and Dayton trotted his horse toward the town of Washington Gulch. He noted a large herd of buffalo in a valley off to his right and suddenly remembered part of his conversation with Dan Moore on the train to Kansas. He'd told Moore that he was going to find the right girl out where the buffalo roam.

Well, there's the buffalo, he thought. *But where's the girl?*

Dayton bottomed out in a low spot on the road and urged the horse for more speed as they started up the hill. Suddenly he heard a series of gunshots ahead. He pushed the gelding even harder, and when he topped the hill, he saw a stagecoach stopped on the road. A man lay on the ground, and passengers were climbing out. In the distance, he saw the gang riding hard toward some dense woods.

Rance skidded to a halt and slid from the saddle near two men and a woman who were bent over the body.

"Folks," Rance said, "I'm Deputy U.S. Marshal Rance Dayton out of the Helena office. Those men were masked, weren't they?"

"Yes, they were," said one of the men. "It was the Phantom Riders, Deputy."

"They robbed us then shot the driver and the shotgunner!" said the woman. "The driver just died."

Dayton raised his eyes toward the spot where he had last seen the gang. "Look, folks, I've got to go after them. Can one of you men drive the stage into Washington Gulch?"

"We'll take care of it, Deputy," said the man who had spoken before. "Go get 'em!"

Dayton vaulted into the saddle and put the bay to a gallop.

Within a few minutes, he caught sight of the galloping gang as he topped a rise. They were in a low spot at the moment, but racing toward the top of a hill.

When Dayton saw the riders again, he was much closer to them, and gaining. They couldn't be more than two miles ahead of him.

Rance wasn't sure what he would do when he closed the gap even more, but somehow he had to keep the gang in sight until they made camp that night. Then he could go for help. Moments later, he was coming up on Washington Gulch when he caught sight of the gang again. They skirted the town and Dayton did the same.

A half-hour passed, and when Dayton crested a hill and saw the gang still riding hard, he was now less than a mile behind them.

When the gang vanished once again, Rance noticed a white ranch house with white outbuildings and a red barn off to his right. The buildings sat in a wide open area dotted with trees.

So far Rance's mount showed no signs of tiring, and he pressed the horse, staying at a gallop. When they came charging over the rise and suddenly encountered an injured buffalo in the middle of the road, there was no chance to change course. The gelding's legs slammed into the buffalo, and Dayton somersaulted out of the saddle. He hit the ground hard and his head struck a large rock beside the road.

Rance Dayton awakened to a world of Montana sunshine…and his head ached something fierce.

He squinted at the bright sunlight coming through a window adorned with lace curtains. He was lying in a bed with pillows propped under his head. He closed his eyes momentarily to ease the intensity of the brilliant light, then opened them again.

Slowly he looked at different objects in the room, and then

his eyes lighted on a young woman sitting in a chair beside his bed. The sun's rays coming through the window made a halo of her golden hair. She was reading a Bible and hadn't yet noticed he had regained consciousness.

Rance studied her for a moment and decided he had never seen such a beautiful woman in all his life.

Rance tried to put it all together. *How did I get here? Why does my head hurt so much? Where—?*

Suddenly it all came back. The galloping horse. The buffalo in the road. Sailing through the air. Rolling on the ground. The rock. The shower of stars. The black whirlpool. And then, sunlight coming through the window with lace curtains.

Rance's mouth was dry, and his neck felt stiff. He moved his head, and pain lanced through it, making him moan.

The girl looked up from the Bible, her eyes widening, and said, "Oh! Hello, Deputy Dayton!" Then she turned toward the open door and called, "Daddy! Mother! He's awake!"

She laid her Bible on a table and got up to stand beside the bed as the sound of footsteps came from the hall.

Rance blinked as he looked at the girl, then let his gaze swing to the door as a couple in their mid-forties hurried into the room.

"Has he said anything, Marcy?" asked the older woman.

"No, Mother."

"Deputy Dayton," said the man, "can you hear me?"

Rance ran a dry tongue over equally dry lips. "Yes, sir."

"Here, Deputy," said Marcy, turning to the nightstand. "Let me pour you a glass of water."

"My name is Mitchell Moran," the man said. "This is my wife, Elizabeth, and our daughter, Marcy."

"I...I'm glad to meet you, sir," said Rance, the slight exertion of speaking sending a lance of pain through his head. It was then that he became aware of the bandage and raised a hand to touch it with his fingertips.

"We fixed you up as best we could," said Elizabeth. "Our son,

Hal, is on his way into Deer Lodge City to bring the doctor. Unless Dr. Hanson is out of town or in the midst of surgery, they should be back in a little while."

Marcy leaned toward Rance with the glass of water. "Here, Deputy…this will help take away that dryness."

Dayton took the water in small sips. When he had drained the glass, he managed a smile and said, "Thank you, ma'am."

"My pleasure," she said.

"We were coming home from Deer Lodge City," said Mitchell, "and were about to turn off the road toward home when Marcy happened to notice a big ol' cow buffalo lying in the road toward Washington Gulch. Just as she called our attention to the cow, we spotted you lying beside the road."

Rance nodded gingerly. "My horse was at a full gallop when we topped the hill. He saw the cow, but it was too late to dodge it. Did you see my horse anywhere?"

"Nope. Just you and the cow. Horse must've run off."

"Mmm…with my saddlebags. My personal things, and my Bible."

Marcy gave her parents a quick glance, then looked away.

"Well, at least my horse must not have a broken leg," said Rance. "I'm glad for that, even if I never see him again. Say! How do you know who I am?"

"We knew by your badge that you're a deputy U.S. marshal," said Mitchell. "We pulled your wallet out of your pocket and found papers identifying you as Major Rance Dayton, II Corps, Confederate Army of Northern Virginia. So we knew your name, and a little about your past."

"My up-to-date identification was in my saddlebags. I'm working out of the U.S. marshal's office in Helena. Just started a few days ago."

"What part of the South are you from, Deputy?" Marcy asked.

"North Carolina. Fayetteville. I was sheriff of Cumberland County before the War."

"I see," she said. "So you put on a badge soon after the War ended?"

"Yes, ma'am. I decided to come west and be a lawman out here."

"Were you chasing an outlaw when you took your spill?" asked Mitchell.

"A bunch of outlaws, sir," said Rance. "Have you heard of the Phantom Riders?"

"Bunch of coldhearted killers! You were chasing them?"

"Yes, sir. My assignment is to trail them till they light somewhere, get help from the local law, and bring them in to hang."

"Well, more power to you, Deputy. We'll have to get you well real soon so you can get back after them."

"Yes, sir. Looks like I'll have to find me another horse though."

"We'll help you do that."

Rance's gaze strayed to Marcy's face. She seemed to be watching him carefully as she spoke. "You…ah mentioned you carried a Bible in your saddlebags, Deputy. Do you read the Bible a lot?"

"Every day," he said. "I noticed you were reading one when I came to."

"Oh, yes. God's given me a real hunger for His Word." She paused expectantly, and Rance smiled at her.

"That's why I read it too," he said. "I've only been saved a couple of years, but walking with Jesus these two years has been wonderful."

"Then you must've gotten saved while you were in the army," said Elizabeth.

"That's right. You all have heard of Stonewall Jackson…I served under him. He was the commander of II Corps. I was saved because of his testimony. General Jackson gave me the gospel many times and pressed home my need to be saved."

"Well, I'll be switched!" said Mitchell. "I'd heard Jackson was a Christian."

"And a very dedicated one, sir," said Dayton. "He won many

of his men to Christ. And what a man of prayer! Often we would hear him praying in his tent late at night...especially when we were going into a battle the next day. He loved his men and prayed earnestly for us."

"Well! What a joy to know that our houseguest is a Christian!" said Elizabeth.

"Tell me," said Mitchell, "is there a Mrs. Dayton somewhere?"

Rance's gaze went to Marcy and she looked down.

"No, sir," he said quietly. "I've not found the right young lady yet. I figure that since I'm now one of God's children, He'll bring her into my life when the time is right."

"That's the way to look at it," said Mitchell, slipping an arm around Elizabeth's waist. "I waited till the Lord sent the most wonderful little gal in all the world into my life, then grabbed her quick!"

Elizabeth's cheeks turned pink. "Oh, Mitch...you say the sweetest things!"

"And I mean every word of it," he said, giving her an extra squeeze.

They heard the sound of pounding hooves outside, along with the rattle of a buggy, and Marcy hurried to the window. "It's Hal and Dr. Hanson," she said.

Elizabeth hurried down the hall and led the newcomers back to Rance's room. She took hold of her seventeen-year-old son's hand and led him toward the bed, saying, "Deputy Rance Dayton, this is our son, Hal. He helped us load you into the wagon when we found you."

Rance extended his right hand, and Hal gripped it firmly.

"Glad to meet you, Hal," said Rance.

"My pleasure, sir," said the handsome youth who looked a lot like his father.

"And this is Dr. Rex Hanson, Deputy," said Elizabeth.

Dayton shook hands with the doctor, then Hanson went to

work. He listened to Dayton's heart with his stethoscope, checked his ears, tested his hearing, examined his eyes, then removed the bandage from his head. Gently he pressed the tips of his fingers to Rance's skull, feeling every square inch.

"Are you having dizzy spells or nausea, Mr. Dayton?" asked the doctor.

"No, sir. Just a powerful throbbing headache."

"Mmm-hmm. I can believe that. You took quite a crack on the head. The rock must've been smooth where you hit it, because the split in the skin is minor and has already stopped bleeding. But you've got something of a knot where it's split on the left side. It'll go down in a day or two."

"Do you think there's a fracture, Doctor?" asked Marcy.

"I'm sure there isn't, Marcy."

"Praise the Lord," she said, smiling.

"I'll leave some powders for you to take, along with directions for dosage, Mr. Dayton," said Hanson. "They should relieve that headache. You do have a mild concussion, so if any kind of complication arises, please send for me."

"Should we have another bandage on his head, Doctor?" asked Elizabeth.

"I don't think it's necessary. You might clean the wound with alcohol a couple of times a day for the next three or four days. But it's already stopped bleeding, so there's no need to bandage it again."

"How soon can I ride, Doctor?" asked Dayton.

"You in a hurry?"

"Well, yes, sir. I was chasing the Phantom Riders when my horse took the tumble and threw me onto that rock."

Hanson's eyes widened. "The Phantom Riders?"

"Yes, sir. My boss at the Helena office has me on their trail. I've got to resume the pursuit as soon as possible."

The doctor scratched his head. "Well, son, with some rest that concussion will clear up in three or four days. But I'd recommend you not ride again for a week."

"But the longer I wait, the more people those murderers will kill."

"I understand, son, but if you try to resume normal activity too soon, it could be dangerous for you. If you collapse, those beasts will keep on killing even longer."

Rance closed his eyes and nodded. "All right. I'll wait a week."

By suppertime, Rance felt like getting up and walking to the table.

Hal seemed avidly interested in the Civil War, and Rance told the family some of his war experiences as they all ate. After supper, Mitch Moran read the Bible and they had a time of prayer. Rance felt right at home.

While Elizabeth and Marcy washed dishes and cleaned up the kitchen, Mitch, Hal, and Rance walked out onto the wide front porch of the ranch house and sat down on wicker chairs. There was a full moon, and the aroma of honeysuckle was in the air, along with the sound of crickets.

The men talked about the Phantom Riders for a while. The conversation had begun to wind down when the women joined them. Soon the beauty of the star-lit heavens captured their attention and they admired God's handiwork.

After a while, Elizabeth said, "Well, Papa, I think it's time we retire for the night."

Mitch agreed, and as they rose to enter the house, Hal said, "Guess I'd better turn in too."

Marcy looked at Rance. "How about you, Deputy?"

Rance drew in the sweet scent of honeysuckle and said, "I think I'll stay up for just a little while and enjoy this night air. My headache is gone, and I want to enjoy the fact that it's not hurting for a change."

"Is it all right if I sit here with you?" she asked.

"Why, of course. I'd enjoy your company."

Marcy turned to her parents and said, "I'll stay here with Mr. Dayton till he's ready to turn in. See you in the morning." She left her chair and moved to the one next to Rance.

The Morans and Hal bid them good night and entered the house.

The moon was now sending its silver light onto the porch, and the breeze toying with Marcy's long tresses made the moonlight seem to dance in her hair. The sight did strange things to Rance Dayton's heart.

"Marcy…" he said.

"Yes, Deputy?"

"Is there a young man in your life? You know, someone special?"

"Not really. There are a couple of nice young men at church that I've dated once in a while…but no one special. What about you? Has…has there ever been someone you were in love with?"

"Well, I was engaged once," said Rance. "But she decided she didn't want to marry a man who wore a badge, so she gave me back the engagement ring and married a doctor."

"Oh, I'm so sorry."

"No need to be," Rance said. "The Lord knew I was going to become a Christian, and He already had a plan for my life. Alicia wasn't in the plan. It kind of hurts when I think of being spurned like that, but it's hurting less all the time."

"I'm glad for that, Deputy."

"Marcy?"

"Hmm?"

"You can call me Rance."

"Oh. All right…Rance."

Dayton took a deep breath of the night air. "It sure is a beautiful night."

Marcy settled back in her chair and gazed up at the twinkling stars. They sat comfortably silent for a while, listening to the cricket concert.

"I sure appreciate your taking such good care of me, Marcy," Rance said after a time.

"We were glad to do it."

"Well, I appreciate what Hal and your parents did, too, but I was referring to you. I mean, it was really something to come out of my unconscious state and see such a…to see you sitting beside the bed. A fella couldn't ask for a prettier lady to take care of him."

Marcy's face tinted. "Well, thank you, Dep—Rance. You're very kind."

"I try to be, but when I said that, it wasn't kindness; it was simply telling the truth. You're a very attractive young lady."

"Well, Rance, I really should turn in. And so should you. I'm sure a good night's rest will help that concussion go away."

"You're right," he said, rising. He looked down into her soft blue eyes and added, "It may sound strange, but I'm glad my horse took that spill. Otherwise I never would've met you. And your family, of course."

Marcy walked Rance to his room, told him good night, and moved on down the hall toward her own room. As she was turning the knob, the door across the hall came open, and Hal whispered, "Hey, Marcy! Did he kiss you good night?"

Marcy glanced quickly toward Rance's door. "Of course not! Hal Moran, why do you ask such a question?"

He grinned slyly. "'Cause I saw the way he looked at you all evening. He really likes you, sis. I thought maybe he—"

"Go to bed!" she snapped. She opened her door and slipped inside, closing it quietly but firmly.

On the fourth day that Deputy U.S. Marshal Rance Dayton had been with the Moran family, Mitch and Hal pulled into the yard after a trip to town and saw Rance at the corral gate, repairing a broken hinge. Hal jumped down out of the wagon before it had come to a complete stop.

"Hey, you're supposed to be resting, Rance!" said Mitch. "What're you doing?"

Rance grinned. "Just thought I should make myself useful around here. I heard Elizabeth mention to you last night that the top hinge on this gate was broken. You said you'd get to it as soon as you could. Well, since the ladies are over visiting your neighbors, I took a look in your toolshed and found a new hinge the same size. 'Bout got it done."

"I'm much obliged, but you didn't need to do that."

"Glad to. I'm feeling much better, and since you're stuck with me three more days, I might as well earn my keep."

Mitch climbed down from the wagon much slower than his son and walked toward the back of the wagon. "We're going to miss you, my friend," he said.

"Well, thank you," said Rance over his shoulder, tightening the last heavy wood screw.

"In fact, just so you won't forget us, Hal and I picked up some gifts for you in town."

Rance turned around to see Mitch holding a beautiful new saddle, and Hal was holding a bridle and a new pair of saddlebags. "Aw, now, you didn't need to go and do a thing like that, Mitch. I—" Rance's gaze riveted on the saddlebags…the initials emblazoned on the sides were R. D. "Well, look at that, will you!"

Rance marveled at the beauty and quality of the saddle and other leather goods, and humbly thanked Mitch.

Just then the women came wheeling into the yard in the family carriage and pulled up to where the men were standing.

"Oh, so you gave them to him early!" said Elizabeth. "You weren't going to give him those until you—"

"Elizabeth! Don't say any more!"

Marcy laughed. "Daddy, you might as well go ahead and do the whole thing."

Rance's brow furrowed. "What whole thing?"

Mitch's features flushed. "Well, you know…day before yesterday you were talking about buying one of my saddle horses."

"Yes."

"And you really like the big gray gelding, don't you?"

"Yes, I do."

"Well, we had a secret family meeting last night after you went to bed, and we decided that since you're such a nice fella, and a lawman and all, we're giving the gray to you. I'd already been to the saddlery in town and bought the saddle, bridle, and saddlebags, and ordered the initials put on. We were going to give you everything at one time, but I just sorta had to go ahead and give you the gear." The older man looked down, a bit embarrassed, then said, "Anyway…the horse and this stuff is our way of saying we appreciate you, Rance."

Rance Dayton shook his head in disbelief. Finally he said, "What does a fella do with people like you?"

Mitch grinned. "Just come back and see us after you get that bunch of killers hanged!"

Rance grinned, then looked at Marcy. "You can count on it!"

The next day was Sunday. Rance thoroughly enjoyed the church services in Deer Lodge City. On Monday and Tuesday he helped Mitch repair the barn roof.

On Tuesday evening after supper, Rance and Marcy took a moonlight walk in the fields. As they strolled slowly in the lush grass, Marcy said, "It's going to be hard to watch you ride away tomorrow."

"Well, I tell you, little lady, it's going to be even harder for me to ride away."

"Rance, I'm praying that the Lord will let you catch that gang soon. Not just because I want them stopped, which of course I do, but…well, because you promised to come back and see us when they were caught."

"There's nothing I want more than to come back and see you," he said softly.

The next morning, as Rance was about to leave, Hal went to the corral, saddled and bridled the gray for him, and left the horse near the corral gate. With his saddlebags draped over his shoulder, Dayton told the family good-bye at the back porch, assuring them he would come visit after the gang was brought to justice. He shook hands with Mitch and Hal, and Elizabeth embraced him affectionately.

Suddenly, all eyes were on Marcy.

"I'll walk you out to your horse, Rance," she said.

When they were halfway between the house and the barn, she stopped and brought her hand from behind her back. "I have something I want to give to you," she said.

Rance looked down and saw a brand-new Bible in her hand. "On Monday, Mother and I visited the neighbors, but we also took a little run into town. I bought you this so you'd have a Bible."

Marcy extended it to him, and Rance took it and captured her hand for a moment. "This means more to me than I could ever tell you, Marcy," he said. "I treasure the Word of God because it's His gift to us, but I will treasure this Bible for an additional reason…because it came from you."

Tears misted Marcy's eyes. "Look inside," she said.

Rance opened to the first page, which was blank except for handwriting that read:

To Rance—

I am so thankful to the Lord for bringing you into my life. Please think of me whenever you read this Bible.

Love,
Marcy

Rance Dayton thought his heart would burst when he read the last two words. He wanted to kiss her good-bye but refrained. Instead, he held the Bible over his heart, and said, "I will think of you every time I read God's Word. And I'll think of you lots of other times too. In fact, probably a thousand times a day."

Marcy raised up on tiptoe and planted a sweet, warm kiss on his cheek.

Rance placed fingertips to his cheek and said, "Marcy, if I'm not careful, I'm going to fall in love with you."

She looked up at him earnestly and said, "Be careful in your pursuit of the killers, Rance, but in your feelings toward me…don't be careful."

"I won't," he said with feeling.

With tears streaming down her cheeks, Marcy Moran watched the man she loved ride away. She didn't move from the spot until he vanished from sight.

TWENTY-TWO

Mitch Moran had provided Rance Dayton a map of Montana Territory. After studying the map Rance rode west, on a hunch, for the town of Phillipsburg.

When he got there he learned that the gang had indeed been at Phillipsburg before him and robbed the town's only bank, leaving a bank employee dead and a customer wounded. Eyewitnesses said they had ridden east out of town.

Rance soon found himself climbing through the Rockies and came upon a small unnamed settlement. The gang had ridden through there two days earlier to water their horses. After following what appeared to be the trail of several horses moving together, he finally came upon a spot where several riders had camped.

He pressed on through the next day and rode down out of the Rockies on the eastern slope. He found another campsite, and by the looks of it, they had been there only a day or so ahead of him. Dayton decided by the distance between camps that the gang was moving slowly. Maybe taking it easy for a while and laying low.

The next morning, Rance stopped in a town called Bedford, but found no one who had seen the gang. He decided to follow the road toward Jefferson City. The road threaded through dense forest, and as he rounded a bend, he came upon a stagecoach.

One middle-aged woman was trying to help another climb up into the box, but her long dress was making it difficult to climb. They paused at the sound of horse's hooves, and peered over their shoulders nervously.

The one on the ground said, "Oh, Myrtle! It's a lawman! See his badge?"

"What happened, ladies?" asked Dayton, as he dismounted.

"A gang of masked men stopped the stage. They killed the driver and shotgunner, wounded our husbands, then robbed us. We have the bodies inside the coach with our husbands. We were going to drive the stage into Jefferson City and find a doctor."

"I'll drive it in," said Dayton. "How long since this happened?"

"About twenty minutes ago."

Rance nodded. "Let me take a look at your husbands."

Both the men had taken bullets in the shoulder, but they were conscious. Rance removed the dead bodies from inside the coach and hoisted them on top. He helped the women inside with their husbands and tied his horse behind, then headed for Jefferson City.

After delivering the wounded men and their wives to the town doctor, Dayton drove the stage to the local marshal's office. The marshal was just coming out the door as Rance set the brake.

"Marshal Naylor?" Rance said, climbing down from the box.

"Yes, sir," said the lawman, who was in his late thirties.

"I'm Deputy U.S. Marshal Rance Dayton, out of the Helena office on assignment to track down the Phantom Riders. They stopped this stage about four miles north of here, killed the driver and shotgunner, and wounded two male passengers. I left them off at the doctor's office up the street, along with their wives, who were unharmed. Will you see that the stage gets to the proper people? I've got to stay after the gang."

"I'll do that, Deputy," said Naylor. "And even more. I'll round up a posse, and we'll go with you."

"I appreciate the offer, Marshal, but Chief Wright only wants one man tracking them because one man is harder to spot on their trail. My job is to locate them when they camp, then obtain help from the nearest local law."

Naylor nodded. "I understand."

"You might see to the people at the doctor's office too," Rance said.

"Will do."

With that, Dayton went to the back of the coach and untied his horse's reins, then swung into the saddle and galloped south out of town.

Marcy Moran sat alone on the front porch of her parents' ranch house near Deer Lodge City, gazing at the rolling hills where she had watched Rance Dayton ride away.

"Lord," she said, "keep Your hand on him. Bring him back to me. Please help him to bring those killers in soon. I want him to know how very much I love him. I must find a way to tell him." She prayed for several minutes, then sat quietly looking across the fields.

"What are you doing, honey?" came her father's voice.

Marcy looked up to see both parents looking down at her.

"I think she's looking for someone to come riding over those hills, Papa," said Elizabeth.

Mitchell grinned and rubbed his chin. "Now, I wonder who that might be, Mother?"

"I don't know his name," she said with a chuckle, "but his initials are Rance Dayton."

Marcy playfully swatted her mother's hand as Elizabeth sat down beside her.

"Well, I'm right now, am I not?"

It was Marcy's turn to chuckle. "Are mothers ever wrong?"

Mitch sat down on Marcy's other side and turned the chair to face her. "You really fell in love with that rugged young fella, didn't you?" he said.

"Yes, I did, Daddy. I just know he's the one the Lord has chosen for me."

"But how does Rance feel about you, Marcy?"

"He as much as said he's in love with me, just before he rode away."

"What'd he say?"

"Mitch, that's private," said Elizabeth. "Don't ask her to tell you."

"I don't mind, Mother. You both saw me kiss him on the cheek."

The parents nodded.

"Well, when I did that, he said 'Marcy, if I'm not careful, I'm going to fall in love with you.'"

"And what did you say?" asked Elizabeth.

"I told him not to be careful in his feelings toward me. And he said, 'I won't.'"

"Sounds like the real thing to me," Mitch said. "You know Mother and I like Rance. We were talking before going to sleep last night, and we both agreed that if what we thought we saw was the real thing, we'd sure welcome it. He's a fine, dedicated Christian young man."

Marcy smiled. "That's the only kind the Lord would send to me, Daddy...and it's the only kind I want."

No one spoke for a few moments, then Elizabeth said, "Honey, do you think you could stand being the wife of a lawman? It's a dangerous profession, and as a deputy U.S. marshal, he'll travel a lot."

Marcy nodded. "With the Lord in our marriage, and the love I feel for Rance, and the love I know he feels for me...I know I could stand it. I'm not saying it would be easy, but the Lord is able to give strength and grace, even to the wife of a lawman."

"Can't argue with that," Mitch said.

Rance Dayton walked into the town marshal's office in Centreville, Montana. When Marshal Ryan Thomas saw the badge on Dayton's chest he rose from his chair, saying, "Welcome to Centreville, Deputy."

Dayton introduced himself, and they shook hands.

"What can I do for you, Deputy Dayton?"

"I was talking to some men on the street out there, and they told me the Phantom Riders were here yesterday."

"Yep."

"I'm on assignment by U.S. Marshal Douglas Wright in Helena to track them down."

"Big job," said Thomas.

"Yes, sir. The men out there said someone had seen the gang members putting their masks on in the alley behind the bank, and he alerted you."

"Sure did."

"What happened then?"

"I recruited some help and gave them a gunfight. We killed two and wounded another in the thigh, but he was able to ride away. One of them was wounded in the shoulder, and the gang rode off and left him."

Rance looked surprised. "It's rare for them to leave one of their wounded behind."

"They couldn't help it," said Thomas. "We were sending so much hot lead after them, they had no choice but to take off. It was late in the day, almost dark, so I didn't form a posse."

"Well, Marshal Thomas, how about letting me talk to your prisoner."

"Be glad to, but I'll tell you right now, he won't give you any information. I tried to get it out of him. Reminded him that his pals ran off and left him to face the law and hang. But it didn't help."

"Well, I have to try. What's his name?"

"He won't tell me. Carries no identification. I understand that none of them do. The dead ones didn't either."

Dayton sighed. "Okay. Well, point me in the right direction."

Twenty minutes later, Rance left the cell block and entered the marshal's office. "You were right, Marshal. I told him the decent thing to do was to give me all the information he could so the killing spree could be stopped. You know…die with his conscience cleared. He just cussed me good and told me to get out."

"'Honor among thieves,' somebody once said," Thomas replied.

The next day, Rance Dayton was riding hard again. Marshal Thomas had told him there were ten outlaws in the gang before the shooting. They were now down to seven, and one of them was wounded.

He headed south toward Toston, which the map showed to be about a mile east of the Boulder River. As he rode, Rance prayed that the Lord would let him catch the killers soon so he could return to Marcy and ask her to marry him.

At sunset, he was about to make camp when he saw a rider-less horse standing in the woods off to the side of the road. There was blood on the saddle. When he drew up, he saw a dead man lying in the bush with a bullet in his thigh.

Rance knelt beside the man and felt the flesh of his face. He was still warm. The gang couldn't be far ahead. Now they were down to six. *Odds are getting even better,* he thought.

Dayton studied the map in the fading light. He could see a pattern to the locations the gang had targeted. They would probably rob the bank in Toston next. And unless they took a day off, they would hit the bank tomorrow.

Rance thought about where he would camp if he were them and decided it would be on the east bank of the Boulder River.

Twilight fell as he headed southeast toward the river. He guided the horse across the river at a point where there was a sharp bend, hoping that if the gang was looking that way, they wouldn't see him. Cautiously, he followed the east bank, walking the gray slowly.

Clouds were gathering as the moon began to rise. Dayton slipped from the saddle and led the gray through the woods along the edge of the river. After about an hour, he caught sight of a winking campfire through the trees.

He tied his horse in thick brush about a hundred yards from the camp. With the breeze rustling the tree branches and the rush of the river, a hundred yards was far enough away if the gray whinnied.

He kept to what shadows the cloud-covered moon allowed and crept up close to the camp. There were six men sitting around the fire, laughing and making jokes. The orange flames allowed Rance to see the horses they had staked out nearby among plenty of grass.

It got quiet for a moment, then one of them brought up the loss of four good men that day. "Shouldn't we go back and break Larry out of jail?" he said.

"Be too risky," said another man. "They just might be waitin' for us to do that."

Rance knew he needed to ride hard for Toston and get what help the local law could give him, but it was night, and the moon was covered. To ride hard now would be dangerous. And it would take quite a while to get to Toston, even at a full gallop. If his horse should fall...

He moved in closer, being careful not to step on a twig. He was almost close enough to make out the features of the three men who faced in his direction. The flickering fire cast dancing shadows on their faces. One of them stood up with a water pan in his hand and said, "Be back in a few minutes, guys."

Rance followed the shadowed figure and watched him kneel beside the stream and dip the pan into the water. The rippling of the river covered Rance's footsteps as he slipped up behind the outlaw and cracked the man on the head with the barrel of his revolver. The man dropped flat on the riverbank, and the pan he had been holding filled with water and sank to the bottom. Rance slipped the outlaw's gun from its holster and threw it in the river.

He then dragged the man into the cover of brush and trees. There, working by feel more than sight, he braced the man in a sitting position against a slender birch and tore up his shirt to make a rope. He used the man's belt to bind his wrists behind the tree, then tied his ankles with the rope and used part of the shirt as a gag.

As Rance moved stealthily back through the trees and brush toward the fire, he saw the shadowed form of another outlaw coming his way. Rance drew up behind a pine tree and waited till the outlaw stepped past him then slammed his gun barrel down on the man's head. He dragged him to a different spot from the other outlaw and bound him to a tree and gagged him in the same manner. Then he took the man's gun and threw it in the river.

The other four were still seated around the fire, eating their supper.

No better time than now, Rance decided. He quietly drew his revolver, cocked it, and dashed in from the surrounding darkness, commanding sharply, "All right, drop those plates and throw your hands in the air!"

Startled, the outlaws jerked their heads up and saw the gun in Dayton's hand and the firelight reflecting from his badge.

"I'm Deputy U.S. Marshal Rance Dayton, and you men are under arrest for murder and robbery! On your feet! I want those guns removed very carefully from their holsters and dropped to the ground."

All four rose slowly to their feet.

Three of the four rose a little bit slower than their fourth comrade, shocked looks capturing their faces. But no one was more shocked than Rance Dayton when he recognized Hank Upchurch, Buford Hall, and Chuck Carney.

Buford released a crooked smile and said, "Well, boys, it's our old pal, Major Dayton! You remember us, Major. We're the guys who saved your life at Antietam."

When no one moved to drop their guns, the fourth man said, "Hey, what's goin' on here? You guys saved this federal man's life in the War?"

Rance Dayton stood there, stunned. He could hardly believe he was looking into the faces of three of the Fearless Four.

"We sure did, Slim," said Carney. "He owes us. It'll be all right now. Everett'll be back any minute. He'll be glad to see the major."

"You are gonna let us go, aren't you, Major?" said Buford. "Like Chuck said, you'd be dead if it wasn't for us."

Everything these men had meant to Rance came rushing back, and he felt torn by the remembrance of their days of glory. For a few moments he let himself weigh the consequences of letting them go. If he took them in, they would be hanged. How could he end the lives of the men who were willing to risk death to save his life? Rance's heart pounded in his chest.

"Major," said Buford, "we can put our hands down now, can't we?"

Rance seemed paralyzed as the cascading thoughts of the War and his friendship with these men filled his mind. His words to them around the campfire after the Battle of Fredericksburg came back with chilling clarity: *I want to thank you guys one more time from the bottom of my heart for laying your lives on the line to save mine. You'll always be very special men in my memories, and in my life. If there is ever anything I can do for any one of you...consider it done.*

"Well, what about it, Major?" pressed Carney. "My arms are getting tired held up like this."

Rance Dayton felt a queasiness in his stomach, but his features took on firm resolve as he said, "It's not Major, Chuck. It's Deputy U.S. Marshal. I'm taking you in."

TWENTY-THREE

Marcy Moran gazed at the distant hills as she stood with her mother on the front porch.

"It'll be two weeks tomorrow since he left, Mother," she said. "I'm afraid something's happened to him."

Elizabeth put an arm around her daughter. "Now, honey, you must trust the Lord in this. He is able to take care of Rance and bring him back to you."

A tear ran down Marcy's cheek and she quickly wiped it away. "I know, Mother. It's just that...well, sometimes my faith grows a little weak."

"Marcy dear, every Christian has those times. When they come, you just hold on to what you know. Right now you can hold on to the fact that God brought that young man into your life for a purpose. Let God work out the details in His own time."

Marcy nodded and gave her mother a smile.

U.S. Marshal Douglas Wright and his deputy, Rance Dayton, turned from the gallows in Helena as the crowd began to disperse.

Wright followed Dayton to the gray gelding and said, "If you do get married while you're there in Deer Lodge, wire me and let me know. After what you did for the people of this territory, you deserve a couple of weeks off."

Rance swung into the saddle. "I'll let you know, sir. If it works out as I believe it will, Marcy and I will be needing a house in Helena."

"Well, there're a few for sale here in town. I'm sure you'll find something suitable."

"Okay. I'll see you soon."

Rance wheeled the gray toward the west, trotted a ways, then drew rein. A lump welled in his throat as he looked back at the gallows and beheld the six lifeless bodies swaying slightly in the morning breeze. He focused on Carney, Hall, Nichols, and Upchurch and bit down hard on his lower lip to keep his emotions in check. But he couldn't blink back the tears that filled his eyes and spilled down his cheeks.

If only things had turned out differently, he thought. If only Stonewall Jackson had not come riding into the Confederate camp in the wilderness on that fateful night. If only the Fearless Four had listened when the other sentries told them not to shoot...

He looked at his former comrades for a long moment, then put the gray to a gallop, heading for the towering Rockies. On the other side of those mountains was the young woman the Lord had chosen for him.

Rance was facing the setting sun as the ranch house came into view. Eager to hold Marcy in his arms, he put the gray to a full gallop.

As he drew near, he thrilled to see her rise from a chair and wave to him. He gave a whoop of excitement and yanked off his hat, waving it in response.

When he drew up and pulled rein, he saw the tears glistening on her cheeks as the glow of the sunset danced in her golden hair.

He slid from the saddle, and Marcy hurried off the porch to meet him, calling his name, her arms open wide.

EPILOGUE

Historians have called the Battle of Chancellorsville "Robert E. Lee's masterpiece, and an almost perfect example of the military arts."

Facing an army of 140,000 with barely 65,000 men of his own, Lee outmaneuvered, out-thought, and out-fought the Union Army of the Potomac. Lee, of course, gave the glory to Stonewall Jackson, whose military genius had been employed to defeat the enemy.

Losses for Major General Joseph Hooker's army were: 1,606 killed, 9,762 wounded, 5,919 captured or missing. Total: 17,287.

Losses for General Robert E. Lee's army were, 1,581 killed, 8,700 wounded, 1,708 captured or missing. Total: 11,989.

When the news of Lieutenant General Thomas J. Jackson's death was released on May 10, 1863, Jackson's one-time aide, young Major Henry Kyd Douglas wrote in his diary: "A great sob swept over the Army of Northern Virginia. It was the heartbreak of the Southern Confederacy."

On Monday, May 11—the day after Jackson's death—General Robert E. Lee issued General Orders Number 61:

With deep grief, the Commanding General announces the death of Lieutenant General Thomas J. Jackson, who expired on May 10, at 3:15 P.M. The daring, skill, and energy of this great and good soldier, by decree of an all-wise Providence, are not lost to us. But while we mourn his death, we feel that his spirit still lives, and will inspire the whole army with his indomitable courage and unshaken confidence in God as our hope and strength.

Let his name be a watchword to his corps, who have followed him to victory on so many fields. Let his officers and soldiers emulate his invincible determination to do everything in the defense of our beloved country.

One historian wrote: "Stonewall Jackson's true value came to light when he began working closely with Robert E. Lee. The calm, resolute, sensitive, and scholarly Lee and the fiery but calculating Jackson formed an almost perfect military team. Jackson's masterpiece came at Chancellorsville where, defying every tenet of military science and history, he led an outnumbered army to victory in a flank march that ranks with Frederick the Great's maneuver at Leuthen as one of the greatest actions in martial records."

Stonewall Jackson's aides dressed his body in a dark civilian suit, then a military overcoat. For a shroud, Jefferson Davis provided the first example of the newly approved Confederate national flag, white with the familiar red-white-and-blue battle-flag design in the upper corner.

The morning after Jackson died, the body was taken to the parlor of the Chandler house. As the Chandlers stood looking down at the coffin, Jim Lewis came in and handed Mrs. Chandler a lock of Jackson's hair that he had cut before the lid was closed.

The coffin was taken to Richmond by train, accompanied by the widow and baby Julia, along with the McGuires, Chaplain Tucker Lacy, Jim Lewis, and Mary Anna's brother, Joe Morrison.

The great general's body lay in state at the Confederate capitol. All the city's businesses were closed, and crowds of tearful mourners—most of whom had never laid eyes on Jackson before—came to pass by the coffin and pay tribute to their national hero.

The body was then removed to Lexington where the funeral was held on Friday, May 15, 1863, at the Presbyterian church where Jackson had faithfully served as a deacon. All Lexington and those in the surrounding countryside followed the coffin to the cemetery, and there the general was laid to rest.

At 1:00 P.M. on June 27, President Abraham Lincoln relieved Major General Joseph Hooker as commander of the Union Army of the Potomac and replaced him with Major General George G. Meade.

The Civil War would go on.